THE RISE AND FALL
OF URBAN ECONOMIES

INNOVATION AND TECHNOLOGY IN THE WORLD ECONOMY
Martin Kenney, Editor
*University of California, Davis and Berkeley Roundtable on
the International Economy*

Other titles in the series:

Andrew Hargadon
Sustainable Innovation: Build Your Company's Capacity to Change the World

Shiri M. Breznitz
The Fountain of Knowledge: The Role of Universities in Economic Development

Martin Kenney and David C. Mowery, eds.
Public Universities and Regional Growth: Insights from the University of California

Mary Lindenstein Walshok and Abraham J. Shragge
Invention and Reinvention: The Evolution of San Diego's Innovation Economy

John Zysman and Mark Huberty, eds.
*Can Green Sustain Growth? From the Religion to the Reality
of Sustainable Prosperity*

Israel Drori, Shmuel Ellis, and Zur Shapira
The Evolution of a New Industry: A Genealogical Approach

Jeffrey L. Funk
Technology Change and the Rise of New Industries

Kaye Husbands Fealing, Julia I. Lane, John H. Marburger III, and
Stephanie S. Shipp, eds.
The Science of Science Policy: A Handbook

Jerald Hage
Restoring the Innovative Edge: Driving the Evolution of Science and Technology

Sally H. Clarke, Naomi R. Lamoreaux, and Steven W. Usselman, eds.
*The Challenge of Remaining Innovative: Insights from Twentieth-Century
American Business*

THE RISE AND FALL
OF URBAN ECONOMIES

Lessons from San Francisco and Los Angeles

Michael Storper,
Thomas Kemeny,
Naji Philip Makarem,
and Taner Osman

Stanford Business Books
An Imprint of Stanford University Press
Stanford, California

Stanford University Press
Stanford, California

Special discounts for bulk quantities of Stanford Business Books are available to corporations, professional associations, and other organizations. For details and discount information, contact the special sales department of Stanford University Press.
Tel: (650) 736-1782, Fax: (650) 736-1784

Printed in the United States of America on acid-free, archival-quality paper

Library of Congress Cataloging-in-Publication Data

Storper, Michael, author.
  The rise and fall of urban economies : lessons from San Francisco and Los Angeles / Michael Storper, Thomas Kemeny, Naji Philip Makarem, and Taner Osman.
    pages cm — (Innovation and technology in the world economy)
  Includes bibliographical references and index.
  ISBN 978-0-8047-8940-0 (cloth : alk. paper)
  ISBN 978-1-5036-0066-9 (pbk. : alk. paper)
  1. San Francisco Bay Area (Calif.)—Economic conditions.   2. Los Angeles Metropolitan Area (Calif.)—Economic conditions.   3. Economic development—California—San Francisco Bay Area.   4. Economic development—California—Los Angeles Metropolitan Area.   I. Kemeny, Thomas, author.   II. Makarem, Naji Philip, author.   III. Osman, Taner, author.   IV. Title.   V. Series: Innovation and technology in the world economy.
  HC107.C22S76 2015
  330.9494'61—dc23
                                                                    2015014231

ISBN 978-0-8047-9602-6 (electronic)

Typeset by Newgen in 10/14 Minion

"When I first came to Los Angeles, I realized nobody had ever painted it."
  David Hockney

"San Francisco beats the world for novelties; but the inventive faculties of her people are exercised on a specialty. Controversy is our forte."
  San Francisco Call, *September 15, 1864*

Contents

Figures, Maps, and Tables

Figures

Maps

Tables

Acknowledgments

T HE RESEARCH ON WHICH THIS BOOK IS BASED WAS FUNDED by a generous grant from the John Randolph Haynes and Dora Haynes Foundation. We would especially like to thank the foundation's director, Bill Burke. Many other people contributed to the project. On a sunny San Francisco afternoon, Arlie Russell Hochschild of UC Berkeley suggested organizing it as a "whodunit" story. Daniel Mazmanian, Edward Leamer, Sanford Jacoby, and Woody Powell provided early precious advice in framing the questions. Many interviewees in both regions also provided clues as to what to look for and made us aware of attitudes and debates in both regions. Participants in the Lusk Symposium at USC, Sciences Po Paris, Stanford University, and UC Berkeley provided valuable feedback. Various parts of the manuscript were read and commented upon by Chris Benner, Martin Kenney, Ed Malecki, Andrés Rodríguez-Pose, AnnaLee Saxenian, and Richard Walker, all leading to major revisions. Margo Beth Fleming of Stanford University Press coached us on sharpening the arguments and improving the organization of the book. The staff of the Luskin School of Public Affairs at UCLA administered our grant funds. The *Centre de Sociologie des Organisations* at Sciences Po provided Michael Storper with optimal conditions to write, as did the *Craft* co-working space on the rue des Vinaigriers and *Graffiti* on La Brea Avenue. The Geography Department at the London School of Economics is a world crossroads of ideas in economic geography and economic development that are drawn upon throughout the book. The Haynes Foundation allowed us to have a weeklong meeting in Barcelona to assemble our manuscript, as that charming city was the shortest distance among our scattered team members at a late stage in the research. Jonathan Storper helped our team make some important contacts in Bay Area leadership circles and provided suggestions of where to have a cocktail following lengthy interviewing in downtown San Francisco. The Burbank Airport was an unexpectedly pleasant early-morning gathering spot for trips north.

Though this book recounts the decline of the Greater Los Angeles economy in comparison to that of the San Francisco Bay Area, it should be remembered that in economics, glory is never forever. The future of both San Francisco and Los Angeles is promising, but not automatic.

THE RISE AND FALL
OF URBAN ECONOMIES

1 The Divergent Development of Urban Regions

FOR THE FIRST TIME IN HUMAN HISTORY, MORE THAN HALF of the world's population lives in urban areas. Eighty-five million people per year are moving to cities worldwide, most of them in the developing world. The most populated six hundred urban areas, or metropolitan regions, concentrate about a fifth of the world's population and about half of world economic output; these proportions will rise to a quarter of the population and more than 60 percent of output in just the next fifteen years (McKinsey, 2011). Indeed, the concentration of economic output in cities is even starker: just 23 mega city-regions (with ten million people or more) produce about a quarter of world economic output. This is not just due to the rapid urbanization in the developing world. Fully 90 percent of U.S. economic growth since 1978 has come from 254 large cities and 50 percent from the 30 largest metropolitan regions. About half of U.S. employment is located on 1.5 percent of its land area.

Even though the world is urbanizing, cities continue to have very different levels of economic development. Within the United States, for example, large metropolitan regions (with more than 1 million people) have average per capita incomes that are 40 percent higher than the rest of the country. On a world scale, residents of larger cities earn incomes that are about four times the global average. Incomes in large urban areas range from about $2,000 per year in Cairo to about $75,000 in cities such as San Francisco, Oslo, and Hartford, Connecticut. Finally, significant differences remain in income levels among metropolitan regions within single countries; in the United States, per capita income in Brownsville, Texas, is $23,000 per year compared to about $75,000 in the San Francisco Bay Area or Washington, D.C., or about a one-to-three ratio.

Economies have forces that sometimes allow development levels to become more similar and others that sometimes pull them apart. The income levels of U.S. states converged from 1880 to 1980, where the richest state (Connecticut) went from being 4.5 times as rich as the poorest (Mississippi) to just 1.76 times. But such convergence came to a stop around 1980 (Ganong and Shoag, 2012). Over the course of that century, U.S. city-regions went up and down the income rankings, fluctuating much more than states. Intermetropolitan per capita income convergence also came to a halt sometime in the 1980s (Moretti, 2012; Drennan and Lobo, 1999; Yamamoto, 2007).

The pattern of income differences between countries and cities changes over time. For countries, economic historians refer to a Great Divergence: China was by far the richest nation in the world in 1492 and still had a higher per capita income than Spain or Britain in 1750. It spent the next two and a half centuries falling behind the West before beginning its climb back up the income ladder in recent years (Pomeranz, 2000; O'Rourke and Williamson, 1999). We now speak of a new "great divergence" in development between city-regions within countries (Moretti, 2012). This means that while it will be essential to promote and sustain urbanization as a key basis for prosperity in the twenty-first century, urbanization alone will not ensure prosperity for every city-region. In the United States, Detroit was the sixth richest metropolitan region in in 1970; it is now 52nd on the list. Boston is now one of the top five American metropolitan regions in income, but it has had many ups and downs in its four-century history and it was down and out as recently as 1980 (Glaeser, 2003).

In this book, we study the divergent fates of two great California city-regions,[1] Los Angeles and San Francisco. In 1970, they had similar levels of per capita income and were fourth and first, respectively, among U.S. metropolitan regions. In 2010, they had almost a one third difference in per capita income and Los Angeles had slipped to 25th place. Throughout history, these kinds of changes in fortune have occurred in the world's great city-regions, often due to war or political change. But in the case at hand, they occurred because of the way that two wealthy, highly developed city-regions entered the New Economy.

In typical lore about these two cities, Los Angeles is said to have fallen on hard times because of the loss of much of its aerospace sector after the end of the Cold War, a flood of low-skilled immigrants from Latin America, and governmental failure. San Francisco won the information age lottery, becoming the world center of that technological revolution and hosting highly skilled immigrants. But none of these factors explain why these two cities diverged from similar starting points, and we will demonstrate in this book that the divergent process of change was principally due to the different ways the two economies reshaped their social and economic networks, the practices of their firms, and the overall ecology of organizations in their economies.

Two Great City-Regions: Los Angeles and San Francisco

By any standard, the Los Angeles and San Francisco metropolitan regions are large, wealthy, and dynamic. Los Angeles, in this context, means the Greater Los Angeles metropolitan region (known officially as the Combined Statistical Area [CSA] encompassing five adjacent, continuously urbanized counties (Los Angeles, Orange and Ventura, and parts of San Bernardino and Riverside). Los Angeles is one of the largest economies in the world. In 2011, its nominal gross metropolitan product was $897 billion, which would make it the world's 16th largest economy, after Mexico (112 million inhabitants) and before Indonesia (220 million).[2] Los Angeles had 18.08 million residents in 2011, making it the second most populous metropolitan area in the United States. Meanwhile, the San Francisco Bay Area generated a gross metropolitan economic output of $575 million, with a population of 7.5 million, making it the world's 22nd largest economy, just after Argentina (35 million) and before Sweden, with 9.6 million people.

Los Angeles is perhaps best known for Hollywood's entertainment industry, though it has a highly diversified economy. Its icons are the palm-lined streets of Beverly Hills and the mansions of Malibu, the hundred-mile string of wide sandy beaches along Santa Monica Bay and the Orange County coastline, its car-and-freeway landscape, and a way of life shaped by its year-round sunny, temperate climate. Los Angeles is frequently characterized as a vast suburban sprawl, but this is something of an illusion. Its settlements include sprawling neighborhoods of single-family houses, opulent villas, rustic canyon settlements, and beachside bungalows but also high-rise corridors and urban neighborhoods of medium-density apartments, all interlaced with

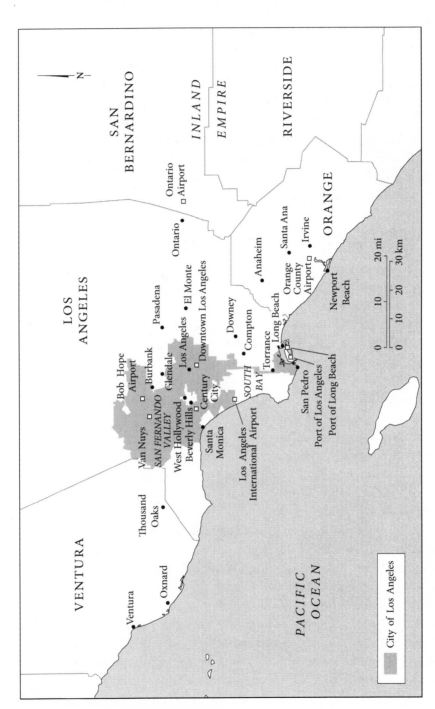

MAP 1.1 Greater Los Angeles

commercial boulevards that stretch for long distances. As a whole, the Los Angeles metropolitan region has a higher average population density than the New York metropolitan area, and its population density is about 20 percent higher than that of the San Francisco Bay Area. Though it has a small downtown for a region its size, Los Angeles has several neighborhoods with double the average density of the City of San Francisco, the Bay Area's urbanized core.

The San Francisco metropolitan area, which is also known as the Bay Area, is a Combined Statistical Area that until 2010 comprised ten varied counties, from the Sonoma and Napa wine country in the north to Silicon Valley and the Santa Cruz Mountains and coast in the south, and from the wild Pacific coastline to the west inland to the mountains separating it from the Central Valley of interior California.[3] With metropolitan expansion, the definition of the region (defined by the U.S. Office of Management and Budget [OMB] as the San Jose–San Francisco–Oakland Combined Statistical Area) was expanded in 2012 to include two inland counties that contain dormitory suburbs in California's interior Central Valley.[4]

The Bay Area is best known for the city of San Francisco: an iconically beautiful, hilly settlement surrounded by water and known worldwide for the Golden Gate Bridge, its waterfront, and colorful neighborhoods of ornate attached row houses. Outside the city of San Francisco, the Bay Area has densely urbanized areas in the East Bay (Oakland) and the low-density suburban megaregion of Silicon Valley. Its settlements are as diverse as those of Los Angeles, from forested rustic neighborhoods through typical California suburbs to dense European-style urban living.

Divergence: The Problem to Be Investigated in This Book

Depending on the method of calculation employed, the overall size of the economy (regional gross output) of the economy of Greater Los Angeles is third or fourth among metropolitan regions in the world, while that of the San Francisco Bay Area is about nineteenth. In terms of per capita income, inversely, San Francisco is consistently in the top five metro areas, and in a more select group of regions with more than 5 million people, it is usually first or second. In that latter group, Los Angeles ranks about 20th. For much of the twentieth century, Los Angeles successfully played catch-up in terms of income to its northern counterpart, all the while absorbing many more

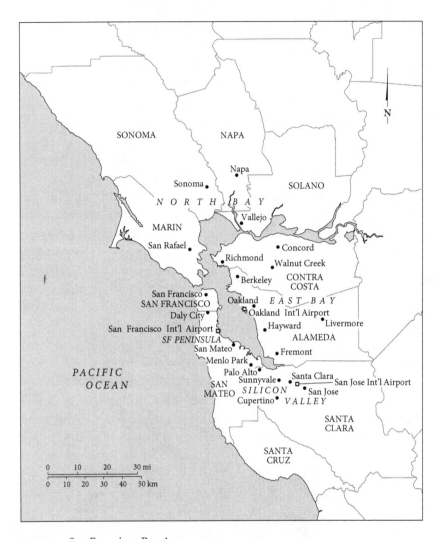

MAP 1.2 San Francisco Bay Area

new people (Rand, 1967). Between 1970 and 1980, Los Angeles's income level began to fall behind that of its northern neighbor. As Figure 1.1 illustrates, in 1970, per capita personal income levels in Los Angeles were 92 percent of those found in San Francisco. By 2012, they amounted to only 71 percent.[5]

As seen in Figure 1.1, Los Angeles has not only failed to keep pace with the Bay Area, but it has been unable to match the performance of many other major American metropolises. In addition to our two California regions, the figure tracks per capita income dynamics between 1970 and 2012 for all other Consolidated Statistical Areas whose populations were over 5 million in 1970: New York–Newark, NY–NJ–CT–PA; Chicago–Naperville, IL–IN–WI; Washington–Baltimore–Arlington, DC–MD–VA–WV–PA; Philadelphia–Reading–Camden, PA–NJ–DE–MD; Boston–Worcester–Providence, MA–RI–NH–CT; and Detroit–Warren–Ann Arbor, MI.[6] To make for a readable figure, incomes are averaged across New York; Chicago; Boston; Washington, D.C.; and Philadelphia, while the Detroit region is presented separately. Across these larger cities, Los Angeles most closely resembles Detroit. The larger story told in Figure 1.1 is that it is not sufficient to observe that the Bay Area is an especially fortunate case among American cities; San Francisco has indeed outperformed most metropolitan areas, but Los Angeles has foundered by that same standard.

Stated another way, the Bay Area and Los Angeles belonged to similar development clubs in 1970. Both regions had more educated workforces

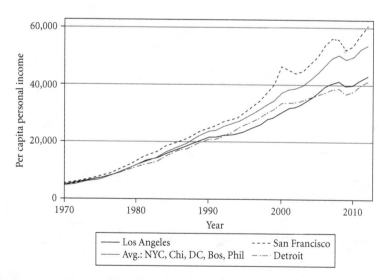

FIGURE 1.1 The evolution of per capita personal incomes in large metropolitan areas, 1970–2012

SOURCE: Authors' calculations using Bureau of Economic Affairs Regional Economic Accounts data.

NOTE: Combined Statistical Area (CSA) definitions are used, with boundaries laid out by the Office of Management and Budget in bulletin no. 13-01, issued February 28, 2013. CSAs represented in this chart comprise the list of regions that had populations over 5 million in 1970.

than the United States as a whole, and they hosted significantly higher proportions of Hispanics than the country as a whole. Both regions developed rapidly in resource-rich California, benefiting from business and financial links to the state's agricultural and natural resources hinterlands. Both nurtured dynamic and variegated manufacturing and service economies. Both benefited from large-scale federal procurement of military hardware from their regional firms. Both were centers of innovation in knowledge-and technology-intensive sectors, producing iconic goods for global markets such as airplanes, semiconductors, communications equipment, and entertainment. Both hosted major scientific research communities, consisting of 6 of the world's top-20-ranked research universities, as well as government research laboratories, independent institutes, large private firms with research and development (R&D) operations, and research hospitals. Migrants were attracted to their natural beauty, excellent climates, and high quality of life, thus sustaining high real estate prices and continued expansion of local markets for nontradable goods and services. Both shared California's relatively progressive governmental structure, institutions, infrastructure, and education policies.

Thus we arrive at the question that is at the center of this book: given similar incomes and wages in 1970 and all of these common developmental characteristics, why did San Francisco surge forward and Los Angeles fall so far behind?

Several Facets of Divergence

Urban and development economics compare economic well-being by correcting money incomes for different levels of local prices, as a way to identify "real" income. Internationally, this involves correcting for purchasing power parity; interregionally, it principally involves correcting for housing prices, the major reason why living costs differ from place to place. For instance, in the years 2007–2008, nominal income in Los Angeles was 70 percent of that of the Bay Area, but its median selling price for homes was 79 percent of that of the Bay Area.[7] Median housing prices are not a precise measure of housing cost differences, because they reflect only costs of new entrants to a region, while most residents are buying and selling within the regional market and paying the difference between past capitalization and present prices. More accurate accounting of effective housing costs should capture the range of situations (immigrants, homeowners, degree of capitalization, income level, renters). Using microdata from the decennial census and the *American Community Survey*, we can calculate such costs for different parts of the population. Annual housing expenditures are estimated by summing annualized rent or mortgage payments, utilities, insurance, condominium fees, property taxes, and other costs where applicable. Each household's housing expenditures are then subtracted from its total wage and salary income to arrive its real income.[8] Since the housing cost information is collected only from 1980 forward, Figure 1.2 presents median values of real (housing-cost-adjusted) income for each region for 1980, 1990, 2000, and 2010.

As the figure shows, from relatively comparable beginnings, San Francisco's real income advantage over Los Angeles grew strikingly, from 14 percent in 1980 to 50 percent by 2010.[9] The broad trajectory and magnitudes of real incomes in Los Angeles and San Francisco reinforce a story in which San

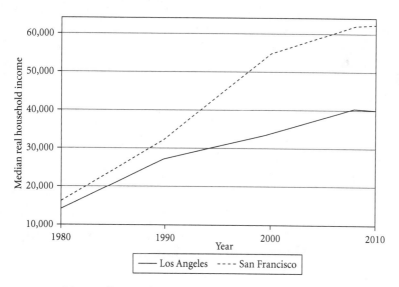

FIGURE 1.2 Metropolitan real median household wage and salary income, 1980–2010

source: Authors' calculations based on a 1 percent IPUMS decennial sample for 1980, 5 percent samples for 1990 and 2000, and a 5 percent American Community Survey sample covering 2005–2010, using CSA boundaries for San Francisco and Los Angeles.

note: Wage and salary income is the total pretax income earned from being an employee.

Francisco has, from comparable beginnings, strongly outperformed its southern neighbor.

Income Growth or Population Growth?

If a region or country increases its income while maintaining a stable population—something like Denmark—we think very differently about it as compared with a place where incomes rise in a context of considerable population growth, as in Chinese cities today, many American Sun Belt cities in recent decades, and California in much of the twentieth century.

Characteristics of the new population matter as well. Consider an economy that grows richer while welcoming only skilled individuals versus another that accommodates a wider variety of immigrants and pulls them up the wealth ladder—a difference we might describe as one of outcome versus opportunity. One economy might increase its per capita income through stricter gatekeeping, whether through formal immigration controls or high housing prices. Meanwhile, a more "welcoming" urban region might receive an influx of migrants whose lower education and skills reduce average income.

Figure 1.3 presents rates of compound annual population and income growth between 1970 and 2012 for the 30 most populous U.S. Combined Statistical Areas. Average values for all U.S. urban regions are documented with solid horizontal and vertical rules. From the figure, we see that the populations of both Los Angeles and San Francisco grew much faster than cities in the Northeast and Midwest, and considerably slower than the Sun Belt metro regions.

Between 1970 and 2012, the Greater Los Angeles economy added more than 8 million people, nearly doubling in size. This makes Los Angeles a distinctly different case from Rust Belt regions like Detroit. Over the same period, the Bay Area grew by about 60 percent, adding more than 3 million people. By the same standard, however, growth rates in both population and income have been slower in Los Angeles than in Houston, Dallas, Atlanta, Miami, Raleigh, Seattle, Denver, Orlando, and Portland.

We could say that Los Angeles has been slightly more welcoming in quantitative terms than the Bay Area. But these different rates of population growth are still both around the national average. Is Los Angeles's weaker income performance evidence of a trade-off between more growth and "better" development? It seems not. The two regions have about the same levels of

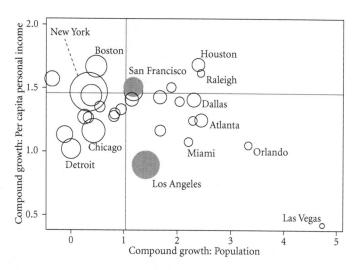

FIGURE 1.3 Population and per capita income, compound annual growth rates 1970–2012, 30 largest combined statistical areas in 2012
SOURCE: Authors' calculations based on BEA Regional Economic Accounts data.
NOTE: Solid horizontal and vertical rules represent average growth rates for population and income among all Combined Statistical Areas. Points are scaled according to population in 2012.

intergenerational income mobility (Chetty et al., 2014, Table III). Moreover, as we will show in Chapter 3, the quality of opportunities—particularly for immigrants—has been lower in Los Angeles than in San Francisco, for every ethnic, age, and educational group and category of immigrants. Concretely, immigrants of all national origins, including recent arrivals and long-term residents, have higher earnings in the Bay Area, even when their educational levels are identical. Los Angeles has not compensated for its relative underperformance in real income by becoming a better "opportunity machine."

Interregional differences in median and (especially) average wage levels could also be partly a function of differences in levels of inequality within regions (their income distributions). The region with higher per capita income could in principle have lower standards of living for many of its people if more of its income goes to the upper tail of the distribution; conversely, a region that is poorer on average could offer better living conditions for the many if more of its income is distributed around the median. Table 1.1 reports the Gini coefficient, using the wage and salary income of census respondents in each region. A Gini coefficient can range from 0 to 1, where 0 indicates that all

TABLE 1.1 Income distribution: Wage and salary income Gini coefficients

Year	Los Angeles	San Francisco	All California
1970	0.448	0.447	0.455
1980	0.463	0.448	0.459
1990	0.482	0.458	0.473
2000	0.508	0.496	0.504
2005–2007	0.506	0.503	0.508

SOURCE: Authors' calculations based on 1 percent decennial IPUMS samples and 3 percent *American Community Survey* sample for 2005–2007.

members of a society earn the same income and 1 characterizes a distribution where one individual has all the income.

Table 1.1 shows that San Francisco and Los Angeles have similar income distributions, with levels of inequality that closely correspond to the entire state of California; by the standards of the developed world, California and its great cities are all rather unequal, and they are increasingly so. But they are not very differently unequal. Los Angeles was somewhat more unequal in 1980 and 1990, though the gap narrows and is nearly eliminated by 2007.[10] If anything, the greater inequality in Los Angeles in the 1980s and 1990s made the gap in per capita income more significant for the average person back then. At every point in each region's income hierarchy, people have higher incomes in the Bay Area than in Los Angeles.

Regions and Subregions

The appropriate scale to analyze employment and incomes is the metropolitan region (the CSA), because communities within a region are parts of a "functional urban region," knitted together economically by dense regional flows of labor between employment and residences, and because firms recruit labor from the regional labor pool. This strong connection is reflected in the fact that labor, land, and housing prices (for a given quality) converge within a metropolitan region and are strongly different from its hinterland.

But there are also higher- and lower-income subregions in both Greater Los Angeles and the Bay Area. There are differences in granularity of counties in the two regions, with the Bay Area made up of ten small-to-medium-sized counties (until 2012) and the Southland having much larger average county size, in both land area and population. The Southland consists of the high-income counties of Ventura and Orange, the low-income counties of River-side and San Bernardino at the region's eastern desert edge, and its histori-cal core in Los Angeles County. Los Angeles County, with almost 10 million people, has the largest population of the 3,144 counties and county authorities in the United States and alone has a greater population than the entire San Francisco Bay Area. Los Angeles County in particular has had a lower rate of job creation in the period under examination than any of the other four counties in its region, and its per capita income, just short of $28,000, lies be-tween that of the two higher-income counties (between $32,000 and $34,000) and the lower-income ones (between $21,000 and $24,000).

The subregional success stories in Greater Los Angeles are limited and fall well beneath Bay Area income thresholds. Orange and Ventura Counties do not play the role in Greater Los Angeles that Silicon Valley does for the Bay Area. The core Silicon Valley counties (San Mateo and Santa Clara) have per capita incomes between $40,000 and $45,000, well above those of Orange and Ventura ($32,000 to 34,000). Orange County would rank *eighth* among the ten Bay Area counties in per capita income. The population of counties in the Bay Area with greater per capita income than Orange County is 6.4 million, about 83 percent of the total Bay Area regional population. Even all the high-income neighborhoods within Los Angeles County, if separated out, would equal about only Santa Clara County and therefore would not compensate for Greater Los Angeles's many poorly performing areas. There is a regionwide income problem in Greater Los Angeles. The Bay Area, by contrast, is success-ful in nearly all of its subregions, and at a level that has only a few equivalent subareas within Greater Los Angeles.

Comparative Regional Economic Development: A Window on Development

If these two regions were two different national economies, much research effort would have been expended and ink spilled in the pursuit of an expla-nation of the causes of this divergence. The divergent economic trajectories of the San Francisco and Los Angeles metropolitan regions have important implications for individuals, families, communities, firms, and governments, just as they would if we were studying two independent countries. Had Greater Los Angeles maintained its position as the fourth wealthiest metropolitan area in the United States, its economic output and per capita income would be almost a third higher today. By extension, its government receipts—at a constant level of taxation—would be much higher, allowing greater per capita investments in education and many other kinds of public goods and services. Over the medium-run time horizon of development that we focus on in this book, most people are raised, are educated, and work in the region in which they started out. And for those who move, it is better to come from or migrate to a high-income region than a poor one. Finding out why one of California's great city-regions has had so much success in entering the New Economy that emerged beginning in the 1970s, and why its other great city has not, is thus a window on the process of economic development more generally.

2 Divergent Development

The Conceptual Challenge

INNUMERABLE FORCES INFLUENCE ECONOMIC DEVELOPMENT. As such it is a very challenging subject for research (Helpman, 2011). Adding to the complexity, research on economic development uses many different methods. Some of it compares large number of cases, using large data sets and statistical analysis (Dollar and Kraay, 2004; Easterly, 2006; Kemeny, 2010). Other approaches use historical and case studies and perform in-depth comparisons of small numbers of cases (Earle, 1992; Mokyr, 1991; North, 2005; Rosenberg, 1982; Acemoglu and Robinson, 2012; Wade, 1990; Amsden, 1992, 2001; Saxenian, 1994). The large-sample studies have the advantage of being able to consider a wide range of possible causes of development (such as education, investment rates, entrepreneurship, institutions, and skills) (Acemoglu et al., 2004). But they may miss the ways these forces interact and combine in different contexts and how they sequence to generate development (Rodrik et al., 2004). Case studies have the advantage of more depth, but they can suffer from being less systematic and their conclusions might not be applicable to other cases. In the present comparison of just two regions, we try to account for these issues by rigorously organizing our case study with questions that draw from the findings of the large-scale empirical studies referred to earlier. In this way, we will have the depth of studying two regions thoroughly, but we do so with a systematic approach that relates the two cases to the concerns of economic development studies everywhere (Tilly, 1986).

Economic development as an academic field contains diverse theoretical elements that can be woven together in very different ways. In this book, we draw on four theoretical streams: international and comparative development theory, urban economics, economic geography, and the study of institutions.[1]

Development Theory

In general, comparative development analysis has been carried out at the scale of countries. At the global scale, if we take nations as units, then per capita incomes range from a few hundred dollars per year in places such as Haiti and certain sub-Saharan nations in Africa to over $80,000 in small, very rich countries such as Norway or Luxembourg and even higher for small petro-states. If we shave off these tails of the distribution, the global international multiple of real per capita incomes in the "players" in the world economy ranges from $1,000 to around $50,000, a 1:50 spread. Between the lower-middle-income countries (about $8,000) and the high-income ones, the spread is 1:6. These are, then, what can be considered the ranges of the "national effect" on per capita incomes.

Interestingly, a strong national effect shows up in international comparisons of cities. For example, if we list incomes of the 50 largest metropolitan regions around the world, about 40 are in the United States, reflecting the imprint of national productivity differences on metropolitan regions (Storper and Bocci, 2008). Thus, Houston might be about as rich, in real per capita terms, as Paris, which is the richest metropolitan region in France, but Houston is not the richest metropolitan area in the United States. Given this national effect, we still want to know why Houston is about 30 percent less wealthy than San Francisco, just as in the case of France, we want to know why Marseilles is about 25 percent poorer than Paris.

In this book, by studying two metropolitan regions within a single country, we can detect causes of divergence that may be overlooked in international comparisons. For example, a major theme in development studies is to identify the influence of trade and barriers to trade on two sovereign countries, but San Francisco and Los Angeles are part of a long-established free-trade zone (the United States). Development studies also looks for how macroeconomic and fiscal factors influence development (savings, investment, and so on), but San Francisco and Los Angeles share a common currency and a strong fiscal union. Development studies examines the roles of differences in how mobile firms and people are in different countries, but San Francisco and Los Angeles are both within the United States and have similar high levels of capital and labor mobility, inward and outward. Institutional differences between countries are also sources of differences in development, but San Francisco and Los Angeles have a single overarching legal and constitutional framework (the U.S. and California constitutions and statutes), and they do not have separate monetary, immigration, exchange rate, and interest rate policies. They also have many shared norms and cultural dimensions that shape social and economic action.

Our choice of two regions with so many obvious structural similarities, but which nonetheless have gone through a powerful economic divergence in a short period of time, effectively controls for a number of the explanatory variables used to account for international differences in development. This does not mean that all those causes are ruled out; instead, the divergence between Los Angeles and San Francisco requires that we use a more finely focused microscope to see if these causes operate in ways that are less obvious. It also opens up the possibility that we will discover causes of divergent regional economic development that are not on the radar screen of the field of international development studies.

International development theory does have a notion that will be central to our comparison of city-regions: that there are structural "clubs" of economies at different levels of development. The most obvious of these are labor-abundant economies of developing countries compared to mature capital- and knowledge-abundant economies, a distinction that maps neatly onto per capita income levels. There is also a strong correlation of real per capita income levels to specialization, education, productivity, infrastructure, the rule of law, and technological capabilities (Acemoglu and Robinson, 2012). High-income economies are systematically different from the club of economies at medium-income levels ($8,000–$20,000 per year) and poor ones (less than $8,000 per year), along all of these lines. The process of development, getting from one club to another, is not smooth, continuous, or automatic because development requires moving all of these things in tandem.

Moving from the poorest club into the middle-income group is selective, known as the "takeoff" problem. It can generally be achieved through abruptly changing the specialization patterns of the economy in question, transitioning from subsistence agriculture or simple commodities into labor-intensive manufacturing. As economies move further up the income ladder, however, a more delicate mix of changes in institutions, education levels, infrastructure, and so on becomes necessary. This is why moving further upward, from the middle-income club to the high-income club, occurs infrequently, so that many countries stagnate in what is known as the "middle-income trap " (Eichengreen et al., 2013). In contrast to these two cases, when countries break into the high-income club, it is rare for them to fall out of it. This is probably because once all these different aspects of development are in place, they mutually support one another and brake shocks in the economy in question, and because rich countries usually have enough innovation capacity to outrun their imitators. The world has had a fairly stable "convergence club" of developed nations for the last century, but over the longer run, the top ranks of countries are more turbulent, as in the Great Divergence between Europe and China after 1750 mentioned in the previous chapter (Pomeranz, 2000).

The club metaphor applies to metropolitan regions within a high-income country such as the United States, but with some modifications. There are regional or metropolitan clubs within the United States: Brownsville, Texas, is in the United States' low-income club, with $23,000 per year per capita income; San Francisco is at the top with about $75,000, and we can say that there is a middle-income group between them, characterized by urban regions such as Phoenix, Las Vegas, and Tampa, on their way up, and Syracuse and Detroit, on their way down. There is also a group of urban regions that are now in the top club—Houston, Dallas, and Atlanta—that broke through the middle-income trap in the last generation. Los Angeles was clearly in the top club in 1970 and is currently somewhere on the borderline between the top-income and the middle-income club, depending on exactly where we place the cutoff. As we shall see, Los Angeles still has significant high-wage activities, such as Hollywood and some of its high-tech sector, but as a city-region, it has an increasing proportion of middle-wage activity that is causing it to converge downward to the middle-income urban regions of the interior West and South and some deindustrializing Rust Belt cities. In general, the fate of city-regions within developed economies is more turbulent in the short run than the fate of national economies. Thus, unlike countries, over a 30-to-40-year period many city-regions within countries can fall out of the top club of cities and others can move into it.

Regional Science and Urban Economics

The analysis of economic development at the metropolitan scale is the central concern of a second theoretical field: regional science/urban economics (RSUE). In its standard account, firms sort themselves among regions according to the factor endowments of each region, which define the region's comparative advantage. As a result, regions come to specialize, as when investment banks locate in some cities, and automobile manufacturing firms in others. Insofar as some industries have some combination of higher productivity, higher skills, better terms of trade, and faster innovation than others, the regions or countries that specialize in them will have higher incomes than others. But the similarity to international development studies ends there. Whereas between countries there are high barriers to the movement of firms and people, such barriers are quite weak between cities within a country. Inside countries, labor, capital, ideas, goods, and services are all highly mobile, and there are much smaller differences between cities in institutions, cultures, languages, and laws than between countries (Helpman, 2011).

Urban economics considers the high mobility of capital, labor, and knowledge to be a strong force for income convergence among city-regions. As firms locate in different regions according to the factor endowments of each region (mix of capital and labor), some regions come to have excess supplies of factors and others have excess demand for them. In response, certain firms will move to areas of excess supply (and hence low price). A pure version of this theory argues that firms may adjust their capital-labor mix to suit the factor endowments of their new locations. This leads to the evening out of the prices of the factors between regions. Since the key factor price that generates per capita income is wages, RSUE predicts a powerful tendency toward interregional income convergence (Glaeser, 2008).

One problem with this predicted convergence is that one of the key assumptions of urban economics is unrealistic in the short to medium run; in most industries, the substitution of capital and labor is quite limited, since production technology (hence use of capital and labor) and quality of products are closely tied to one another. Production, in other words, are only moderately malleable in response to the availability of factors in different regions, in the short run. Another problem is the assumption that certain firms and industries can easily relocate to those places where factors of production are abundant or relatively cheap. Instead, some firms are highly constrained to co-locate with other firms, in a phenomenon known as clustering or "agglomeration" (Duranton and Puga, 2004). Agglomeration, in this view, could lead to durable income divergence to the extent that different types of firms are stuck to one another in a region (Thisse, 2010).

To respond to these issues, urban economists train their attention on two other mechanisms that could generate income convergence: the movement of people, and differences in the cost of living. This is where urban economics models really distinguish themselves from international development approaches and make their most plausible claims. Regions that host concentrations of highly paid skilled workers will drive up the regional cost of living, especially through pressure on the housing market. This rise in living costs can be strong enough to offset interregional differences in *nominal* (money) income. In other words, the salary of a worker in New York City may be much higher than of a similar worker in Omaha, but after accounting for regional differences in the cost of living (especially housing), the New Yorker's overall well-being ("total utility") will be no higher than that of her counterpart in Omaha (Glaeser, 2008). Thus, the appearance of different income levels is an optical illusion; underneath it is the reality of equalized real income or equalized overall quality of life between regions, according to the theory.

The main process that brings about this equalization or convergence is migration of people and firms. RSUE holds that people vote with their feet by leaving expensive places or places with low quality of life or unpleasant climates. When they do this they increase labor supplies in attractive regions, which initially creates downward pressure on their wages. This then attracts more firms (employment) away from the high-priced areas, generating increases in unemployment there and leading labor to have to tame its wage demands. Rising employment in arrival locations then starts to exert upward pressure on local wages. Urban economists contend that these forces lead to interregional convergence in economic well-being (in either nominal or real income). Such movements of people and firms shape specialization patterns, in a feedback between factor markets, factor prices, and the locations of firms.

However, even when we rigorously control for housing costs, real incomes have not tended to converge among metropolitan areas in the United States in recent decades, even for workers with similar demographic and skill profiles (Kemeny and Storper, 2012; Moretti, 2013). As noted earlier, there is a spread of about 1:3 in nominal income among American city-regions. When we account for differences in living costs, the top club of cities in the United

States remains on average about 15 percent richer than poorer ones; this gap is widening all over the United States and in many other developed countries (Moretti, 2012). The contrasts between San Francisco and Los Angeles are even starker. In Figure 1.2 we learned that there is an almost 50 percent real income gap between Los Angeles and San Francisco *after* carefully controlling for housing costs. Additionally, in Figure 1.3 we saw that both regions are just above the U.S. average for population growth, and we will see that the overall amenity levels of the two regions are quite similar. The real income divergence has occurred in spite of all the offsets that RSUE says should operate to smooth money income differences into similar real income or overall utility levels.

New Economic Geography (NEG)

A third field, New Economic Geography (NEG), provides tools to resolve some of the puzzles described earlier.[2] Economic geographers generally approach the problem of economic development from the vantage point of industries and firms. NEG centers on one of the foundational questions of economic development: why are economies specialized? Why, for instance, are so many jobs in the finance sector concentrated in Lower Manhattan, as opposed to having each city, town, and village host its own investment banking firms? In the context of the current case study, why is so much employment and production in the entertainment industry concentrated in the Los Angeles region, even though people around the world consume the output of this sector? And why does the Bay Area play host to so many businesses working in high technology? In contrast to the RSUE view, that firms are like free agents, seeking the capital and labor wherever the best combination of those may be located, NEG holds that—for certain industries, and especially high-wage innovative ones—the main criterion for a firm's location is where other similar or closely related supplier firms are located. Its core model is a theory of clustering as a principal reason for regional economic specialization.

NEG builds on early theories of specialization. In 1817, David Ricardo observed that Portugal's pleasant climate and fertile soil justified its specialization in the production of port wine. With recourse to such accidents of geography we can explain that Odessa, Texas, could no more become a transshipment hub than Duluth, Minnesota, can anchor a local oil and gas industry. But natural resource endowments do not help us understand the evolution of regional economic specialization of Los Angeles and San Francisco. Nothing in the natural world can convincingly explain why Los Angeles has retained Hollywood, the world's leading agglomeration of the entertainment industry.[3] Natural endowments tell us little about why the Bay Area is the location for the Silicon Valley information technology (IT) cluster.

Subsequent amendments to the theory of comparative advantage, in the context of the nineteenth-century industrial revolution, came to emphasize the uneven distribution of technology and knowledge (Mokyr, 1991; Rosenberg, 1982). Technology and knowledge are, in turn, considered to be embodied in people. Thus, one might argue that Los Angeles and San Francisco are differently specialized because their workers are differently endowed with abilities and knowledge—traits that researchers call "human capital." This is certainly true in a descriptive sense: San Francisco can sustain a dynamic high-technology sector because a large number of people skilled in information technology call the Bay Area home, while Los Angeles has so many entertainment workers. But we need to understand what *gives rise* to these differences and why Los Angeles, which had the world's biggest concentration of PhD engineers in 1970, has not been able to maintain its position as a lure for human capital.

Clustering makes industries geographically lumpy and relatively hard to move. The principal force that makes activities geographically sticky is known formally as "agglomeration economies" (Krugman, 1991a, 1991b; Fujita et al., 1999; Fujita and Thisse, 2002). Viewed through the lens of the lumpiness that comes from agglomeration, both Hollywood and Silicon Valley persist, in no small way, because firms in these industries tap into large regional pools of labor with specific types of skills, their developed business networks, their supply chains, and the exchange of new ideas that abound in these communities of entrepreneurs and workers (Puga, 2010). Returning to the contrast between NEG theories and RSUE theories, NEG suggests that the possibility of outward mobility of labor and capital of highly clustered industries is limited—even when the cost of living rises steeply—because the advantages of staying are much greater than the gains from leaving. In turn, this limits the forces of interregional income convergence that are at the heart of RSUE theory.

Leamer (2012) points out, in this regard, that the classical modern theory of comparative advantage and economic development (what is known as the Stolper-Samuelson model, the basis for RSUE) suffers from an internal contradiction. On the one hand, it holds that the underlying characteristics of places—notably their technologies and factor endowments—are fixed; on the other hand, it holds that capital, labor, and knowledge are mobile. The realistic picture is that the mobility of such factors is gradual—it takes a long time and a lot of such mobility to even out development between regions, such that at any given moment, jobs and firms are unevenly distributed. Moreover, the economy is continually inventing new activities that are lumpy; young, highly innovative industries that pay high wages are more clustered than the economy as a whole. Innovation disrupts tendencies to evenness of incomes across regions and countries in an ongoing way. In contrast to innovative industries, older industries have more stable markets, less rapidly changing technologies, and bigger firms, so they can divide themselves and their production chains out into different regions and countries, becoming less clustered (Norton and Rees, 1979; Grossman and Rossi-Hansberg, 2008; Blinder, 2009). The pattern of development is the outcome of this ongoing contest between convergence and divergence forces, in which neither one ever wins (Storper, 2013; Kerr, 2010; World Bank, 2009).

This observation leads us back to Leamer's (2012) point that any theory of development has to have its time frameworks right. Agglomeration economies don't change very fast. If one is trained to work in a particular sector that is concentrated in only a few locations, the choice set of potential migration destinations is limited, unless the worker is willing to retrain and change professions (A. Scott, 2010a, 2010b). In the medium run, there will also be wage spillovers from the lumpy and sticky regional core to rest of the regional service economy (Balassa-Samuelson effects) (Moretti, 2012). Wage and income inequality between metropolitan regions—divergence in real and nominal terms—will thus be significant and persistent. We will see that diverging quality of specialization is indeed behind diverging incomes in Los Angeles and San Francisco and that this divergence in specialization has to be explained.

Institutions and Regional Development

Institutions is a term that refers to many things, including the formal rules (such as constitutions, laws, and governments) that shape economies, informal routines (such as rules of thumb and conventional ways of doing things), and the principal public and private organizations that bring people together to carry out collective action in an economy. Institutions are also included in what economic sociologists call "social practices" and "social structure" (Granovetter, 1985, 2001). Institutions shape the ways economies operate (North, 1990; Granovetter, 2005; Hall and Soskice, 2001). Most of the research on institutions and economic development compares institutions of different countries, contrasting constitutions and legal frameworks, the structure and performance of governments, and the politics of decision-making and interest groups. These forces shape labor markets, entrepreneurship, and the growth of firms (Acemoglu et al., 2004; North, 2005). Some economists hold that institutions are as important to development as economic geography and trade (Rodrik et al., 2004).

As we noted in the previous chapter, city-regions within a country are subject to the common sovereign powers of their national government. When we turn to powers not reserved to national governments, and hence to institutions that might be regional in scale, the problem is that they are not obvious to the naked eye. In the United States, city-regions do not exist as scales of government; they are instead governed by a kaleidoscope of cities, counties, and special-purpose agencies; even these are sometimes just pass-through agencies for policies of states and the federal government. Some of the key interest groups that strongly impact regional politics and policies (such as business leaders or labor unions or even nongovernmental organizations [NGOs]) are not entirely local.

An early institutionalist analysis of differences in regional development is economist Benjamin Chinitz's (1961) comparison of New York and Pittsburgh. Chinitz observed that dominant local industries can strongly affect the cost and supply of labor, capital, and entrepreneurship available to other industries in the region. These feedbacks ultimately become institutionalized, in the sense that they attract in or crowd out distinctive types of labor, capital (firm organization), and entrepreneurial and managerial practices.

A rich literature on regional differences in institutions that attach to specific industrial sectors has also emerged. Saxenian (1994) showed that the San Francisco Bay Area conquered the IT sector in the 1980s because its firms were more flexible, less hierarchical in their management style, and more networked together than the early computer firms in Boston. Kenney and Mowery (2014) emphasize the different ways that business and research institutions network in regions, as the relational infrastructures that shape innovation and entrepreneurship. This insight is closely linked to research in organizational sociology that examines the evolution of organizations (such as firms) but also the genesis of new types of organizations, practices, and economic agents—known as "organizational fields" (Powell et al., 2012; Powell and Sandholtz, 2012; Padgett and Powell, 2012). Interregional differences in the emergence or reshaping of organizational fields will influence which activities regions generate or capture, thus shaping the landscape of economic specialization.

Widening the institutional arc, in the last 20 years scholars have investigated regional economic and civic networks. Feldman and Zoller (2012) quantify interregional differences in brokers and deal makers, such as venture capitalists, as a force in shaping the geography of knowledge-intensive industries. A different, "new regionalist" current argues that the strength of bridges between business leadership networks and civic networks (NGOs, community organizations, churches, etc.) shape the direction and strength of regional adaptation to external shocks (Safford, 2009; Benner and Pastor, 2014). Others argue that regional adaptation is a function of both the strength of major groups and how well they construct informal "bridges" or formal coalitions, with both coalescence and competition important to regional dynamism (Storper, 2005; Rodríguez-Pose and Storper, 2005).

It is not just the structure of networks, but the content of what they do that matters to development. Storper (1995) argued that the practices that coordinate firms, labor markets, universities, and other elements of an industry's organizational ecology are highly variable and often are tacit, informal, or conventional; they are the industry's "untraded interdependencies." Another aspect of content is how networks of people form their beliefs and worldviews about economic change. Do some networks of leaders and groups generate worldviews that are appropriate to successful economic transformation, while others block them? Or can worldviews change practices and encourage successful transformations? Where do such worldviews come from? Storper and Salais (1997) treat this subject in detail, and since then it has become part of the regional development literature under the rubric of the role of "epistemic communities" in economic transformation. There may also be a role for path-breaking individuals or "robust actors" to alter practices and perceptions of what is possible and hence to change what their networks do collectively (Padgett and Ansell, 1993).

Another key question for institutionalist approaches is how entrepreneurs emerge, what kinds of entrepreneurs emerge, and whether they flourish or are blocked by the regional economic environment (Acs et al., 2010; Fairlie,

2013; Chatterji et al., 2013; Kirzner, 1979). Capturing promising new industries involves the nurturing of the entrepreneurs who come up with breakthrough innovations or products, and transforming older ones involves spin-off firms who help the major existing firms remain dynamic (Klepper, 2009). Do some regions do this systematically better than others? Do the existing networks investigated by Chinitz shape these processes?

Taking all these institutional forces together—existing firms, innovation, networks and leadership, conventions and worldviews, entrepreneurship— economic sociologists speak of the emergence of "organizational fields" or ecologies that are hospitable to some types of activities and hostile to others (Powell et al., 2012; Padgett and Powell, 2012).

Organization of the Book

The four theoretical fields discussed in this chapter are summarized in Table 2.1. We draw on them in framing the investigation in this book, and by doing so we will shed light on how well they do as frameworks for explaining economic development. We have therefore organized the book as a sort of detective story. We consider all the prime suspects, drawn from development theory, RSUE, NEG, and institutionalism. In this "whodunit" story, we will track down clues, keep the evidence that is confirmed, exclude other hypotheses, and finish by connecting the dots.

Chapter 3 considers the evolution of the industrial composition of the two economies—regional economic specialization. Chapter 4 does the same for the workforce and its skills and the kinds of jobs carried out and wages. In these two data analysis chapters, we show that much of the seeming similarity among economies dissolves away when we disaggregate capital (industries and firms) and labor (skills, tasks, individuals). Chapters 3 and 4 draw heavily on economic geography and urban economics.

Chapter 5 changes the style of investigation from mostly deductive reasoning and statistical evidence to historical case studies. It shows how key tradable industries in the two regions emerged and how they responded very differently to challenges and opportunities generated by the decline of the postwar economy and the advent of the New Economy. The two regions developed very different basic organizational ecologies in the period under examination.

TABLE 2.1 Four theoretical frameworks for the study of economic development

Theoretical frameworks	Basic causes of development	Convergence/ divergence	Sorting (external causes) versus interaction (local causes)
International development studies (IDS)	Factors, institutions, trade, factor mobility, policy, technology	Trade, factor mobility for convergence; but many institutional, cost, technology barriers	Both
Regional science/ urban econom- ics (RSUE)	Sorting of people, housing mar- kets, factor costs; congestion costs; amenities/ environment	Emphasizes conver- gence; "real" wage/ utility convergence; population versus income tradeoff	Sorting more than interaction; interaction of individuals more than firms
New Economic Geography (NEG)	Trade and transaction costs of industries; agglomeration forc- es; local ("home") markets; specializa- tion of production; institutions and history matter	Tension between con- vergence forces from mobility and diver- gence due to innova- tion, new industries and clustering	Interaction among firms, between firms and local environment as important as sorting
Institutions/ economic sociology	Creation of skills; entrepreneurship and innovation; business and civic networks; organi- zational forms and practices; world- views, epistemic communities	Institutions gener- ate divergence by influencing specialization	Mostly local (feed- backs and inter- actions), but can be influenced by external forces

We then examine institutional forces in more detail. In Chapter 6, we consider the most obvious dimension of this: economic development policies and the role of local governments. In Chapter 7, we turn to how the major organized actors in the two regions perceived their problems and opportunities and defined their policy agendas. Chapter 8 quantifies the structures of business and civic networks, or what we call the "relational infrastructure" of the two regions.

The final section of the book pulls the analysis together and extends it. Chapter 9 connects the dots and argues which forces made the decisive contributions to divergence. In Chapter 10 we offer some reflections on how Los Angeles and San Francisco can maintain or improve their performance, lessons that are applicable widely to city-regions everywhere. The final chapter then comes full circle to the four theories discussed in the present chapter, to think about what we have learned about the academic field of economic development analysis in general. It suggests several ways that theory and methodology can be improved in the field of economic development.

3 The Motor of Divergence

High-Wage or Low-Wage Specialization

Understanding Specialization

Modern economies have a core set of activities whose output they export to other places. In turn, they import specialized goods and services from their trading partners. This division of labor between specialized regions and countries is a key source of development. Specialization raises productivity and enables more varieties of products and services to be generated than would be possible in the absence of specialization and trade. Surrounding the core of tradables is the local activity for home consumption. Tradable industries sometimes use nontradable local inputs (the film industry uses local carpenters), and nontradable final output industries sometimes draw on imported inputs (dry cleaners use imported chemicals and machinery). But in the final analysis, economies are highly identified with, and their development shaped by, their core specializations.

Consider the film industry in Los Angeles. Producing movies in Hollywood (essentially, product development) is a labor-intensive process, but once a movie is created, it can be very cheaply exported to consumers worldwide. Thus, employment growth in Hollywood depends not so much on the desire of Angelenos to consume filmed entertainment as on global consumer demand for Hollywood films. This stands in contrast to one's neighborhood dry-cleaning establishment, whose market is limited by the local population's income and preference for dry cleaning. It is prohibitively costly for a resident of Oakland to have her dry cleaning performed in Cincinnati. For similar reasons, gyms, K–12 schooling, the construction industry, and restaurants serve mainly local customers and depend largely on regional demand and income levels. The growth of nontradables in the long run can come either from increasing their productivity (hence stimulating local demand through lower prices) or from increasing regional income. The growth of tradable activities is not constrained by the size of the local economy but by evolution of global demand in conjunction with the region's share of global production, which is determined by the proportion of global production capacity that is clustered in the region.

The relationship between employment in the tradable sector and the size of the nontradable sector is known as the "multiplier effect." Multipliers vary widely. For example, in recent years, when the traditional manufacturing sector adds one job, 1.6 jobs are in turn added in the regional nontradable sectors. The New Economy—meaning innovation-oriented high-technology work— has a higher multiplier, generating almost five additional local jobs for each new core tradable job. This is because such workers in such industries are highly paid and because the industry itself uses more locally clustered inputs and services for each unit of output (Moretti, 2010, 2012). Thus, specialization causes incomes between city-regions to diverge by combining two effects: the differences in their core tradable wages and the different multipliers that they generate.

Across the developed world, due to the selective expansion of New Economy industries in certain regions since the 1980s, the income gaps between prosperous and struggling regional economies have widened. This stands in contrast to the 1960s and 1970s, where interregional differences in incomes in most countries diminished, as Old Economy industries matured and spread out. Of course, no region can enjoy the effect of high incomes from its clusters of high-wage industries forever; all regions ultimately face downturns as industries mature, become more routinized and cost-competitive, and spread out.

The dot-com boom of the 1990s provides a dramatic example of how specialization can shape regional economic performance. Galbraith and Hale (2008) demonstrate that the bulk of national income growth in the United States between 1994 and 2000 was driven by large income gains in just *five* of the country's 3,144 counties: Santa Clara County, California; San Mateo County, California; San Francisco County, California; King County,

Washington; and the borough of Manhattan, New York.[1] These are very specialized local economies. The three Bay Area counties, as well as King County (Seattle) in Washington housed the core agglomerations of the U.S. high-technology boom, while Manhattan is a principal center of the global financial system.

Bringing all this together, the best effects of specialization on regional per capita income emerge in regions that contain a high proportion of tradable sectors, and where a high proportion of the tradables are in turn innovative and based on nonroutine and highly skilled work. By contrast, regions that specialize in activities with low innovation or skill levels or routinized work will have relatively low per capita income.

Researchers have long debated whether it is better, in the long run, for an economy to be diversified or specialized (Beaudry and Schiffauerova, 2009). Diversification is said to offer more resilience when principal activities turn down, but there is no empirical evidence for the proposition that more diversified regions have better long-term growth prospects, whether in quantity of employment or income levels. Glaeser's (2003) long history of Boston's economy suggests that it is successive respecialization in new tradables that is the key. Most major American urban regions are today about equally diversified in broad terms; it is not their *overall* level of specialization that is so different as much as the *type* of specialization and the skills and wages of the jobs they generate (Kemeny and Storper, 2014).

There is considerable confusion about how to appropriately measure specialization and for what purpose. First of all, specialization can be measured as a *share* of the local economy ("relative specialization") or considered as the *absolute size* of any sector in the local economy. Relative versus absolute specialization generate very different rankings of regions, because a small region can have a large local share of an industry with a very small local cluster compared to a big region, where a small share can represent a big cluster. What fragmentary evidence we do have suggests that in the economy as a whole, bigger clusters have higher wages when compared to smaller clusters *within the same industry* (Kemeny and Storper, 2014). However, for any given region, it could still be better for per capita income if a high share of local employment is in high-wage industry, even if its local cluster is smaller in absolute terms than those of bigger regions.

Analysts also frequently use a measure of relative specialization that compares the local economy's shares in activities to their shares of the national economy; this is known as a location quotient (LQ). This can be interesting in descriptive terms, to see what regions do compared to other regions in the country. But it says nothing about the per capita income effects of specialization, since a region could have a high LQ in something that is low-wage, or it could have a high LQ in an industry that is mostly quite spread out, leading to a high LQ in a local cluster that is too small to seriously impact local per capita income. The most sensible way to see the effects of specialization on per capita income is to identify the tradable industries that are the most important local employers and then analyze the type of jobs and wages they offer.

There is an additional challenge to understanding specialization concerning the definition of industries. If data categories are used that are too broad, then they will lump together different activities and make regions appear more similar than they really are, but if data categories are too detailed, they will separate activities that are closely related and miss their clusters. In order to generate an accurate picture of specialization, we need to do a deep dive into the data to solve both these problems.

Specialization of the Los Angeles and San Francisco Regional Economies

At first glance, when looked at in a broad way without much detail, the overall economic structures of San Francisco and Los Angeles appear quite similar. According to data from the U.S. Bureau of Economic Affairs, services and manufacturing each made up around 23 percent of total employment in Los Angeles and San Francisco in 1970. In contrast, service activities now make up half the jobs in both regions; government is now the second largest source of employment at just over 10 percent, followed by retail, then manufacturing, and finally finance and real estate.[2]

Mirroring a trend evident throughout the richest economies in the world, manufacturing employment has declined because of automation and relocation of firms to regions in the South and West of the United States or offshored to developing countries (Grossman and Rossi-Hansberg, 2008; Blinder, 2009; Blinder and Krueger, 2013). The Greater Los Angeles region remains an important manufacturing center in terms of the absolute number of workers employed, but manufacturing's share is now less than 10 percent in both the Bay Area and Los Angeles. However, Los Angeles's loss has been much greater than San Francisco's, because its share at the beginning of deindustrialization was higher.

In the United States, industries are described using the North American Industrial Classification System (NAICS), which replaced the Standard Industrial Classification (SIC) in 1997.[3] In both systems, general industry groups, such as manufacturing or construction, are indicated using two-digit codes (under NAICS, these would be 31–33, and 23, respectively). With each additional digit, more specificity is captured. The two-digit industry "construction" contains three-digit industries such as 236, "construction of buildings," which in turn contains four-digit industries such as 2361, "residential construction"; six-digit sectors such as 236115, "New Single-Family Housing Construction (except For-Sale Builders)"; and all the way to ten-digit sectors. The NAICS codes are thus like a system of Russian dolls, each level nested within the higher, bigger category. Unless fairly detailed sectors (four digits or more) are analyzed, there is a high risk of lumping together activities that are dissimilar in wages, growth prospects, products, and linkages to other sectors in the economy. Imagine, for example, that we compare the two-digit finance, insurance, and real estate (FIRE) sector in New York; Hartford, Connecticut; and Los Angeles. The three metropolitan areas have similar shares of this two-digit industry. But FIRE means different activities in the three cities, dominated by high-level investment banking and securities in New York City, the insurance industry in Hartford, and the residential real estate lending industry in Greater Los Angeles. If we were instead to show the four-to-six-digit FIRE subsectors, we would see that the three regions are differently specialized, leading to a completely opposite conclusion from the two-digit analysis. Ranking the three cities in their share of two-digit FIRE activity is ranking apples and oranges.[4] Much research on large numbers of city-regions uses these aggregated industry categories, however, because using more detailed ones greatly increases the amount of data needed to depict specialization and causes problems with modeling. The advantage of our deep dive into two regions is that we can deal with this complexity and obtain more accurate results.

And yet there is such a thing as too much detail or disaggregation when it comes to identifying specialization. Individual activities can be functional components of larger regional agglomerations that are closely interrelated through supply linkages, sharing of a labor pool, information spillovers, and co-growth over time. When these close relations correspond to geographical clustering, the regional tradable cluster will involve a coherent specialization that cuts across many NAICS codes, making it easy to underestimate the size of a specialized cluster. Consider, for instance, the ten largest tradable sectors in San Francisco and Los Angeles in 1970 and 2010. In 1970, the Bay Area already employed large numbers of workers in the production of semiconductors and electronic capacitors. The SIC system classified these activities into a number of seemingly disparate industries, yet in the San Francisco region they are obviously part of a single information technology industry that shares labor, inputs, and knowledge. By treating each separate industry as if it were a distinct specialization, we would significantly underestimate the scale of and strength of the Bay Area's high-tech specialization.

Following this logic, we group together closely related industries to capture the full extent of specializations. Table 3.1 (see below) presents the results from the standard, narrowly defined sectors.[5] Table 3.2 (see below) then reports the more accurate picture of specialization, where related activities have been combined. In 1970, both Los Angeles and San Francisco hosted an array of high-technology industries. In Los Angeles, high technology jobs were chiefly found in aerospace. The aircraft sector alone in Los Angeles accounted for nearly 3 percent of regional employment in 1970, while "Aircraft equipment" also ranked in Los Angeles's ten largest tradable sectors by employment.[6] Table 3.2 combines the sectors pertaining to the production of vehicles, subsystems, and components that are necessary for atmospheric or space flight, into the "Aerospace" agglomeration (Stekler, 1965). The "Aerospace" agglomeration in Los Angeles in 1970 employed over 100,000 workers, nearly 3.5 percent of the regional labor force. According to complementary (but more aggregate) data from the Bureau of Economic Affairs, just over 350,000 workers were employed in related industries of the "Aircraft and parts," "National security," and "Ordnance" sectors in Los Angeles in 1970, out of a total employment base of approximately 4 million—nearly 8 percent of the workforce.

By 1970, high-technology manufacturing in San Francisco was already concentrated in sectors related to information technology, including "Electronic computing equipment," "Electronic components NEC," "Semiconductors," and "Communication transmitting equipment." This was the nascent Silicon Valley. However, in 1970 Los Angeles was also specialized in information technology. In 1970, San Francisco employed 38,621 workers, or 2.7 percent of its workforce in this area, while Los Angeles employed a comparable proportion

TABLE 3.1 Specialization: The ten largest tradable industries by employment, 1970 (SIC) and 2010 (NAICS)

Los Angeles, 1970 (4-digit SIC)		San Francisco, 1970 (4-digit SIC)	
Tradable industry	Employment share (%)	Tradable industry	Employment share (%)
Aircraft	2.7	Trucking, except local	1.5
Trucking, except local	1.2	Semiconductors	0.9
Electronic components NEC*	0.8	Business consulting services	0.9
Communication transmitting equipment	0.8	Wholesalers NEC	0.7
Business consulting services	0.8	Electronic components NEC	0.7
Aircraft equipment	0.8	Electronic computing equipment	0.6
Wholesalers NEC	0.7	Truck equipment	0.6
Electronic computing equipment	0.7	Communication transmitting equipment	0.5
Truck equipment	0.6	Commercial machines and equipment	0.5
Motion picture production, except TV	0.5	Electric measuring instruments	0.5
Total	**9.6**	**Total**	**7.3**

Los Angeles, 2010 (6-digit NAICS)		San Francisco, 2010 (6-digit NAICS)	
Tradable industry	Employment share (%)	Tradable industry	Employment share (%)
Motion picture and video production	1.4	Software publishers	1.9
Hotels and motels	1.4	Custom computer programming services	1.8
General warehousing and storage	0.6	Electronic parts and equipment wholesalers	1.7
Computer systems design services	0.5	Computer systems design services	1.6
Custom computer programming services	0.4	Hotels and motels	1.5
Freight transportation arrangement	0.4	R&D in physical, engineering, and life sciences (not biotechnology)	1.5
Women's clothing wholesalers	0.4	Computer and peripheral wholesalers	0.9
Women's, girls', and infants' cut and sew apparel contractors	0.4	Data processing, hosting, and related services	0.6

(continued)

TABLE 3.1 *(continued)*

Los Angeles, 2010 (6-digit NAICS)		San Francisco, 2010 (6-digit NAICS)	
Tradable industry	*Employment share (%)*	*Tradable industry*	*Employment share (%)*
Other aircraft parts and auxiliary equipment	0.3	Semiconductor and related device manufacturing	0.5
Electronic parts and equipment wholesalers	0.3	Wineries	0.4
Total	**6.1**	**Total**	**12.4**

SOURCE: Data from *County Business Patterns.*

NOTE: 1970 and 2010 data are imperfectly comparable due to the switch from four-digit SIC codes to six-digit NAICS codes in 1997.

*NEC: Not elsewhere classified.

TABLE 3.2 Tradable industry groups (agglomerations) in 1970 and 2010

Group	Los Angeles, 1970		San Francisco, 1970	
	Employees	*Employment share (%)*	*Employees*	*Employment share (%)*
Information technology	81,872	2.6	38,621	2.7
Aerospace and defense	108,083	3.4	455	0.03
Logistics	39,851	1.3	21,313	1.5
Entertainment	22,978	0.7	2,171	0.15
Apparel	56,965	1.8	7,806	0.06

Group	Los Angeles, 2010		San Francisco, 2010	
	Employees	*Employment share (%)*	*Employees*	*Employment share (%)*
Information technology	153,524	2.7	255,334	10.2
Aerospace and defense	47,960	0.9	735	0.02
Logistics	129,651	2.3	23,505	0.9
Entertainment	141,025	2.5	14,686	0.5
Apparel	50,788	0.9	819	0.03

SOURCE: Authors' calculations based on collections of four-digit SIC codes (1970) and six-digit NAICS codes (2010) using *County Business Patterns* (the precise definitions of these agglomerations are available from the authors).

of its workforce, which amounted to just over 80,000 workers. In other words, both regions were strongly specialized in IT equipment, and in terms of absolute jobs, Los Angeles's agglomeration dwarfed that of the Bay Area.

Table 3.1 reveals some other key areas of focus for each economy in 1970. In Los Angeles, these consisted of logistics ("Trucking, except local") and the film industry ("Motion picture production, except TV"). Greater Los Angeles also had a big apparel industry, which had no single component large enough to be listed in Table 3.1, though the cluster of interrelated apparel activities employed nearly 2 percent of Los Angeles's workforce. As befits major urban centers, Los Angeles and San Francisco were both focused on business services ("Business consulting services"), as well as some Old Economy manufacturing ("Truck equipment," and in the case of San Francisco, "Commercial machines and equipment"). All in all, the Greater Los Angeles economy in 1970 had large clusters in knowledge-intensive industries such as aerospace, IT, and entertainment. San Francisco showed signs of an emerging focus on information technology, but not in a manner that strongly distinguishes it from Los Angeles. Overall, Greater Los Angeles had a bigger and more concentrated tradable sector.

The situation reversed dramatically over the following decades. By 2010, seven of the ten largest six-digit NAICS industries in San Francisco were integral parts of Silicon Valley's information technology cluster.[7] The information technology agglomeration, documented for 2010 in the lower panel of Table 3.2, came to account for over 250,000 jobs in the Bay Area and over 10 percent of total regional employment.

Greater Los Angeles followed the opposite trajectory. By 2010, it had become a less specialized regional economy than in 1970, and the region appears much less focused on high-wage New Economy activities than San Francisco. The Southland's largest single industry in 2010 was in "Motion picture and video production," which employed 1.4 percent of its workforce. Though aerospace defined the Los Angeles economy in 1970, by 2010 the "Other aircraft parts and auxiliary equipment" was only the ninth largest sector and employed a mere 0.3 percent of the regional workforce. Even the broader Los Angeles aerospace agglomeration in 2010, documented in the lower panel of Table 3.2, employed less than half the workers it did in 1970, while in relative terms it shrank to less than 1 percent of the regional employment base.

Los Angeles retained its foothold in information technology, as evidenced by its considerable employment in such categories as "Computer systems design services," "Custom computer programming services," and "Electronic parts and equipment wholesalers," with the IT agglomeration employing about 150,000 workers, or about 3 percent of the regional workforce (compared to its 10 percent share of the Bay Area). Los Angeles developed a larger logistics industry ("General warehousing and storage" and "Freight transportation arrangement"). Logistics activity is organized around the expanded Los Angeles–Long Beach port complex and the inland warehousing, dispatching, and rail freight forwarding industries. Defined in terms of the number of 20-foot equivalent containers,[8] Los Angeles County boasts the largest container seaport in the United States and the seventh largest in the world. As a result, by 2010, logistics employed nearly 130,000 workers, making up just over 2 percent of regional employment.

The Quality of Specialization: Wages

The two regions also had diverging quality of their respective specializations. Table 3.3 presents estimates of average annual wages for the tradable six-digit NAICS specialization of each region in 2010. Workers in the principal tradable sectors in the Bay Area earned considerably higher wages than those who worked in the largest sectors in Los Angeles. The best-paid large sector in Greater Los Angeles is "Computer systems design services," where the average worker in 2010 earned $90,874. In the Bay Area, the best-paid large sector in the Bay Area is "Software publishers," where the average worker earned $169,432. In 2010, eight of the ten largest tradable sectors in the Bay Area had salaries over $100,000, while not a single one of the top ten in Greater Los Angeles reached that baseline.

Equally importantly, average wages vary considerably across the two regions even within the same detailed sectors (for instance, "Computer systems design services," "Electronic parts and equipment wholesalers," and "Custom computer programming services"). Even when we break them down into fine subsectors, the two regions' electronics industries are very different. Orange County in Greater Los Angeles hosts a large high-technology agglomeration, accounting for as much as 10 percent of the county's total employment, and is one of the biggest high-technology clusters in the United States.[9] But the data here suggest that though both regions produce computer equipment, Silicon Valley is involved primarily in high value-added activities such as design, while Orange County is doing more routine work that demands less skill and pays lower wages.

TABLE 3.3 Average wages in ten tradable sectors with highest employment, 2010

Greater Los Angeles		San Francisco Bay Area	
Industry	Wages ($)	Industry	Wages ($)
Motion picture and video production	69,016	Software publishers	169,432
Hotels and motels	26,217	Custom computer programming services	111,648
General warehousing and storage	40,878	Electronic parts and equipment wholesalers	139,661
Computer systems design services	90,874	Computer systems design services	111,312
Women's clothing wholesalers	50,931	Hotels and motels	30,260
Custom computer programming services	89,295	R&D in physical, engineering, and life sciences (not biotechnology)	133,834
Freight transportation arrangement	50,684	Computer and peripheral wholesalers	155,961
Women's, girls', and infants' cut and sew apparel contractors	18,548	Data processing, hosting, and related services	120,464
Other aircraft parts and auxiliary equipment	65,685	Semiconductor and related device manufacturing	131,059
Electronic parts and equipment wholesalers	77,947	Wineries	54,954

SOURCE: Authors' calculations based on data from *County Business Patterns*.
NOTE: Sectors featured in both regions in italics. Wages are in nominal 2010 dollars.

If we take the regional economies as a whole, Angelenos earned wages that were, on average, 70 percent of the average worker in the Bay Area. This overall gap is smaller than what we have just observed within the tradable sector. This is because wages in locally serving nontradable sectors are closer together than are the wages in their specialized, tradable sectors.[10] But this only reinforces the importance of differences in the tradable part of the economy. Such differences were too small to be decisive in 1970. Major divergence emerged in average regional wages in subsequent decades, propelled by powerful divergence in wages in the tradable sectors.

Specialization and Innovation Rents

Another way to gauge the nature of a region's specialization pattern is to examine its innovations. Highly innovative industries have high wages. The

newness of their products allows them to have prices based on rarity, a phenomenon known as "economic rents." Regions that host sectors in which
there is considerable innovation will therefore do better than regions that do
not (Storper, 2013).

Patent data shed light on the innovation-intensity of our two regions' industries. Patents are a reliable but incomplete measure of innovation. Patents
do not directly indicate the market value of inventions; in practice, some
patents represent innovations worth untold fortunes, while others are largely
worthless.[11] Despite these limitations, patents provide a useful paper trail for
the production of new ideas.

Figure 3.1 shows that until around 1990, Los Angeles had a higher total
number of patents than San Francisco. After the early 1990s, patents granted
in the Bay Area grew dramatically. By 2005, nearly three times as many patents were granted in San Francisco as in Los Angeles. In 1970, the Bay Area
produced 40 patents per 100,000 inhabitants, increasing to 153 in 2005. Comparable figures for Los Angeles are 30 in 1970, declining to 24 in 2005. On a per
capita basis, Los Angeles thus patented at 75 percent of the Bay Area's rate in
1970, but this moderate difference grows dramatically in the twenty-first century, with Los Angeles's rate dropping to only 15.6 percent of the Bay Area's.

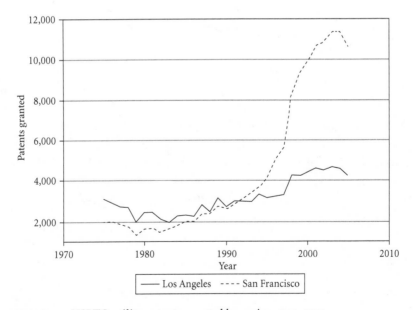

FIGURE 3.1 USPTO utility patents granted by region, 1975–2005

Patent counts might overstate the gap in innovation, because many innovations in filmed entertainment and other creative sectors in Los Angeles are not patentable. But this is also true of one of the Bay Area's specializations, software, so there could be understatement of the Bay Area's advantage as well. There is no doubt, however, that the Bay Area has achieved a dramatic lead over Greater Los Angeles in commercially valuable innovations.[12]

Looking inside specific sectors confirms this interpretation.[13] Figure 3.2 provides counts of patents granted in two IT industries: Computers and Communications, and Electrical and Electronic. In each patent class, the two regions produced a roughly similar number of patents until the mid- to late-1980s. After that point, the Bay Area overtook Los Angeles. In computers and communications San Francisco produced four times as many patents as Los Angeles in 2005; on a per capita basis, the Bay Area was ten times as inventive as Greater Los Angeles.

The Work of Regions: Specialization by Task Content

Another way to confirm that the Bay Area's economy is focused on more sophisticated activities than that of Los Angeles is to examine the nature of tasks embodied in its mix of occupations. Since the 1930s, the U.S. Department of Labor has described and codified the task content of occupations in its *Dictionary of Occupational Titles* (DOT).[14] Researchers have subsequently distilled this task information into higher-order concepts like routineness and abstract thinking. When combined with data describing the mix of occupations in industries, regions, or nationwide, these data can reveal the evolving shape of labor demand (Autor et al., 2003; Autor and Dorn, 2013). Distinctions between routine or nonroutine activities, as well as between cognitive or manual work are of particular interest.[15] Jobs consisting of nonroutine work involve complex environments with few universal rules, whereas routine work is guided by the application of rules and protocols. Manual work is chiefly physical, while cognitive work is more mental. Combining these dimensions, we can say, for instance, that the job of a stockbroker requires a lot of nonroutine cognitive work, specifically in terms of interacting with others and quantitative analysis; equally, from the DOT we learn that this particular occupation has a low proportion of routine manual and cognitive tasks.

In the late twentieth and early twenty-first centuries, the economies of wealthy nations have seen a steady increase in the wage premium for workers

a) Computers and communication

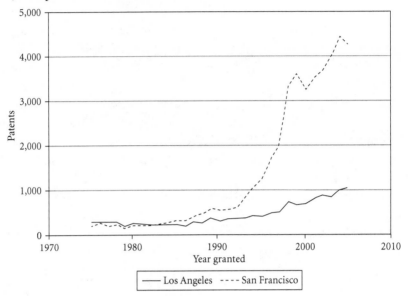

b) Electrical and electronic

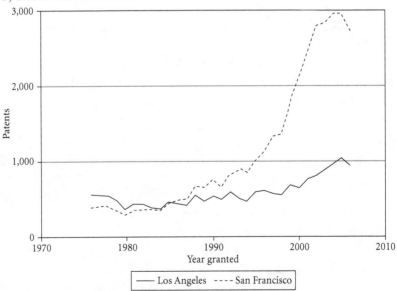

FIGURE 3.2 USPTO utility patents granted by region in two industries, 1975–2005

SOURCE: Authors' calculations based on National Bureau of Economic Research patent data, as cleaned and organized, from Sonn and Storper, 2008.

in occupations requiring performance of nonroutine cognitive tasks (Autor et al., 2003; Goos and Manning, 2007). Because jobs of this kind are hard to embed in simple rules, they require considerable education; for these same reasons, such jobs are not easily automated and replaced by machines (Autor et al., 2003).[16] They also often require face-to-face interaction and are therefore resistant to being offshored (Storper and Venables, 2004; Kemeny and Rigby, 2012; Ebenstein et al., 2009; Blinder and Krueger, 2013). Some of these same features are also present in nonroutine manual work, such as that performed by skilled tradespeople. These occupations are not as highly remunerated as nonroutine cognitive work, but they are on average better-paid than routine manual jobs, especially in relation to the relatively low formal education levels they require.

Routine work, whether chiefly manual or cognitive, requires less education and training and tends to be found in industries that are capital-intensive, where machines more easily replace workers. In addition, in many such industries, firms operate on a large scale, producing standardized products that can be cheaply shipped to distant markets. As a result, these activities are also often located in areas where land and/or workers are relatively cheap, and in general they are less clustered than sectors with a high level of nonroutine cognitive work content. All these circumstances combine so that workers in routine occupations are less well paid than workers who perform nonroutine tasks.

Building on the approach taken by Autor and Dorn (2013), we use data from two sources. To capture occupation-specific measures of the extent to which a particular occupation demands abstract tasks—our proxy for cognitive nonroutineness—we use data from the 1991 revision of the DOT. We merge this with snapshots of regional occupational structure, using population data from the Census Bureau.[17] These data permit the construction of summary measures of the nonroutineness of an entire regional economy, as well as of a particular local agglomeration. Table 3.4 presents a comparison of several industries in which both regions are specialized.[18] Higher values indicate more nonroutineness. The table shows that within these industries, San Francisco's occupational structure implies greater nonroutine thinking than in Los Angeles.[19] The nonroutineness gap is quite large for "Computers/data processing services" and "Electrical machinery," which are areas of particular specialization in the Bay Area. For comparison, differences in nonroutineness are modest in "Legal services" and "Insurance," in which neither

TABLE 3.4 Nonroutine cognitive task intensities in selected regional industries, 2006–2008

Sector	Nonroutineness		
	Los Angeles	*San Francisco*	*United States*
Computers/data processing services	5.21	6.11	5.54
Electrical machinery	3.63	4.70	3.64
Legal services	2.92	2.99	2.95
Insurance	3.66	3.67	3.72

SOURCE: Authors' calculations based on IPUMS 3 percent *American Community Survey* sample for 2006–2008, using person-level sample weights.

NOTE: Higher values of nonroutineness indicate that the occupational mix in an industry is tilted toward jobs that require greater nonroutine interaction and analytics. Each outcome reported here had an acceptably small linearized standard error. T-tests indicate that the difference in mean task values for computers/data processing and electrical machinery are statistically significant at a 5 percent level; the differences are not significant for the other two selected sectors.

region specializes. Notice that the two regions differ in the type of work done even *within* their industries, underscoring our earlier point about the importance of observing these economies by disaggregating them in a finely grained way.

Does this different level of nonroutine tasks predominate in the two regional economies as a whole? We answer this question by constructing regionwide nonroutineness indices, taking into account the all the industries in each metropolitan area. Equation 3.1 builds this measure as follows:

$$NR_{jt} = \sum_i \overline{nr}_{jit} \left(e_{jit} \bigg/ \sum_i e_{jit} \right) \qquad (3.1)$$

where regions are indexed by j and time by t; $\overline{nr}$ is the mean requirement for nonroutine cognitive activity among all sampled workers in industry i in a region; and e indicates total employment. Hence, NR is a weighted sum of the level of nonroutine cognitive requirements in each industry and region, where the weight is the employment share of each industry in the overall regional economy in question. NR therefore gives an overall sense of the sophistication associated with the job mix of each region.

Table 3.5 shows that in 1970, the economies of the Bay Area and Los Angeles had similar levels of sophistication, as measured by nonroutineness.[20] Both regions' task mix was more nonroutine than that of the United States as

TABLE 3.5 Aggregate regional nonroutine cognitive task indices

Region	1970	1980	1990	2000	2006–2008
Los Angeles	2.58	2.54	2.78	2.88	2.82
San Francisco	2.61	2.68	3.11	3.57	3.47
United States	2.40	2.41	2.75	2.99	2.95

SOURCE: Authors' calculations based on IPUMS 1 percent 1970 metro sample; 5 percent 1980, 1990, and 2000 samples; and the 3 percent *American Community Survey* sample for 2006–2008.
NOTE: In each case, person-level sample weights are used to estimate task means. Higher values of nonroutineness indicate that the occupational mix in a region is tilted toward jobs that require greater nonroutine interaction and analytics, here taken as a proxy for sophistication. Each outcome reported here had an acceptably small linearized standard error.

a whole; this indicates that in terms of labor endowments, both should have been well positioned to enter the New Economy. San Francisco and Los Angeles then diverged strongly between 1980 and 1990, and though Los Angeles improved in absolute terms, it fell below the U.S. average by 1990 and never again rose above it. Meanwhile, the Bay Area's sophistication surges ahead of that of Los Angeles and the United States, sagging a bit in the dot-com bust of the early 2000s, along with the country as a whole. The Bay Area's lead is large from somewhere in the 1980s onward.

A region's overall level of nonroutine cognitive work is a combination of how much it specializes in industries where nonroutine cognitive work is especially important, in software as opposed to logistics for instance, and whether the region's firms in that industry are positioned in particularly nonroutine segments of the industry in question. Equation 3.2 controls for differences due to interindustry specialization patterns by using national industry averages of industrial nonroutineness combined with region-specific employment weights in each industry to see whether there is a difference between the real and expected levels.

$$\overrightarrow{NR}_{jt} = \sum_i \overrightarrow{nr}_{USAit} \left(e_{jit} \Big/ \sum_i e_{jit} \right) \qquad (3.2)$$

In Figure 3.3 a score of 1 indicates a level of nonroutine tasks precisely in line with national averages; higher values point to greater-than-average regional sophistication. In 1970, both regions are more sophisticated than one would expect on the basis of the industries in which they are specialized. Los Angeles's deviation from the expected value is just slightly below the Bay

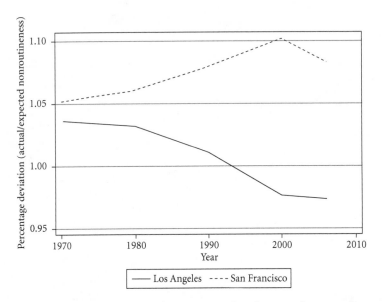

FIGURE 3.3 Percentage deviation between actual and expected nonroutineness

Area's. Between 1980 and 1990, Los Angeles's actual nonroutineness premium begins to decline relative to that of the United States, and then it turns sharply down in the 1990s. By the end of the period, Los Angeles is less sophisticated than what we would expect from its industry mix, while the Bay Area is well above its expected level.

Thus, Los Angeles and San Francisco differ not only in terms of the average sophistication of jobs in the industries their economies host, but also in the specific sophistication of the regional versions of those industries. From yet another angle, we clearly see the evolution of the gap in the quality of specialization of the two regions.

Alternative Measures of Specialization: Technological Relatedness

We noted earlier that one potential limitation of using standard industrial classifications is that either they might lump together unlike or unrelated activities, or the opposite, they might miss close relationships between activities. We have already corrected for the first potential error, by disaggregating into four- and six-digit NAICS industries. To deal with the second problem, we have to identify hidden relationships that are not identified in NAICS codes (Powell et al., 2012; Frenken et al., 2007; Hidalgo et al., 2007).[21]

One way to do this is to map connections among the knowledge bases that underlie industries. When patents of different kinds tend to be found in the same region, we can say they are more likely to rest upon a common knowledge base. Ó hUallacháin (2012) examines concentration and co-location patterns in U.S. cities of 35 groups of patents between 1995 and 1999, with groups defined on the basis of underlying technological similarity. San Francisco emerges as the most inventive region, leading the United States in shares of patenting in semiconductor devices (29 percent), information storage (33 percent), computer peripherals (25 percent), computer hardware and software (25 percent), biotechnology (16 percent) and nuclear/X-rays (14 percent). The Bay Area is also the most inventive region in electrical lighting, miscellaneous electrical and electronics, surgery and medical instruments; electrical devices; coating; measuring and testing; and power systems. By contrast, innovation activities in Los Angeles are dispersed over many more areas, with weaker leadership in any: it ranks among the top five metropolitan areas in 26 of 35 subcategories, but it leads only in the broad category "amusement devices." The most highly related knowledge bases among all patents are in fact electronics technologies, confirming our point that they form part of a single regional specialized agglomeration. No equivalent focus exists in the Greater Los Angeles economy.

Rigby (2012) builds indices of knowledge relatedness among 438 primary patent classes to characterize the technological coherence of regions on the basis of their patenting activity. A patent class is closely related to another class when the patents in different classes cite each other often. Relatedness index values for 1975 find Los Angeles with a slightly more cohesive knowledge base than San Francisco. By 2005, however, the situation has reversed: the Bay Area has become considerably more specialized than Los Angeles in its knowledge space. Given evidence of this kind, San Francisco appears to have both higher levels and greater internal relatedness of its patenting activity; it is therefore not only better specialized but much more focused than Los Angeles.

Conclusion: Focus and Sophistication

The Los Angeles and San Francisco regions started out with many similarities in their economies and shared roots in technology-intensive production. In

1970, both regions had strong clusters in tradable manufacturing activities, including aerospace, defense, and electronics, with Los Angeles somewhat more specialized overall. In both relative and absolute terms, the largest set of tradable clusters was located in Los Angeles, encompassing the aerospace, defense, and entertainment sectors. In relative terms, the Bay Area had a fairly large concentration of employment in communication technology fields and a high level of innovation. In absolute terms, however, employment in these sectors was considerably smaller than the Los Angeles agglomeration.

Sharp divergence in their levels of specialization in tradable industries and the type of tradables emerged in subsequent decades. The Bay Area grew into a more and better specialized regional economy, focused on knowledge economy activities that require sophisticated tasks. After the end of the Cold War, Los Angeles never re-established its previous levels of focus in technology-related industry. Indeed, rather than strongly respecializing in *any* other sectors, the Greater Los Angeles regional economy lost its focus. It now resembles a pointillist painting. Moreover, Los Angeles has developed higher shares of low-wage sectors like textiles and developed bigger middle-wage, middle-skill activities in port-related logistics and international trade.

We also showed that typical methods of analysis would miss many of these differences. If examined using the usual broad sectoral categories (two- and three-digit NAICS) and typical indices of diversification, these two regions would mistakenly appear to resemble one another and neither would seem exceptional compared to other major metropolitan regions. Considered with disaggregated categories, corroborated through data on wages, patents, the sophistication of work tasks, and patent relatedness, we can be confident that the two economies have sharply diverged in the level and nature of their specializations. These results call into question many of the statements commonly made about regional economies, and especially the rankings of regions in different industrial sectors.

Interestingly, leaders in Los Angeles do not clearly understand how far they have slipped down the ladder of sophistication, nor how poorly the region has done in capturing the key tradable knowledge economy functions and activities that have emerged since 1980. One business leader we interviewed claimed that Orange County could be considered the most important high-tech cluster in America, in terms of diversity and patenting.[22] On the basis of patents, this is certainly incorrect. Moreover, in contrast to what leaders in Orange County think of their high-tech economy, entrepreneurs and elites in Silicon Valley as well as most academic experts on the subject do not consider Orange County to rank highly in the hierarchy of American regional technology clusters.[23]

Nor can the mediocre performance of the Greater Los Angeles economy be pinned principally on the decline of the aerospace cluster. Estimating this involves a complicated counterfactual, because gains or losses in direct labor demand involve gain or loss to employment of residents what would have been increased employment of in-migrants, and therefore employment change has impacts on population. Moreover, direct employment gains or losses induce counterpart gains or losses in the locally serving industries (multiplier effects) whose growth or decline also involves a combination of in-migration or out-migration.

Direct employment loss in aerospace in the 1990s was 147,000, of which 60 percent out-migrated (Scott, 2010b). Using figures from the U.S. Bureau of Economic Affairs and *County Business Patterns*, the per capita effect can be estimated. The reported actual personal income of Greater Los Angeles was $496 billion in 2000. Had all the aerospace jobs stayed and paid an average of $88,000 per year, Los Angeles personal income would have been almost $13 billion higher in 2000. In addition, assuming a multiplier of 2 to local employment and an average wage of $40,000 per local service job, we can derive an alternative regional personal income of $521.243 billion in 2000. Real population of the region was 16,426,322 in 2000. The 2000 population would have been higher by the 60 percent of those who lost their jobs and migrated out of the region, multiplied by their households (roughly a 1:2 ratio of employed to population), or 176,400. It would also have included additional population from the induced (multiplier effect) jobs (311,000), at a ratio of 80 percent taken by in-migrants (thus, 311,000 jobs add 248,800 to the baseline population). Combined with the retention of the direct employees who left the region, we derive an alternative year 2000 population of 16,851,522. The nominal per capita personal income of the region would have been $30,931, compared to its reported figure of $30,214. Per capita income, in other words, was about 2.37 percent lower in 2000 in Greater Los Angeles from what it would have been without the aerospace shock. This is a big shock. But it is a rather small fraction of the actual divergence in the per capita incomes of the two regions that occurred in the 1990s.

The problem in Los Angeles is thus broader and deeper than the aerospace shock. Even after controlling for its industrial mix, Los Angeles has an occupational structure that has become systematically less sophisticated than one would expect given its specialization pattern. On this measure, it is underperforming not only the Bay Area, but also the nation as whole.

By global and national standards, both Los Angeles and San Francisco are city-regions of the first order. Yet over the last 40 years, one has established itself at the pinnacle of the global knowledge economy, while the other is neither sufficiently sophisticated to generate top-rank average wages and per capita income nor sufficiently cheap to compete for routinized activities that go to regions in lower-income development clubs.

4   The Role of Labor in Divergence

Quality of Workers or Quality of Jobs?

DIFFERENCES IN AVERAGE REGIONAL WAGES IN THE BAY AREA
and Los Angeles grew from a small 5 percent in 1970 to a very
large 35 percent in 2010 (Table 4.1).[1] Accounts of regional fortunes often call
attention to the quality of the workforce in determining both regional specialization and regional wages. In this chapter we consider whether growing
wage and income gaps can be explained principally due to the characteristics
of the labor force (the supply of education and skills) or to the characteristics
of the jobs that are available in the region (labor demand), and how changes
in the two relate to one another over time. Most importantly, we have to identify which of these forces set off the divergence or generated a switching point
in the development of the two regions.

To begin with the supply side, the principal indicator of labor skills is educational attainment. Education is a sensible but not perfect signal of human
capital. Many studies confirm that differences in educational attainment correspond closely to variation in wages among countries and cities (Barro, 1997;
Benhabib and Spiegel, 1994; Moretti, 2004).

In both regions and for the United States as a whole, education levels have
been rising (Table 4.2).[2] While in 1970 mean educational attainment among
workers in Los Angeles was 1 percent below the U.S. average, it fell to 2 percent
below the average by 2010. In 1970, educational attainment in the Bay Area was
2 percent above the national average, and by 2010 it was 8 percent higher than
the U.S. average such that by the end of our study period the average worker

TABLE 4.1 Mean wages for workers active in the labor market

	1970	1980	1990	2000	2005–2010
Los Angeles	$7,326	$13,703	$25,770	$31,713	$40,708
San Francisco	7,708	14,738	29,568	47,476	62,086

SOURCE: Authors' calculations using data on wage and salary income from IPUMS Census extracts: 1 percent metro samples in 1970 and 1980, 5 percent samples in 1990 and 2000, and a 5 percent sample combining 1 percent American Community Survey samples for 2005–2010. Unless otherwise specified, all IPUMS data in this chapter will use these same data.

NOTE: In order to account for all workers active in the labor market, we estimate a worker's annual wage on the basis of reported wage income, usual hours worked per week, and number of weeks worked in the current year. We exclude data on individuals who are self-employed, as well as workers below age 16 and above age 65.

TABLE 4.2 Mean years of schooling for workers active in the labor market

	1970	1980	1990	2000	2005–2010
Los Angeles	11.95	12.49	12.58	12.34	12.73
San Francisco	12.38	13.26	13.57	13.69	14.02
United States	12.08	12.72	12.77	12.65	13.00

SOURCE: Authors' calculations using IPUMS data.

NOTE: The IPUMS data on education do not provide a simple count of years of schooling; instead they group some years under a single code and others get their own number. We recode the EDUC variable as follows: 6 is added to EDUC values 3 through 11; a value of 6.5 is assigned to 2; code 1 is assigned a value of 2.5; and a code of zero is set to zero. This requires some assumptions about code values at the low end of the educational spectrum, for instance assuming that grades 5 through 8 are equally well represented in code 2. However, this scheme comes closest to measuring schooling years in a manner that permits sensible interpretation of city-average values. It is also worth noting that the underlying educational data are top-coded, with four years of college being the highest recorded. This could bias the results if one region has a larger proportion of its college graduates that have additional years of schooling.

in the Bay Area had two years of college under his or her belt. In contrast the average worker in Los Angeles had attended less than one full year of college. Additionally, a consistently larger share of workers in the Bay Area has earned at least a four-year college degree, 19 percent in 1970 and 49 percent in 2010. In Los Angeles, fourteen percent of workers held at least a bachelor's degree in 1970 and 27 percent by 2010.

In order for these important differences to be considered an independent cause of the wage gap, they would have had to change prior to the wage gap. The Bay Area started out with a very small educational lead, and the wage gap opened up more and more from 1970 onward. Does this mean that education gaps caused the differences in specialization and job quality documented in the previous chapter? Or did the development of different quality specializations cause the regions to offer increasingly different types of jobs, in turn leading them to attract a different quality of workers? This chicken-or-egg question is central to understanding divergent economic development (Muth, 1971; Combes et al., 2008). There are many dispersed clues to follow before we will be able to connect the dots, which we do in the conclusion to this chapter.

People: Gender, Ethnicity, Foreign-Born

Widening gaps in the ethnic, gender, age, and national origin of people in each region's labor force could drive the wage gap, if they are associated with systematically different education and skill levels (Glaeser and Maré, 2001). Gender affects average wages as a result of gendered wage discrimination (Blau and Kahn, 2000), and indirectly through gendered differences in experience and education. However, the share of women in the workforce in Los Angeles and San Francisco has evolved in tandem, rising from 38 percent in 1970 to around 48 percent by 2010. Ethnic makeup could also have implications for average wage levels. Ethnicity is correlated with differences in educational attainment between groups, sometimes due to discrimination in access to education or, in the case of immigrant groups, different average educational levels in the country of origin. Workers of different groups are also paid differently for equivalent work, which is direct wage discrimination.

Table 4.3 describes the ethnic composition of each region's workforce, based on responses to the U.S. Census and the *American Community Survey*. While the labor markets in both regions are dominated by workers who self-identify as white in 1970, thereafter the proportion of whites declines consistently, falling from close to 90 percent to just below 60 percent. Concomitantly, the share of workers identifying themselves as Asian grows in both regions, while the proportion of blacks has remained stable in Los Angeles and declined by half in the Bay Area. In Los Angeles, the share of Hispanic workers more than doubled, from 9 percent in 1980 to nearly 20 percent in 2010. In the Bay Area, the share of Asian workers grew by a factor of six over this period. Almost the entire difference in composition is due to the difference in share of Asians in the Bay Area, which almost exactly offsets the lower shares of black and Hispanic workers there compared to Los Angeles. Hispanic and black workers have an average education level below the national average.[3] Caution should be exercised here, since within any of these

TABLE 4.3 Race and ethnicity of workers active in the labor market

	White (%)	Hispanic (%)	Black (%)	Asian (%)
Los Angeles, 1970	90	—	7	3
San Francisco, 1970	87	—	7	5
Los Angeles, 1980	76	9	8	6
San Francisco, 1980	77	5	8	10
Los Angeles, 1990	67	16	6.5	9.4
San Francisco, 1990	70	6	4	19
Los Angeles, 2000	57	22	8.5	11
San Francisco, 2000	60	9	4	26
Los Angeles, 2010	59	18	7.5	14
San Francisco, 2010	58	6	3	31

SOURCE: Authors' calculations using IPUMS data.
NOTE: Hispanic figures are not reported for 1970 because this category was not identified in the 1970 decennial Census.

groups—white, Hispanic, black, and Asian—are subgroups, differentiated by educational attainment.

These are regionwide figures; thus, for example, the percentage of Latinos in Los Angeles County is higher than for Greater Los Angeles as a whole. Moreover, the figures are for the *active workforce*, rather than the total population. The Hispanic workforce, for example, has grown more slowly than the share of Hispanics in the total population, and historically blacks have had lower labor force participation than whites.

Each racial and ethnic group has some immigrants and some native-born workers, so we will examine immigrants separately later in this chapter.

The Contribution of Education to Wages

The contribution of education to the increasing regional wage gap should reflect both interregional differences in education levels and interregional differences in reward levels for a given level of education. Table 4.4 compares wages for each education level between the two regions. Highly educated workers in Los Angeles were once paid more than their counterparts in the Bay Area. Angelenos with at least four years of college enjoyed a 5 percent wage premium over similarly educated workers in the Bay Area in 1970. From

TABLE 4.4 Wages by educational attainment among workers active in the labor market

	1970	1980	1990	2000	2005–2010
Los Angeles, college graduates	$11,705	$20,408	$40,317	$54,115	$68,730
San Francisco, college graduates	11,127	19,981	41,397	69,807	90,102
Los Angeles, some college	7,631	14,128	25,690	31,959	37,936
San Francisco, some college	7,432	14,057	26,027	38,354	43,608
Los Angeles, HS graduates	6,789	12,319	20,557	24,601	29,727
San Francisco, HS graduates	7,059	12,886	21,191	28,631	32,830
Los Angeles, some HS	5,762	9,782	14,177	16,050	19,690
San Francisco, some HS	6,041	9,328	14,447	15,402	19,452

SOURCE: Authors' calculations using IPUMS data.
NOTE: College graduates are defined as workers with at least four years of college.

1990 forward, skilled workers did consistently better in the Bay Area. By 2005–2010, college degree holders in the Bay Area earned about one third more than their counterparts in Los Angeles.[4] The only educational group where Angelenos are better paid is the very bottom of the skill hierarchy (but the difference is small and within the statistical margin of error).

In other words, the wage gap is associated with a widening gap in education levels, but also by a widening interregional gap in wages at identical levels of education. This is the first clue that the wage gap cannot only be due to the composition of the labor force.

The Role of Labor Demand: Different Jobs, Different Wages?

When regions are specialized in different tradable industries, their labor requirements will also be different. Manufacturing and financial services, for example, require different mixes of labor skills. To see this effect on Los Angeles and the Bay Area, we again use the DOT and Census to classify workers depending on the extent to which their occupation demands routine or nonroutine cognitive tasks, but this time we do so for each education level (Table 4.5).

Los Angeles had *higher* levels of nonroutine tasks than San Francisco at all education levels of its workforce in 1970 and 1980 (Table 4.5). This turned

TABLE 4.5 Nonroutine cognitive task intensity by education level

	1970	1980	1990	2000	2005–2010
Los Angeles, college graduates	4.94	4.40	4.76	4.85	4.74
San Francisco, college graduates	4.72	4.36	4.88	5.42	5.24
Los Angeles, some college	2.97	2.79	2.99	2.98	2.80
San Francisco, some college	2.72	2.68	2.92	3.09	2.77
Los Angeles, HS graduates	2.28	2.21	2.15	2.13	2.14
San Francisco, HS graduates	2.21	2.15	2.08	2.17	2.08
Los Angeles, some HS	1.57	1.31	1.25	1.31	1.27
San Francisco, some HS	1.53	1.23	1.16	1.20	1.21

SOURCE: Authors' calculations using data from IPUMS samples and the *Dictionary of Occupational Titles*.

NOTE: Higher values of nonroutineness indicate that the occupational mix in an educational category is tilted toward jobs that require greater nonroutine interaction and analytics. See Chapter 3 for a fuller description of the construction of task indices.

around by 1990 for college degree holders in the Bay Area; by 2000, workers with at least a college degree in San Francisco were engaged in more work consisting of nonroutine cognitive tasks.[5] This is our second clue: workers with *similar* education levels earned more in the Bay Area beginning in the 1980s because they performed less-routine tasks than their Los Angeles counterparts. Wage differences, by this account, cannot be due only to differences in the characteristics of the workforce; they have to be due at least partially to the different characteristics of jobs.

This interpretation does not sit comfortably with standard urban economics, as outlined in Chapter 2. RSUE predicts that any systematic differences in demand should stimulate growth in labor supply through migration or education, resulting in a strong tendency for interregional convergence of wages for similarly educated workers. One possible explanation for this discrepancy is that other forces prevent or slow the migration process that would equalize wages between metropolitan areas. We return to this idea shortly. It is also possible that our measures of human capital are not picking up even more subtle skill differences between the workers of San Francisco and Los Angeles. For example, two individuals who have earned bachelor's degrees can deploy different skills that could make one more productive than the other. To take an extreme case, Mark Zuckerberg (the founder and CEO of Facebook) is a college dropout, but he is different from his fellow dropouts in ways that are economically important but that don't easily show up in the Census (other than in his reported wages, but we cannot use data on his wages to explain the causes of his wages). The productivity of two similarly educated individuals could also differ according to their effort (ambition, work ethic), innate talent, acquired experience (on the job and in life), or the extent to which formal levels of education (such as a bachelor's degree) are "big tents" that mask very different real educational acquisition.

Why Do People Go Where They Go? The Determinants of Sorting and Migration

If we assume that, for each measurable educational category, San Francisco has an endowment of systematically more productive workers (more Zuckerbergs), we then need to know why more such high-skill workers have come to be concentrated there than in Los Angeles, especially in light of the similar starting points in the 1970s. Does the Bay Area school system produce particularly highly skilled individuals at each level of educational attainment? Does some aspect of regional culture generate better-motivated or better-trained workers? These are possibilities, but many of San Francisco's workers are not native sons and daughters. What forces sort the Zuckerbergs to the Bay Area and not to Los Angeles, or for that matter to some other region of the United States and beyond? Mark Zuckerberg relocated from Cambridge, Massachusetts, to Silicon Valley because the Bay Area hosts a uniquely dense and innovative cluster of Internet technology firms, along with an unparalleled ecosystem of such things as venture capital financing and young technologists. This ecosystem in the Bay Area attracts skilled and ambitious IT professionals from around the world; for the same reasons, aspiring screenwriters, actors, producers, and agents flock to Los Angeles. To the extent that these ecosystems generate different labor demands, the supply follows, and in this way, two distinctive regional labor forces come into being.

In contrast to this demand-led view of the sorting of people into regions, many urban economists argue the opposite: that people do not go to places chiefly for jobs but to satisfy a wide range of preferences for where to live (Roback, 1982; Rappaport, 2007; Graves, 1980; Partridge, 2010). They look for regional lifestyle features, or "amenities." Amenities include physical, social, and cultural aspects of places; the term covers both things people pay to experience, such as restaurants, entertainment, and sporting events as well as regional characteristics that are freely available to them, such as the weather or landscape. According to many urban economists, people decide where to live and work in order to maximize some combination of amenities and money income. More money income is not their only goal, because some places offer living costs and access to amenities that stretch the satisfaction that can be obtained with a given budget. Applying this theory, urban economists commonly claim that a principal reason that many workers relocated from the former industrial heartland of the Northeast to the South and West after the 1950s was not because jobs moved from North to South. Instead, they moved to better enjoy a free amenity they valued: warm, sunny winters, which became more appealing as a result of the advent of air-conditioning to offset uncomfortable hot and humid summers (Graves, 1980; Glaeser and Tobio, 2008). Other scholars, examining the revitalization of formerly dilapidated central cities in the 1980s and 1990s, consider that cultural amenities like tolerance, hip restaurants, and music festivals have drawn "creative" people back in (Florida, 2002). They argue that highly skilled workers in particular prefer these amenities and can afford them. Following this line of reasoning, did the Bay Area get ahead of Los Angeles because its amenities drew in more of these people, and then the high technology industries followed them?

These arguments are the subject of vigorous debate (see, for instance, Scott and Storper, 2009; Kemeny and Storper, 2012; Partridge, 2010; Gabriel and Rosenthal, 2004). But in comparing San Francisco and Los Angeles, these arguments add little to the explanation of divergence. Both regions enjoy pleasant, sunny climates with mild winters, and they boast ready access to mountains, the Pacific Ocean, and other forms of natural beauty; both regions are also major regional centers of high and popular culture. Assuming that people move primarily to satisfy their desire for certain amenities, and that highly skilled workers disproportionately prefer sunny Januarys, art galleries, pop culture, and opera houses, neither the Bay Area nor Los Angeles has the edge.

Urban economics also highlights the importance of how money wages get adjusted into "real" wages through differences in the cost of living, principally due to differences in housing costs (Albouy, 2008; Glaeser et al., 2005, 2006; Saks, 2008). Local governments create land use regulations that affect housing supply (more or less restrictive regulations), and this determines how much the housing supply changes in response to demand. Consider, for instance, a city where many new migrants have chosen to settle. In the absence of restrictive regulation, housing construction will add supply to meet the growth in demand. Regulation or "not in my back yard" (NIMBY) politics make housing supply less elastic; instead of adding sufficient supply, growing demand will raise housing prices and drive certain people away from the region. Restricted housing supply could also force local firms to raise money wages to compensate their workers for higher housing costs, or it could cause them to move away in order to keep their wages lower. Or it could cause workers in the restrictive region to substitute smaller or less desirable housing. In this perspective, land use regulation can significantly shape migration and hence the regional labor supply.

Following this line of reasoning, one hypothesis about why the Bay Area has a better educated and more productive workforce goes as follows. Assume that local governments in the Bay Area enact highly restrictive laws regarding land use. Without such restrictions, rising demand for housing would lead builders to construct new homes, but in the context of a restrictive land use regime it leads to high prices for existing housing units. Because of the high housing costs, lower-income workers are effectively priced out of the region. The outcome is a Bay Area regional economy increasingly biased toward highly productive workers earning high wages and living in expensive homes, but where overall population levels grow slowly. By contrast, more permissive regulation in Los Angeles would allow more housing to be built, keeping housing prices down, and in turn allowing a higher proportion of less educated workers with lower wages to live in the region, as well as more population growth.

This story has some superficial plausibility, but closer inspection reveals fatal problems with it. Figure 1.3 showed that the two regions are situated just above the national average for metropolitan population growth. The populations of both Los Angeles and San Francisco nearly doubled over our study period, and while in absolute terms this means many more migrants entered Greater Los Angeles, the difference is modest, not one of orders of magnitude. Indeed, one of the reasons why the San Francisco region is so intriguing as an example of high-income economic development is that—unlike successful older cities such as New York or London—its population and its income level have *both* grown so much.

Land use regulation can take a wide variety of forms, from city council bylaws to environmental assessments to zoning boards and even practices that are not on the books. While one might readily compare a given type of restriction across locations, the breadth of regulatory mechanisms makes it challenging to compare restrictiveness at the level of municipalities or metropolitan areas. Urban economists have employed a variety of strategies to overcome this problem. Some researchers consider that the gap between the marginal cost of producing a unit of housing in a particular location and the current market price of a comparable unit reveals the strength of the regulatory regime (Glaeser et al., 2005, 2006). By this price-cost metric, where costs include the prices of land, construction labor, materials, and other relevant factors, major cities in our two regions—the municipalities of Los Angeles, San Francisco, Oakland, and San Jose—were *the* most highly regulated cities in the United States in 1998–1999.[6] According to Glaeser and colleagues (2005, 2006), the housing prices are between one third and one half higher than they would be without restrictions. To provide some comparison, this figure is only around 10 percent in other major cities like Boston, New York, and Washington, D.C. But in any event, according to this method of calculation, the Bay Area is not more restrictive than Los Angeles.[7]

We can buttress this interpretation by directly measuring restrictiveness. Saks (2008) combines secondary survey data in which city planners, government development officials, and others are asked to report their views about local land use regulation. The data were originally gathered across several years, though they are clustered chiefly between the mid-1970s and early 1980s. In theory, then, these data are a snapshot of differences in restrictiveness at a sufficiently early time period such that they could generate subsequent economic divergence in our study regions.

Table 4.6 presents results from Saks's index of housing supply regulation for major subregions of our two regions, as well as population-weighted regional averages. There is a fair degree of variability of regulation among cities *within* each region. For instance, San Francisco and San Jose appear to be quite restrictive, whereas regulation is lower in the Vallejo-Fairfield-Napa area (higher index values indicate greater restrictiveness). Some of the index differences reflect physical and political geography. For instance, San Francisco is the most highly restrictive city in the Bay Area. There is no single city in Greater Los Angeles the size of the City of San Francisco that is as restrictive. But there are many smaller municipalities as well as neighborhoods within the City of Los Angeles that are as restrictive as the City of San Francisco (West Hollywood, Beverly Hills, Santa Monica, Agoura Hills, Pasadena). This is because Los Angeles and its neighboring cities do not contend

TABLE 4.6 Regional land use regulation levels

Metropolitan area	Raw score	Weighted score	Regional weighted sum
SAN FRANCISCO AREA			
San Francisco	2.1	0.632	
San Jose	1.65	0.432	
Oakland	0.1	0.036	
Vallejo-Fairfield-Napa	−0.27	−0.022	
Total			**1.078**
LOS ANGELES AREA			
Los Angeles-Long Beach	1.21	0.787	
Riverside-San Bernardino	1.73	0.235	
Ventura	1.15	0.053	
Orange County	−0.32	−0.054	
Total			**1.021**

SOURCE: Authors' calculations based on Saks (2008) and 1980 U.S. Census data (the latter used for population weights).

NOTE: Higher index values indicate greater restrictiveness. Some metropolitan areas in the San Francisco region did not have available data. In the calculations shown, these are not included in the regional weighted sums; however, some sensitivity testing was performed to investigate whether, if such regions were highly restrictive, it would appreciably change results. Because these are not highly populated metropolitan areas, even restrictiveness levels approaching those found in San Jose do not importantly change the results. Though the calculations do somewhat magnify the greater restrictiveness in the Bay Area, the two regions remain closely comparable along this index.

with the physical restrictions of the City of San Francisco, bounded as it is by water on three sides. However, what is most important in all of this is that the weighted sums for the San Francisco and Los Angeles regions are nearly identical. As with the price-cost ratio described earlier, by this measure both have highly restrictive real estate markets that drive up prices in both of them.[8]

To bolster confidence in this interpretation, we examine two additional indices. The first is the Wharton Residential Land Use Regulation Index (WRLURI) (Gyourko et al., 2008), which measures a variety of local and state regulatory factors for 2,600 municipalities in the United States. WRLURI scores are larger for cities in which regulation is reported higher. In order to identify a regional value of land use restrictiveness, we create a weighted sum of municipal WRLURI values, where the weight is each municipality's

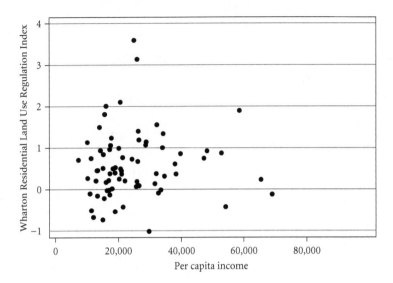

FIGURE 4.1 Land use restrictiveness and per capita income, cities,
Greater Los Angeles
SOURCE: Data from Wharton Residential Land Use Regulation Index.
NOTE: Correlation coefficient = 0.044; p = 0.65

share of regional population. The index is standardized with a mean of 0
and a standard deviation of 1. The overall WRLURI value for Los Angeles is
1.22, while for the Bay Area it is 0.83. On this measure, while both regions are
highly regulated by national standards, the Los Angeles metropolitan region
is somewhat *more* restrictive than the Bay Area.

Beneath the regional average, as we remarked earlier, individual cities have
very different levels of restrictiveness. To illustrate this point, Figure 4.1 plots
municipal WRLURI scores against per capita personal income for cities in the
Los Angeles region. The lack of a clear linear pattern in the plot suggests that
more land use restrictiveness does not lead inexorably toward a city excluding
low-income people. To take an example, Beverly Hills and Covina (a lower-
middle-income eastern suburb of Los Angeles) have nearly identical levels of
land use restriction as measured by the Wharton Index, yet average income
levels in Beverly Hills are about three times as high as in Covina.[9] In other
words, the principal forces behind local differences in housing prices are in
structural processes, such as the sorting of population by income level (class
segregation) and the environmental quality of neighborhoods, race, and
proximity to employment (Combes et al., 2008). But the sum total of these

differences at the regional level do not explain overall *regional* average housing price differences.

As a final indicator of land use restrictiveness, we consider the number of building permits issued in the region. Using annual data between 1980 and 2007, we scale this figure on a per capita basis to control for differences in population size. The growth in building permits likely reflects a mix of demand and supply forces; they are therefore a noisy measure of restrictions. Nonetheless, assuming that demand for housing has been comparably high in each region, Figure 4.2 suggests that there have only been small interregional differences in the elasticity of housing supply. While the number of permits issued per capita fluctuates over time, overall trends in the San Francisco and Los Angeles regions closely track one another, with San Francisco appearing somewhat more restrictive between 1982 and 1991, then becoming more permissive during the 1990s and again more restrictive in the first decade of the twenty-first century.

Based on the preceding evidence, overall interregional differences in the ability to develop land and housing do not appear to have played an important role in the population dynamics of the two regions. Indeed, by the logic

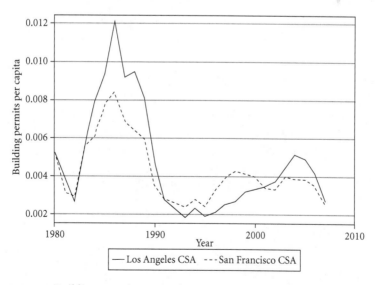

FIGURE 4.2 Building permits per capita, 1980–2007
SOURCE: Data from the *State of the Cities Data Systems* (U.S. Department of Housing and Urban Development, 2010).

of the land use hypothesis, high levels of land use regulation in both regions ought to have generated sufficiently large housing price increases to considerably limit population growth in both. Both regions have added considerably to their populations, and yet they added people with different average levels of skills.

If higher housing prices in the Bay Area did not emerge because of tighter regulation or significantly lower growth of housing supply there, then it stands to reason that much of the difference in housing prices is the result of high incomes in the Bay Area, not the cause (Carruthers and Mulligan, 2012; Moretti, 2013). This does not mean that land use regulation and housing supply never play an important role in regional development. Regulation certainly influences the order of magnitude of housing costs in both San Francisco and Los Angeles, but not their wage differences or capacity of their residents to afford housing.

The Role of Immigration in Workforce Composition and Wages

Foreign-born workers comprise a large, growing, and comparable overall share of the labor force of Greater Los Angeles and the Bay Area (Table 4.7; Waldinger and Bozorgmehr, 1996). This means that we will need to see how the composition of immigration in each region affects wages.

Immigration is heavily tilted toward less educated Latinos in Greater Los Angeles and more toward more highly educated Asians in the Bay Area (Saxenian, 2002, 2006). Among foreign-born workers in Los Angeles, the largest number are Mexican-born; by 2010, one in five non-native workers in Los Angeles originated there. Salvadorans and other Latin American immigrants are also present in Los Angeles in relatively large numbers. In San Francisco in 1970, the largest cohort of immigrants arrived from China. By 2010, Mexico was the most common immigrant birthplace in the Bay Area, just slightly

TABLE 4.7 Proportion of immigrant workers active in the labor market

	1970 (%)	1980 (%)	1990 (%)	2000 (%)	2005–2010 (%)
Los Angeles	11	20	32	40	38
San Francisco	11	16	28	37	39

SOURCE: Authors' calculations using IPUMS data.

TABLE 4.8 Educational attainment among immigrant workers active in the labor market

	1970	1980	1990	2000	2005–2010
Los Angeles	10.6	10.5	10.7	10.9	11.6
San Francisco	11.4	12.5	12.5	12.9	13.5

SOURCE: Authors' calculations using IPUMS data.

TABLE 4.9 Immigrant wage premiums

	1970	1980	1990	2000	2005–2010
SAN FRANCISCO REGIONAL WAGE PREMIUM BY BIRTHPLACE					
Foreign-born wage premium	6%	18%	27%	60%	65%
Native-born wage premium	5%	5%	10%	45%	47%
WAGES OF HISPANIC IMMIGRANT WORKERS					
Los Angeles	$5,085	$9,005	$14,493	$20,231	$26,465
San Francisco	5,960	11,102	17,383	24,252	31,669

SOURCE: Authors' calculations using IPUMS data.
NOTE: The regional wage premium represents the percentage excess earned by workers in San Francisco over those in Los Angeles.

ahead of China and the Philippines. Though Mexicans are currently the most common in San Francisco, they account for less than 7 percent of the total immigrant population—much less than in Los Angeles. Table 4.8 shows how these differences are associated with a widening interregional gap in average educational attainment of immigrants.

In Table 4.9, we show that these gaps are in turn reflected in immigrants' wages: like their Bay Area native-born counterparts, foreign-born workers in the Bay Area have consistently earned higher wages than those who have settled in Los Angeles. The gap between immigrant wages in San Francisco and Los Angeles has grown considerably faster among immigrants than among natives of the two regions. This fits the conventional narrative. If San Francisco is absorbing highly skilled workers, and Los Angeles's immigrants are on average less skilled than average native-born residents there, then interregional wage disparities among foreign-born residents ought to be larger than interregional disparities among native-born residents.

The question then becomes: are different immigration streams causes or consequences—once again, chicken or egg—of diverging specialization and labor demand? Were the influxes of less skilled immigrants into Los Angeles and highly skilled immigrants into the Bay Area causes of diverging specialization? Or are immigrants chiefly responding to evolving differences in job opportunities? To put this another way, is it the case that a substantial number of low-skill immigrants chose Los Angeles because it was *already* on an economic low road? And were highly skilled immigrants drawn to San Francisco because the Bay Area was creating so many high-skilled, nonroutine jobs?

To solve this puzzle, we need to think about why different immigration streams to these regions got started and reinforced. One common account of the sources of immigration emphasizes the proximity of the Los Angeles region to the border. Los Angeles is situated a mere 130 miles north of the San Ysidro port of entry, which divides San Diego and Tijuana and is the busiest land border in the United States (Bureau of Transportation Statistics, 2012). Immigrants may thus settle in Los Angeles because of geographical convenience. But immigrants travel hundreds or even thousands of miles to get to the border, and once they cross it many continue their journey to distant places. For instance, there are large groups of Latin American immigrants in U.S. regions far from the border, including Chicago and New York City. And between 2000 and 2010, the Hispanic population (of which over half were foreign-born) grew fastest in North Carolina, South Carolina, Arkansas, and Alabama.

In this context, Hispanic immigrants in the Bay Area earn more than their counterparts in Los Angeles (Table 4.9). The Hispanic immigrant premium in the Bay Area over Los Angeles is surprisingly large and durable: 17 percent in 1970; 23 percent in 1980; and 20 percent in 1990, 1990, and 2005–2010. Given this ongoing disparity, why wouldn't Hispanic immigrants persevere for the additional 360 miles it would take them to arrive in San Francisco in hope of earning higher wages?

To the extent that proximity matters today, it may reflect the past when distance was more costly to people. This argument refers to the historical presence of Mexicans in the Los Angeles area. California was part of Mexico until 1848, when California was ceded to the United States after the Mexican-American War. Both San Francisco and Los Angeles had considerable Spanish, Mexican and mixed *Californio* communities at that time. By virtue of history, both San Francisco and Los Angeles ought to have been, and have in fact long been, destinations for migration from Mexico. The more relevant question is therefore: what explains the much higher recent inflow of less skilled Latin-American migrants into Los Angeles as compared to San Francisco? The clue that emerges is that Asians are attracted to the Bay Area because more high-skilled jobs are created there, and Latin Americans are attracted to Los Angeles and its abundance of low-skilled labor demand.

Moreover, once immigrants arrive in the two regions, they seem to use and develop their skills differently. Table 4.10 shows that highly educated immigrants to Los Angeles earned higher wages in 1970 and 1980 than their Bay Area counterparts, but they fell behind by 1990. Subsequently a large disparity in pay emerged among workers who have attended at least some college. The gap is widest among immigrants who hold a college degree. In that category, immigrant Angelenos earned only three quarters of the wages of their counterparts in San Francisco during 2005–2010. Among the least well-educated immigrants, wages are consistently higher in the Bay Area throughout the study period.

How can we explain why immigrants with the same education levels earn such different wages in the two regions, particularly over the past 20 years? One possibility is that education levels do not capture more subtle forms of worker differences (motivation, effort, or on-the-job experience). In this way of thinking, immigrants with college degrees in Los Angeles could be systematically less skilled or ambitious or hardworking than those in the Bay Area. Among all the immigrants with college degrees, the question then becomes: why would more of those with systematically higher levels of human capital (*Los Zuckerbergs!*) go to the Bay Area and not Los Angeles? Once again, the

TABLE 4.10 Wages of immigrant workers by educational attainment

	1970	1980	1990	2000	2005–2010
Los Angeles, college graduates	$10,153	$17,981	$33,503	$45,561	$61,171
San Francisco, college graduates	9,313	17,773	37,081	64,433	87,026
Los Angeles, some college	7,114	12,441	21,695	28,105	35,477
San Francisco, some college	6,913	12,807	23,107	33,890	41,289
Los Angeles, HS graduates	6,233	10,904	16,396	21,649	27,319
San Francisco, HS graduates	6,393	11,351	17,726	24,853	30,238
Los Angeles, some HS	5,908	8,713	12,853	17,650	22,079
San Francisco, some HS	6,029	9,584	14,343	19,198	23,850

SOURCE: Authors' calculations using IPUMS data.
NOTE: College graduates are defined as workers with at least four years of college.

signs point to gaps in specialization and labor demand driving the sorting of different types of immigrants to the two regions (Saxenian, 2006). A higher level of high-skilled immigration—especially in the science, technology, engineering, and math occupations—to the Bay Area probably has positive effects on native-born workers in these occupations. Peri and colleagues (2014) estimate that a rise in the growth of such foreign-born workers by one percentage point increases the growth of native-born college-educated workers by seven to eight percentage points.

This interpretation is backed up by our evidence that immigrant workers with similar education levels and origins perform jobs that are different. In the Bay Area, a higher proportion of immigrants at all education levels perform nonroutine tasks than in Los Angeles. Though we cannot measure them, there are probably different on-the-job learning-by-doing processes in the two regions. These "experience effects" enlarge initial differences and thus drive a growing wedge between Bay Area immigrant earnings and those of their Angeleno counterparts (De la Roca and Puga, 2012; Burdett and Coles, 2010). All in all, the clues add up to a story where immigration, while contributing to wage divergence, is not an independent cause of it but in large measure a response to divergent labor demand.

A final consideration is that immigrants in both regions are not just workers, but also significant numbers of them are entrepreneurs. We analyze entrepreneurship in Chapter 7. For present purposes, we can note that both regions have many immigrant entrepreneurs. Their experiences range from low-income ethnic entrepreneurship in the nontradable part of the economy to high-value entrepreneurship in tradables (such as in Silicon Valley). Entrepreneurs earn much income through profits rather than wages. Per capita income figures capture all reported sources of income. In both regions there might be unreported income of many sorts, but there is no reason to suspect any regional bias that would alter the picture of divergent returns to skill painted by the preceding data.

Poorer Now, but a Better Opportunity Machine?

Economies move forward through time, and the benefits of development are captured not only in a snapshot but in a long motion picture covering different generations and regions. Denmark is a wealthy small country with little population growth, and it transmits its high standard of living to successive, equally-sized generations. China was a poor country that is incorporating hundreds of millions of people into development and higher incomes, and its task is therefore not only to increase the number of jobs but to improve them and to widen this circle of improvement to more and more people over time. With this in mind, it is worth considering the fact that Greater Los Angeles is more than twice the size of the Bay Area. For much of the twentieth century, Los Angeles incorporated many more newcomers than the Bay Area, and it did so while raising levels of skill and real incomes for the newcomers.

Even if Los Angeles has been a bigger opportunity machine than the Bay Area, it is certainly not a *better* one. The quality of integration of low-skill immigrants in recent decades has been better in the Bay Area. In Table 4.11 we confirm this by examining the wages of recent immigrants within skill categories, where "recent" is defined as someone who arrived in the five-year period prior to each wave of data collection. In 1970, recent immigrants residing in Los Angeles who held a high school diploma and those with some college earned more than their counterparts in the Bay Area. But after 1970, recent immigrants in San Francisco across the education spectrum enjoyed higher earnings than their counterparts in Los Angeles. Hence, in the early years of their presence in the United States, workers in the Bay Area have generally done better no matter what their initial skill level.[10]

Unfortunately, we lack detailed data on the economic performance of second-generation immigrants in our two regions, but Chetty and colleagues (2014) show that intergenerational income mobility is about equal for the two

TABLE 4.11 Wages of recent immigrants by educational attainment

	1970	1980	1990	2000	2005–2010
Los Angeles, college graduates	$6,506	$12,954	$23,292	$34,596	$41,493
San Francisco, college graduates	6,966	13,839	28,254	58,221	60,295
Los Angeles, some college	5,066	8,488	14,510	19,495	19,763
San Francisco, some college	4,607	9,859	16,007	27,507	24,640
Los Angeles, HS graduates	4,658	8,296	11,545	15,620	16,774
San Francisco, HS graduates	4,440	9,297	12,208	18,834	18,394
Los Angeles, some HS	4,732	6,259	8,904	12,128	14,430
San Francisco, some HS	5,299	6,689	10,498	12,775	14,983

SOURCE: Authors' calculations using IPUMS data.
NOTE: College graduates are defined as workers with at least four years of college.

TABLE 4.12 Wages of nonrecent immigrants by educational attainment

	1970	1980	1990	2000	2005–2010
Los Angeles, college graduates	$11,690	$19,963	$35,915	$47,310	$56,625
San Francisco, college graduates	10,282	18,913	39,284	66,230	83,595
Los Angeles, some college	7,513	13,520	23,180	28,980	32,446
San Francisco, some college	7,358	13,513	24,538	34,763	37,133
Los Angeles, HS graduates	6,570	11,710	17,890	22,502	25,561
San Francisco, HS graduates	6,776	11,938	19,233	26,227	29,306
Los Angeles, some HS	6,151	9,782	14,512	18,624	21,096
San Francisco, some HS	6,208	10,715	15,755	21,095	26,779

SOURCE: Authors' calculations using IPUMS data.
NOTE: College graduates are defined as workers with at least four years of college.

regions. In addition, we can measure the wages of the first generation that have lived in the United States for longer periods. Table 4.12 estimates average wages for immigrants who have lived in the United States for more than five years. In 1970 and 1980, more highly skilled nonrecent immigrants earned slightly higher wages in Los Angeles than in the Bay Area. Less skilled nonrecent immigrants earned somewhat more in San Francisco. But from around 1990 onward, an immigrant at any skill level who has lived in the United States for at least five years and who lives in the Bay Area has a higher expected income than a comparably educated immigrant who lives in Los Angeles. As with workers in general, in recent years this expected wage gap is particularly large for the most highly skilled workers. Thus, although Greater Los Angeles has offered opportunity to a larger absolute number of immigrants, San Francisco has taken on a broadly similar proportion of immigrants relative to total population for many decades, and it has mostly offered them a greater quality of opportunity, in the form of higher wages and real incomes.

Is the Immigration Effect Temporary?

Immigration to Los Angeles from Latin America appears to have peaked between 1990 and 2000 (Myers et al., 2010). While immigration is still on the rise in the United States and many cities in the South, mass immigration began earlier to gateway cities such as Los Angeles, San Francisco, and New York (Painter and Yu, 2009). It is not surprising that immigration has peaked in

TABLE 4.13 The timing of immigration and the immigration peak

	Recent in all immigrants, 1980–1990 (%)	Recent in all immigrants, 1990–2000 (%)	Recent in 1990 population (%)	Recent in 2000 population (%)
Los Angeles	29.7	17.5	8.1	5.4
San Francisco	26.0	22.5	4.2	6.1
New York City	24.0	21.7	4.7	5.3

SOURCE: Painter and Yu, 2009.

these initial gateways but continues to rise elsewhere. Annual immigration into Los Angeles County in 2009 was 20 percent lower than in 1980, whereas over that same period it became 82 percent higher for the United States as a whole and 20 percent higher for California. Table 4.13 shows that, as compared with that of San Francisco, the immigration wave in Los Angeles ramped up more steeply in the 1980s and then dropped off more steeply during the 1990s.

Myers and colleagues (2010) point out that the age and origin structure of California immigrants is changing rapidly as a result of the passing of the immigration peak: immigrants in the state are aging, they are increasingly English-speaking, and their levels of homeownership and income are rising. By contrast, in the key new-immigration states and cities in the South and Southwest and on the eastern seaboard, immigration is still on the rise, with indicators of integration lagging behind California. To what extent could the peak and decline of the immigration wave from Latin America influence the interpretation of the economic divergence between Los Angeles and San Francisco? As the pace of immigration declines, any downward effect on wages from the arrival of people with low education levels from Latin America will also decline in both San Francisco and Los Angeles. This explains little about income divergence, since the earlier timing of the peak in Los Angeles should have helped Los Angeles catch up to San Francisco, as a higher proportion of its immigrants have had more time to integrate and acquire more skills. There is little reason to believe that Los Angeles has diverged downward from San Francisco because of its earlier peak of low-skilled foreign immigration.

Regional Wage Spillovers

Theory suggests another possible dimension of wage divergence. The high wages in the core tradable specializations of the regional economy might affect the wages of workers in other tradable sectors; this was one of the themes of Chinitz (1961) that we discussed in Chapter 2. Bartik (2012: 556) confirms this for U.S. metropolitan regions in general:

> [W]hen 1 percent extra of the local population gets a college education, the average earnings per capita in the local economy go up over twice as much as would be expected from direct earnings effects on those whose education increased. What's going on here? Within firms, worker skills may have positive spillovers. Stronger skills for my fellow workers make it easier for my employer to introduce new technology, thereby increasing my wages. Across firms, worker skills may have positive spillovers due to agglomeration economies. A local cluster may raise workers' wages due to firms stealing ideas from other firm's workers or firms benefiting from a network of skilled suppliers.

Spillovers may also occur between the tradable industries' wages and those in the locally serving sectors, a phenomenon known as the Balassa-Samuelson effect (Balassa, 1964). Colloquially, it answers the following question: why does a haircut in New York cost so much more than in Shanghai (assuming that hairstylists in New York and Shanghai are equally efficient at performing haircuts)? The accepted answer is that New York is specialized in tradable outputs that have much higher average wages and productivity than in the tradable sector of Shanghai. Subsequently, through the complex mechanisms of setting exchange rates between the two economies, nominal wages in the *locally* serving sectors are also much higher in New York than Shanghai. The Balassa-Samuelson effect is thought by some economists to operate at the regional scale through the interlocking effects of higher wages in the tradable sector and land and product prices that everyone faces (Moretti, 2012). The evidence presented in this chapter is consistent with such an interpretation that overall wages in the Bay Area economy are rising through spillovers from that region's bigger and higher-wage core than in Los Angeles.

Conclusion: Specialization and Labor Demand Generate Wage Divergence

In this chapter, much as a detective investigates a case using forensics, we have examined how differences in the labor markets of metropolitan Los Angeles and San Francisco contribute to their wage divergence. Drawing on a wide range of hypotheses from urban economics, labor economics, regional science, and other fields, we have tracked down the clues. The bulk of the evidence points to a conclusion that divergence in labor demand—specialization—set off divergence in opportunities for workers in the two metropolitan areas, which subsequently shaped each region's immigration dynamics as well. Demand changes were the chicken and supply changes are mostly eggs in this process.

As Los Angeles's high-technology sectors declined after the 1980s, and as Silicon Valley emerged as the premier New Economy hub, the returns to education in the Bay Area shot ahead and have widened over time. This interpretation is consistent with evidence for a large sample of regions; not only will a positive labor demand shock generate in-migration, but some of the shock will translate into higher long-term employment rates and long-term wage increases (Bartik, 2012: 553). The Bay Area's capture of the New Economy is the primary reason why similarly educated workers are now paid so differently in our two economies. Moreover, the only sensible reason why the Bay Area ought to have a growing gap in supply of motivated and productive workers is that they migrated there in response to perceived opportunity in the New Economy of the Bay Area. Differences between the Bay Area and Los Angeles in terms of the quality and quantity of their cafés, sunshine, and real estate are nowhere near strong enough to have meaningfully shaped the differential migration patterns. And though differences in the overall composition of immigration streams correspond to differences in wages, they cannot be thought of as an independent causal force behind the divergence. Also, San Francisco is not a unique case of enjoying this positive snowball process of creating its regional labor force as a response to its positive conversion of its productive base. Boston, New York, Seattle, Minneapolis, and Washington, D.C., are similar cases.

Finally, there is a major possible source of divergence that we cannot measure directly: experience and learning within each regional labor market (De la Roca and Puga, 2012). In technical terms, although in our empirical analysis we control for observable individual-level differences in productivity—ethnicity, age, gender, immigration status, education, and so on—it is possible that experience in each regional labor market helps even initially similar people acquire progressively different real skills and drives wages increasingly apart.

If we bring all these pieces of the puzzle together, the Bay Area and Los Angeles now offer different developmental opportunities to significant groups of workers. This reminds us of a point we made in opening this book: where people are located matters. The quality of an economy's specialized tradable sectors exercises durable effects on people's life chances and personal development (Sampson, 2012; Moretti, 2012).

5 Economic Specialization

Pathways to Change

INDUSTRIES, FIRMS, AND ENTREPRENEURS IN THE BAY AREA AND
Los Angeles did not plan the divergence that emerged. They faced
challenges from the restructuring of the Old Economy and benefited from
new opportunities in the New Economy. But they did so very differently.
Their successes and failures widened the income gap between the two regions,
which was reflected in both what the regions do—their specializations—and
the quality of those specializations.

In what follows, we present comparative case studies of entertainment,
aerospace, information technology, logistics, and biotechnology. Our aim is
to identify critical turning points in the development of these sectors and to
show how the economic agents in each regional economy responded to them.
In information technology, there was a difference in how skills and organizational practices were influenced by predecessor industries: aerospace in Los
Angeles and communications in the Bay Area. In biotechnology, a new form
of science-based capitalism emerged in the Bay Area, but not in Los Angeles.
In the entertainment industry in Los Angeles, a new form of project-based,
networked capitalism emerged as the industry reinvented itself in response
to external shocks. In logistics, Los Angeles built an effective public policy
coalition and cemented Los Angeles's position as the West Coast's principal
international transport hub.

West Coast High Technology

Greater Los Angeles's slippage down the ranks of metropolitan regions accelerated in the 1990s along with a sudden and sharp drop in business for its aerospace industry, as the U.S. Defense Department scaled back its needs after the end of the Cold War. Table 3.2 showed that the aerospace agglomeration in Southern California employed over 100,000 workers directly and accounted for nearly 3.5 percent of the regional labor force in 1970, which by 2010 had declined to less than 50,000 and only 0.9 percent of the workforce. A more inclusive definition of the aerospace cluster suggests that about 350,000 workers were employed in closely linked sectors or activities in 1970, about 8 percent of the regional workforce, declining to 271,000 in 1990. By 2011, however, this was cut to only 88,400 (a 68 percent decline) for a loss of 142,000 mostly well-paying jobs. Twenty-five percent were engineers or scientists in 1990 (Thomas and Ong, 2002).

Although the aerospace industry is intrinsically volatile because of the lumpiness of Pentagon contracting, its downturn since 1990 has been more durable and deeper than in the past and now seems as if it could be permanent (Dardia et al., 1996; LAEDC, 2012). At the end of the Cold War, from 1988 to 1996, national defense outlays fell from $334 to $240 billion. The share of national aerospace jobs in Southern California (including San Diego County) fell from 25 percent to 14 percent in 2011, as the sector was geographically restructured to the benefit of Washington, Texas, Arizona, Georgia, Ohio, and Illinois. Schoenie and colleagues (1996) found that 63 percent of aerospace workers laid off in California earned higher wages in their next jobs and that 9 percent of aerospace workers left the state to find employment elsewhere. In 2010 there were still several large military hardware programs in the region, such as Boeing's C17 aircraft (which ended in 2015), the F35 Joint Strike Fighter Jet fuselage construction, and the F-18, 40 percent of whose value of construction is located in Greater Los Angeles. There is still a large parts industry that feeds into military and civilian aircraft and missile construction located in other regions, and a growing drone industry that builds on the region's technological capacities and offers some hope for job creation (Kleinhenz et al., 2012). In 2011, the average aerospace worker in Los Angeles County still earned $88,000, about double the average wage for the county as a whole. The direct role of the aerospace decline in Los Angeles's per capita income problem is often exaggerated. Chapter 3 shows that Los Angeles's per capita income would have been 2.37 percent higher had the region not suffered the aerospace cutbacks of the 1990s. But we will now show that the decline of aerospace is a sign of a broader failure of the Los Angeles economy to adopt the organizational practices that are required to perform at the higher end of the New Economy. Until the shock of the 1990s, firms in the aerospace cluster in Greater Los Angeles aggressively seized technological and commercial market opportunities. The Los Angeles County aerospace cluster was a leading-edge innovator in the technologies that generated the computer revolution, notably in semiconductors for uses in missile and aviation guidance systems and communications.

What changed in the 1990s that prevented successful adaptation? To answer this question, we go back to the roots of high technology in Southern California.

The Roots of Aviation and Aerospace: Los Angeles's High-Tech Powerhouse

The military equipment industry in Los Angeles had its roots in the aviation industry, a precision mechanical engineering sector. Inspired by the invention of the Wright brothers in Ohio, in 1909 Glenn Martin designed and built his own airplane in Santa Ana (Simonson, 1968). Martin went on to form his own company, the Glenn Martin Company, and in 1915, Martin's company hired Donald Douglas, a young engineer from the East Coast. Martin's firm then merged with the Wright Brothers to create an Ohio-based company. Douglas later on returned to Los Angeles to found his eponymous company. In 1916, the Loughead brothers, flight hobbyists and natives of Northern California, moved to Los Angeles, where they founded the Lockheed Aircraft Company in Hollywood in 1926 (Cunningham, 1951). They hired Jack Northrop, another East Coast–based engineer, who would later revolutionize the design of aircraft frames with his monocoque approach (Simonson, 1968; Bloch, 1983).

Civic boosters in the region recognized the potential of the aircraft industry. At the turn of the century, Harry Chandler (of the family that founded the *Los Angeles Times*), had been a central figure in organizing for construction of the Port of San Pedro, as well as the Owens River aqueduct (which brings water from central California to the City of Los Angeles), and the development of the San Fernando Valley. After World War I, Chandler and his cohort began efforts to lure the aircraft industry to Los Angeles. Chandler's efforts included promoting the region's climate to plane makers and raising capital for the formation of Douglas Aircraft Company, an early example of what we would today call venture capital financing (A. Scott, 1993; Lotchin, 1992). A Chandler syndicate also financed Western Air Express, which would later become TWA. The Los Angeles Chamber of Commerce pressured the city into creating a "super airport" consisting of both an airfield and manufacturing facilities, where LAX now stands. LAX still abuts the major engineering and manufacturing belt of the aerospace industry, from El Segundo to the Los Angeles County south beach cities. Another example of civic leadership came in 1927, when Robert Millikan approached the Guggenheim Foundation for funds to create the Guggenheim Aeronautical Laboratory of the California Institute of Technology (GALCIT). This would later become the Jet Propulsion Laboratory (JPL) in Pasadena. Millikan, convinced that Los Angeles could become a major center of the aircraft industry, recruited Theodore von Karman to Caltech, where he began work on rockets and rocket-assisted take-offs. In 1944, von Karman was directed to write the "Towards New Horizons" report for the Army Air Corps, calling for the maintenance of a "permanent interest of scientific workers in the problems of the Air Force" (Rae, 1968: 1196). Von Karman's report laid the foundations for Air Force Project RAND, created under the aegis of Douglas Aircraft in 1946, and in 1948 spun off as an independent nonprofit corporation located in Santa Monica to pursue technical and strategic research under contract to the Air Force (Kucera, 1974).

The decisive turning point that led to Los Angeles County becoming the world's leading aerospace agglomeration consisted of two technological breakthroughs in aircraft design: Lockheed's L-10 Electra, introduced in 1933; and in 1935, Douglas's DC-3 (A. Scott, 1993; Scott and Storper, 1987). These two aircraft were greatly superior in efficiency and speed to existing aircraft, and the market for commercial aircraft responded accordingly. Lockheed's planes accounted for 10.6 percent of all aircraft sales in 1933 and Douglas's for 1.2 percent. By 1937, Lockheed's machines accounted for 32.8 percent, while Douglas's accounted for 59 percent. When demand for aircraft increased during World War II, Los Angeles became the central provider to the War Department. Employment in aircraft industries in Los Angeles increased from 15,000 workers in 1939 to 190,700 workers in 1943 (A. Scott, 1993). At the end of World War II, the aircraft industry went through the first of what would be many external shocks. Nationwide, the government canceled $21 billion worth of contracts (Leslie, 1993). By 1948, regional employment in the aircraft industry had fallen to 44,600, a decrease from the wartime peak of 76.6 percent (A. Scott, 1993).

This decline, however, was quickly broken by the onset of the Cold War, as bombers were the mainstay of atomic delivery capacity in the early 1950s. The Korean War also generated new demand for fighter aircraft.

Defense technology went through a revolution in the early 1950s. In 1953, the defense establishment in Washington concluded that missiles would be the technology of the future, since the thermonuclear weapons that were emerging at that time were lightweight enough to be transported by missile rather than bomber aircraft. Secretary of defense Charles Wilson set up a group known as the Teapot Committee to report on the feasibility of producing intercontinental ballistic missiles (ICBMs). Faced with this opportunity, Los Angeles's aviation industry made its first great skills transposition from airframes into missiles and their guidance systems.

Two types of skills were transposed from aviation to aerospace: from airframe to missile construction and from aviation communications to missile guidance. Hughes Aircraft Company employed Simon Ramo and Dean Woolridge, who built up the advanced electronics capacity within the firm, such that Hughes came to house the largest concentration of technical college graduates, including the greatest number of PhDs in any single industrial facility of that period except for the Bell Telephone Laboratories in New Jersey. By the end of the 1950s, Hughes alone was responsible for 20 percent of the electronics business in California (A. Scott, 1993). Ramo and Woolridge left Hughes to create Ramo and Woolridge (later TRW), to provide systems engineering and technical guidance to the ICBM program. They subsequently developed Titan, the Atlas-boosted guidance system, and the intermediate range Thor missile. RAND, located in Santa Monica, would dominate the strategic planning for the Cold War, which was reflected in the expansion of the Atlas, Titan, Thor, and Jupiter programs, most of them in Los Angeles–based firms. Guidance systems for these missiles required semiconductors, and engineers in the industry transposed their skills to making custom chips. In 1960, Los Angeles firms manufactured more semiconductors than did the Bay Area, using in-house designs for sophisticated chips (Klepper, 2010; Kolko, 2002).

Aerospace and aviation were located across the Greater Los Angeles region.[1] Aerospace interests and culture were pervasive in Southern California, just as later on, IT would become a pervasive element of leadership and economic considerations in the Bay Area. The industry also generated a wealth of spinoff innovations that were not planned as dedicated components of aviation and missiles and that pervaded the regional economy (Klepper and

Sleeper, 2005). For example, ICBMs required satellites, but satellites were subsequently used for other purposes, much in the same way that semiconductors were developed by Western Electric to solve switching problems in the American telephone system but subsequently became useful for computing (Flanigan, 2009). The region also developed space probes for NASA, which required advanced communication systems enabling the probes to relay information back to Earth. Improving the quality of these signals led to the creation of cellular telephony and wireless communications. This dynamism and complexity is largely ignored by many oft-quoted authors who have argued that the defense industry structure of the 1940s was not organizationally adaptive, or that its technological output was restricted to what the Department of Defense commands (cf. Kaldor, 1982; Markusen et al., 1991).

The Roots of Bay Area High Technology: Communications

The Silicon Valley electronics industry has its roots in radio hobbyists at the turn of the twentieth century (Sturgeon, 2000; Lécuyer, 2006; Rao and Scaruffi, 2011). In 1908, Cyril Elwell, a radio enthusiast and graduate from Stanford University, acquired the U.S. patent rights for the arc transmitter, which had been invented in Denmark. The arc transmitter produced clearer signals at greater distance than existing radio technologies, just ten years after Marconi's first transmission in England. Elwell's company, the Federal Telegraph Company (FTC), partly funded by Stanford University, had stolen a march on other radio producers in the United States and was in a position to provide the U.S. Navy with their key ship-to-ship and ship-to-land communication system during World War I (Sturgeon, 2000; Lécuyer, 2006).

Four years after inventing the vacuum tube in Chicago in 1906, kicking off the "age of electronics," Lee de Forest moved to San Francisco, where he would further develop his technology. His invention overcame many of the problems of range and quality of arc transmitters. During the 1930s, Eitel-McCullough and Litton Industries emerged as the major producers of power tubes and, later, microwave tubes. These electrical components had become the basis of radar systems, in addition to their use in radio communications (Lécuyer, 2006). Frederick Terman—a central actor in the nurturing of Silicon Valley, about whom we say more shortly—was close friends with Charles Litton, Sr. and developed a program at Stanford University in vacuum tube engineering. Terman hired Litton to teach courses about vacuum tube making, while Litton supported the program by donating $1,100 to Stanford's electrical engineering department. Terman also financed two of his students—David Packard and William Hewlett—to start up their own firm.

During his time at Stanford, as a professor and then as the dean of engineering, Terman pioneered three major institutional changes in academia. First, he encouraged Stanford to create the Stanford Research Institute (today renamed SRI International), whose purpose was "to pursue science for practical purposes [which] might not be fully compatible internally with the traditional roles of the university" (Saxenian, 1994: 23). However, the first attempt to create the institute occurred in August 1945 in Los Angeles, when Maurice Nelles, Morlan A. Visel, and Ernest L. Black of Lockheed proposed creating it under the name Pacific Research Foundation. A second attempt was made by Henry T. Heald, then president of the Illinois Institute of Technology. In 1945, Heald wrote a report recommending the establishment of a research institute on the West Coast in close association with Stanford University, with an initial grant of $500,000 ($15 million today), but the idea was not implemented. The third and successful attempt was made by Terman at Stanford, creating the SRI.

Terman's second major innovation was to persuade Stanford to open its classrooms to local companies through the Honors Cooperative Program. Terman's third major innovation was to push for the creation of the Stanford Industrial Park, which was the first university industrial park, an organized incubator for firms created by researchers. Terman is what sociologists Walter Powell and John Padgett call a "robust actor": someone who transforms an organizational field through his actions, with effects that often go well beyond his intentions (Powell and Sandholtz, 2012; Padgett and Ansell, 1993).

There were other robust actors in the Silicon Valley case. In 1948, three scientists at Bell Laboratories in New Jersey, among whom was William Shockley, invented the first small device for semiconducting electrical signals. Transistors—miniature wire-based circuits—started substituting for vacuum tubes in a wide variety of products, but the goal was to achieve thinner, more powerful versions of semiconductivity. By 1954, it was clear that the next form of such devices would be based on new electrical resistance materials (such as germanium or silicon) and that the circuits would be embedded in them. In 1955, Shockley relocated to Palo Alto, where he created Shockley Transistors. Legend has it that he wanted to be closer to his aging mother, who lived in Menlo Park. In what is perhaps one of the most powerful recent examples of unintended consequences in the geography of economic development, Shockley drew a number of highly talented engineers to his firm. However, disenchanted with Shockley's style of management—among other things, Shockley was a temperamental character who was known to hold public firings—the so called "traitorous eight" left Shockley to create Fairchild Semiconductors in 1957. The eight defectors were keen to find employment together as a group and remain in the Bay Area. When they could not find an employer for the entire group, they were offered the opportunity to start their own firm by Arthur Rock, a New York–based banker, who linked them to investor Sherman Fairchild, from Rochester (Lécuyer, 2006). This was the precursor to Silicon Valley's subsequent institutionalization of high levels of job-hopping, considered a source of its strength because it encourages the circulation of knowledge (Fallick et al., 2006).

Fairchild transformed the semiconductor industry and the Bay Area with it. The company had an impact on the region in two major ways. First, like Lockheed and Douglas for aircraft in Los Angeles several decades earlier, Fairchild made a breakthrough innovation. Transistors until this point had been made from germanium, but silicon components were much better at resisting high temperatures. Fairchild pioneered the planar manufacturing process using silicon, and it created the integrated circuit. Second, Fairchild was responsible for 24 spin-offs, the biggest of which were Intel, National Semiconductor, and AMD.[2] And thus were born the twin characteristics of Silicon Valley, spin-off and labor mobility.

Silicon Valley stands apart from both Los Angeles and the rest of the nation's high-tech clusters due to the rate of its spin-offs. Over the period 1957–1986, there were 91 spin-offs in the semiconductor industry nationwide, and Silicon Valley accounted for 79 of them (Klepper, 2009). In 2010, the San Jose–Sunnyvale area ranked first in the United States among large metropolitan areas in the per capita rate of IT start-up firms, a position it already held in 1990. Contrast this to Orange County, which was in fifth place in 1990, but not even among the top 20 regions by 2010 (Stangler, 2013).

Until the 1970s, the primary consumer of semiconductors in both the Bay Area and Los Angeles (indeed, nationwide) was the Department of Defense. Defense Department demand was unstable and proved to be a source of vulnerability in the 1960s, during a defense build-down known as the "McNamara Depression," after then secretary of defense Robert McNamara (Kucera, 1974). As early as the 1960s, Silicon Valley firms actively sought commercial clients, in stark contrast to their counterparts in Los Angeles County. In the early 1960s, Fairchild was principally a semiconductor firm looking for markets, whereas Los Angeles semiconductor producers were aerospace/aviation firms engaged in making custom chips for engineering guidance and communication systems. Unlike their Los Angeles counterparts, Silicon Valley firms actively sought to make semiconductors cheaper, to commoditize them, and to make them suitable for a wide variety of end uses.

The Consolidation of IT Leadership in the Bay Area from the 1970s Onward

Intel's invention of the microprocessor in 1971 ushered in the era of smaller computers affordable by private users. It stimulated Silicon Valley's next big transposition of its skills, from chips to computers. Further downsizing of computers happened with the personal computer, the earliest forms of which are traced to the Alto, a product created but never produced for market by Xerox's research lab, PARC, in Palo Alto, followed by IBM's commercialized IBM PC. Xerox was an early investor in Apple Computers, and the avant-garde Alto shaped the design of Apple's Macintosh.

The IBM PC revolutionized computing, selling one million units within three years of its launch in 1981. Several decisions made by IBM had far-reaching consequences for the industry. First, having experienced antitrust lawsuits, IBM decided to make its computer from off-the-shelf components. IBM also made the specifications of its machines available to its competitors, enabling its competition to reverse-engineer and replicate its machines. Overall, the wide availability of generic parts and machine designs fostered the emergence of a PC-clone industry. In this way, a variety of Silicon Valley–based companies, including Hewlett Packard and Sun Microsystems, got into the PC business, along with manufacturers outside the region, including Commodore, Compaq, Dell, IBM, and Olivetti (Saxenian, 2000).

With computing, of course, came an explosion in demand for operating systems and software. It was not obvious where the software industry would agglomerate. Los Angeles had an early presence in the software industry. In the late 1960s, Los Angeles–based Computer Science Corp. was the largest software company in the country and was the first software company to be listed on the New York Stock Exchange. IBM also bought an operating system for its PC, 86-DOS, from a young Seattle programmer, Tim Patterson. In

1981, Bill Gates bought the rights to 86-DOS and hired Patterson to develop it into MS-DOS, which would become the operating system for the IBM PC. In the early 1990s, IBM was the leading software company nationally, with headquarters in upstate New York. Microsoft, located in Seattle, owned the industry-standard operating system for which software would be developed. In spite of these leading firms located elsewhere, Silicon Valley became the biggest software cluster in the United States. The Bay Area has a supply structure for software that is unparalleled, such that the big companies frequently source their software inventions from the Valley and then take routine development in-house (Saxenian, 2000).

The Emergence of Venture Capital

New ideas create bottlenecks in industrial systems, because the services and inputs they need often do not exist. They stimulate entrepreneurial start-ups to meet these needs. This is not limited to direct production. Sometimes the entrepreneurial process grows to the point that new types of organizations and actors are needed to make the emerging production systems work (Ferrary and Granovetter, 2009; Samila and Sorensen, 2011; Kenney and Patton, 2005). These organizations emerge through trial and error, by bringing together different types of human, financial, technological, and management resources and skills. These new combinations of resources and skills are often assembled by new types of intermediaries or dealmakers (Feldman and Zoller, 2012). In Silicon Valley, venture capitalists are key dealmakers; in Hollywood, as we shall see shortly, the dealmakers are agents, specialized lawyers, and some independent investors. In 1995, 23 percent of total venture capital investments in the United States occurred in Silicon Valley; by 2013, this share was about 40 percent. In Los Angeles, the share was about 5 percent in the early 1990s, and about 6 percent in 2013.

Four firms are commonly held to have pioneered modern venture capital: J. H. Whitney, ARDC, Industrial Capital Corporation, and Pacific Coast Enterprises. The first two were from the East Coast and the second two were located in the Bay Area. Since the 1930s, the founder of Whitney had been investing in such industries as motion pictures, orange juice production (Minute Maid), and food processing. In 1946, George Doriot created ARDC (American Research and Development Corporation) in Massachusetts, and his success came from backing Digital Equipment Corporation (DEC) in Boston in 1958. ARDC was the first institutional venture capital company, not financed by wealthy investors. Doriot went on to many other activities, including founding the top-ranked French business school INSEAD. Fairchild, initially backed by an individual wealthy investor (Sherman Fairchild), was subsequently recapitalized by Venrock in 1959, which was also funded by wealthy individuals (it was initially known as Rockefeller Brothers and Company). Other firms came from East Coast financiers in the early 1960s, including William Draper and Sutter Hill.

The Valley was therefore an early magnet for venture capitalists from elsewhere, but the process of spin-off and emulation initially became increasingly localized. The early wins of those who invested in high technology—such as Doriot's bet on DEC and Venrock's on Fairchild—illustrated the possibilities that were opening up with the advent of the semiconductor industry. However, the process of emulation became increasingly localized. Fairchild acted as a venture capital petri dish. Former Fairchild employees Eugene Kleiner and Don Valentine founded Kleiner Perkins and Capital Management Services (later to become Sequoia Capital) in 1972 on Sand Hill Road (Castilla, 2003). Sequoia, in turn, was the early investor in Apple and Atari. The initial pull of demand attracted the venture capitalists into the Valley; initial successes reinforced interest in the tech industry; insider knowledge of the industry led to local spin-offs, and their successes in turn led to more emulation and geographical concentration in the Valley, especially in Menlo Park (Zook, 2002). This process never took off in Los Angeles. In the late 1950s and early 1960s, the vibrant tech sector in Los Angeles was composed of large companies that did not require outside capital.

The Rise of the Internet

In the early 1960s, Leonard Kleinrock of MIT; Paul Baran, an engineer at the RAND Corporation (in Los Angeles); and Donald Davies at the National Physical Laboratories in the United Kingdom, worked together to develop the basic idea for a communications network for the Defense Department, known as ARPANET. The idea was to create a distributed communications system that would not collapse via an attack of any of its individual nodes. Kleinrock was responsible for the development of the key technological component for such a network, the digital packet switch (which enables information to be moved by being cut up into different packets and shunted around any available node in the network). Kleinrock moved to UCLA in the mid-1960s. This led to the initial network being set up to connect three universities (UCLA, UC Santa Barbara, and the University of Utah), a consulting firm (BBN), and the Stanford Research Institute. Kleinrock's computer at UCLA became the host for the first Internet transmission in 1969 (Mowery and Simcoe, 2002). Los Angeles was also an early leader in developing a wider set of early practices of the Internet. As Mowery and Simcoe (2002: 1374) put it:

> The diffusion of the Internet relied on the creation of a set of flexible and responsive governance institutions. Most of these institutions trace their origins to an informal correspondence process called request for comments (RFC), which was started in 1969 by Steve Crocker, a UCLA graduate student in computer science. The use of RFCs grew quickly and another UCLA student named Jon Postel became the editor of the series of documents, an influential post that he would hold for many years.

The subsequent phase of proto-Internet development, however, took it away from Los Angeles. The development of the technical protocol for email (TCP/IP) was achieved in 1972, and this allowed the spread of electronic messaging. There were technically advanced European networks for sending messages, as well as the defense network and the National Science Foundation's NSFNET in the United States. As the American networks were bigger, they created exponentially more traffic and demand for a technology of servers to break the emerging bottlenecks. The bottleneck was solved by the open platform represented by TCP/IP and Ethernet. Cisco, Bay Networks, and 3Com, all new entrants into the industry, built large businesses selling products based on this open network architecture. These firms were all located in the San Francisco Bay Area. Then, in the late 1980s and early 1990s, the protocols that restricted the use of the proto-Internet to noncommercial or public clients were relaxed. At this point, a British engineer, Tim Berners-Lee, working at CERN in Geneva, combined the notion of hypertext with the domain name system and TCP—all existing ideas—and thus created what he called the World Wide Web. Berners-Lee wrote a markup language to create web pages, called HyperText Markup Language, or HTML, along with prototype browser and server software. Since the firms that specialized in mass processing of data and data switching were already located in Silicon Valley, these breakthrough innovations disproportionately benefited its firms, particularly Yahoo! and Netscape.

Yet another bottleneck to be opened up was how to enable Internet users to efficiently find what they needed online. Early search engines such as Excite, AltaVista, and HotBot all advanced web searching; none managed to be profitable. In 1996, Stanford doctoral students Larry Page and Sergey Brin pioneered a new search tool that they would later call Google. Unlike other search tools, which ranked pages according to how many times a search term appeared on each page, Google determined relevance by measuring the amount and quality of links for a given page.

Information Technology: Why Not Los Angeles?

Silicon Valley's story of creating and solving problems, appropriating and incorporating advances made elsewhere, and wrapping them into a system for commercialization—over and over—is a breathtaking one, the iconic economic development story of the last half century. It is frequently said that "the victors write history," which in this case refers to a temptation to make the Silicon Valley development pathway seem inevitable. And yet, as our examination of high technology in Los Angeles has illustrated, the region's firms were early leaders in semiconductivity. Early leadership was also true, to some extent, of the Boston region for semiconductors and computing (Saxenian, 1994), and—in the case of the Internet—a number of European firms and research organizations.

In retrospect, it can be seen that Los Angeles's current modest position in information technology has much to do with the organizational practices that developed in the transition from aviation to aerospace, which was based on the "weapons system" concept of procurement that was adopted in 1955. With this method, the major or "prime" contractor not only developed and produced the airframe but also integrated guidance and other systems and assembled and tested the entire system (Harlan, 1956). The weapons system approach was in turn coupled to a procurement system known as "concurrency," involving the simultaneous completion of all parts of the weapons system, hence requiring centralized management and consultancy. Such concurrent and complete systems contracts were extremely lucrative, driving the region's other major aircraft producers, such as Douglas and Hughes, to diversify into missile production as well as electronics (Peck and Scherer, 1962).

From 1955 onward, the organizational structure of the Greater Los Angeles high-technology complex and the behavior of its firms were oriented toward large-scale, vertically integrated research, development, and production, and away from the highly diversified open contracting and subcontracting networks that had developed in the aviation period. This change in organizational form and practices benefited the Los Angeles economy immensely but would also sow the seeds of its difficulty in entering the IT economy in the 1970s. This was not complete vertical integration in the classical sense of the term, but rather a hierarchically organized and centrally planned project system, involving prime contractors at the top, with control over any project, and associated prime contracts and subcontractors working for them in a highly structured way. This organizational form, however, could not be more different from the flexible open interfirm networks and dealmakers, with high levels of interfirm mobility that were emerging in Silicon Valley (Kenney and Florida, 2000a; Fallick et al., 2006).

It has frequently been claimed that U.S. government expenditures and, more specifically, Cold War science and procurement were largely responsible for their high-technology economies (O'Mara, 2005; Markusen, 1991). But military procurement boosted what already existed in Los Angeles, following Donald Douglas's breakthrough innovation and the industry-building actions of Ramo and Woolridge, Howard Hughes, and Jack Northrop. Likewise, Silicon Valley arose because it broke away from the organizational practices of Cold War procurement and "went civilian."

The Hippie Connection: Regional Culture and Relationships at Work

Thus far, we have seen that Silicon Valley and Los Angeles have contrasting histories in the IT age because Silicon Valley had robust actors, some favorable accidents, the "snowball" effect of growing agglomeration economies, and less monopoly of its resources by the existing aerospace industry. But in the Bay Area's success in IT, there was more: the people who pioneered the IT industry drew on social networks, and hence worldviews, that were not present in the world of Los Angeles.

In 2005, not long before his death, Jobs gave a commencement speech at Stanford University, and toward the end of the speech, he said the following:

> When I was young, there was an amazing publication called *The Whole Earth Catalog*, which was one of the bibles of my generation. It was created by a fellow

named Stewart Brand not far from here in Menlo Park, and he brought it to life with his poetic touch. This was in the late 1960s, before personal computers and desktop publishing, so it was all made with typewriters, scissors, and Polaroid cameras. It was sort of like Google in paperback form, 35 years before Google came along: it was idealistic, and overflowing with neat tools and great notions. (Jobs, 2005)

The Whole Earth Catalog was a serialized publication of the late 1960s and early 1970s, central to the Bay Area counterculture (Turner, 2006). It advocated development of "appropriate" technologies for a better, more empowered life and the solution of social problems through technology and tools. Some of its acolytes also used it as a vehicle for social critique, through the notion of an efficient and ecological rather than ostentatious material life (Roszak, 1969). This echoed previous American movements for aesthetic purity and, in some cases, austerity.

Another of the figures deeply involved in early Silicon Valley, Jaron Lanier, also stresses the influence of the Bay Area counterculture on Silicon Valley technoculture: "There is no single explanation for why tech culture has come to be as it is. However, Apple exemplifies one strain of influence that is particularly underappreciated: the crossover between countercultural spirituality and tech culture" (Lanier, 2013: 205). Lanier continues:

It's hard to overstate how influential this movement was in Silicon Valley. . . . The Global Business Network was a key, highly influential institution in the history of Silicon Valley. It has advised almost all the companies, and almost everyone who was anyone had something to do it. Stewart Brand, who coined the phrases "personal computer" and "information wants to be free," was one of the founders. (Lanier, 2013: 206)

The movement was so important at the time that the State of California created an Office of Appropriate Technology at the top of its executive branch, in its governor's office.

This alternative culture was "a heavy burden to bear for skeptics in Palo Alto in the 1980s," that is, for the more conventional engineering leaders of the Valley (Lanier, 2013: 205; cf. Turner, 2006). But in spite of the skeptics, social networks between people like Brand and Jobs facilitated cross-pollination between these two worlds. The cross-pollination shaped one of the Valley's key strengths, enshrined in Jobs's astute mix of beauty, technological performance, and the use of elite commoditization to lead mass commod-itization. The Bay Area's unique mix of counterculture critique of the main-stream, utopianism, elitism, and technocracy formed the strengths of Silicon Valley, foreshadowing the zeitgeist of the IT age itself. Indeed, the most recent wave of San Francisco Bay Area technology leadership—the "app makers" of San Francisco—are inspired by alternative, out-of-the-box cultures of work and life, just like their forebears in the 1980s (Foege, 2013a, 2013b). As it was put in an account of this milieu in 2013: "The youth, the upward dreams, the em-phasis on life style over other status markets, the disdain for industrial hier-archy, the social benefits of good deeds and warm thoughts. . . . It is startling to realize that urban tech life is the closest heir to the spirit of the sixties" that was so strong in San Francisco itself (Heller, 2013a: 67). Counterculture circles existed elsewhere, and the Bay Area was not the only (but it was perhaps the strongest) outpost of the alternative/appropriate technology movement, but it was the place where the relational infrastructure allowed these worlds to talk to one another and generate new forms of action and innovation. As Mark Pisano put it to us: "Steve Jobs would have never evolved out of Southern California" (Pisano, 2009).

We have just described a unique type of social and business network in the Bay Area that did not exist in Los Angeles. Networks of relations—what we will call the relational infrastructure of regions in Chapter 8—widely influ-ence pathways of economic development.

Southern California in the Age of IT: A Second- and Third-Mover Region

Greater Los Angeles is the fourth largest high-technology region in the coun-try in absolute terms (153,000 employees compared to 255,000 in the Bay Area), but IT accounts for a much smaller proportion of regional employment in Greater Los Angeles (2.5 percent) than in the Bay Area (10 percent), Wash-ington, D.C. (8 percent), Seattle (7 percent), and several other regions. The region has three main high-technology clusters (A. Scott, 1993). In the South Bay Area of Los Angeles County (from LAX to the Orange County border, along the coast), there remains a large defense electronics and communica-tions technology sector. In central Orange County, to the south (centered on Irvine), there is a large cluster in high tech, mostly involved in computer component manufacture, medical devices, and various other manufacturing activities that incorporate electronics into sophisticated devices. In Los Angeles County as well, there is a recent IT cluster centered on application development and content provision for Internet media, centered in Santa Monica and Venice. Los Angeles County ranks seventh in high-tech employment (but first in population) out of the more than 3,000 counties in the United States, and Orange County ranks fourteenth. But Orange County has a lower percentage of high-tech employment compared to the key high-tech clusters in suburban counties around Seattle or Washington, D.C.

Average wages within IT are much lower in Greater Los Angeles than in the Bay Area (Table 5.1). Part of the difference reflects the different mix of 43 subsectors of the IT area of the economy, each with different wage levels. But even *within* these narrow subsectors, wages are lower in Los Angeles than in the Bay Area. The Bay Area's higher wages are thus due to a combination of being more oriented toward high-wage subsectors and of higher wages within subsectors, showing that the Bay Area is higher up the technological ladder than Orange County, mirroring the data on the different proportions of nonroutine work of the two regions in Chapter 3.

Why are the electronics sectors of southern Los Angeles County and Orange County not as high up the ladder of IT industry wages or degree of nonroutineness as their counterparts in the Bay Area? One factor may be, indeed, the heritage of aerospace. Oden and colleagues (1996) found that firms specializing in missiles systems had difficulty converting their output to civilian

TABLE 5.1 Average wages in information technology sectors, 2010

	Average wages: Greater Los Angeles ($)	Average wages: Bay Area ($)
OVERALL IT AGGLOMERATION		
Information technology agglomeration (43 six-digit sectors)	86,169	128,216
SELECTED SIX-DIGIT SECTORS		
Software publishers (511210)	128,583	169,432
Custom computer programming services (541511)	89,295	111,648
Computer systems design services (541512)	90,874	111,312
Computer equipment and software merchant wholesalers (423430)	80,416	155,961

SOURCE: Authors' calculations based on data from *County Business Patterns*.
NOTE: Wages are averages expressed in nominal 2010 dollars.

markets, that is, their technologies could not easily be converted to civilian use. There are also significant organizational barriers for defense firms seeking to switch to civilian markets in the form of high organizational overheads (due to procurement regulations) and secrecy requirements. Moreover, while aerospace was still booming, until the late 1980s, the commercial electronics and medical device industries did not have a slack labor supply to draw from in Greater Los Angeles. They had to draw in new labor, and most of the top engineering and entrepreneurial talent was going to the more exciting and higher-wage IT agglomerations in Silicon Valley, Boston, and Austin. However, none of this fully explains why the firms in Greater Los Angeles occupy product and technology niches that are well below those of Silicon Valley firms on the quality and price ladder.

Later on, in the early 1990s when aerospace laid off more than 100,000 engineers, a large new potential labor supply was created but, as we noted earlier, it seems that most of them were a poor fit to the market-oriented IT industry. Thomas and Ong (2002), based on interviews, concluded that the prevailing opinion among recruiters was that displaced aerospace engineers were ill-matched for the technological and organizational needs of electronics firms operating in the commercial marketplace.

A high-technology agglomeration has been emerging in the Santa Monica/Venice area in the core of Los Angeles County known as Silicon Beach. MySpace was created in 2003, and along with Friendster it was an early leader in social networking, offering its users the chance to connect with their friends, posting music and video. When MySpace was sold to News Corp in 2005, a number of the founding members decided to stay in Los Angeles and form other enterprises. Co-founders Chris DeWolfe and Josh Berman led the way, and at least six start-up companies have been formed by previous MySpace employees.[3] Since 2010, a number of technology giants have set up offices in the neighborhood, including Facebook, Google, Microsoft, Netflix, and YouTube, while Amazon is negotiating a deal that will see it open a major Los Angeles office.[4] Much of this is just the normal process of industry growth, and Los Angeles is getting branches of these major firms as they become mature multilocational corporations, just like most of the world's principal cities. But another part of the momentum for Silicon Beach can be traced to the marriage of Internet and entertainment. Netflix, for example, has a wealth of data on the type of programming consumers desire and has recently turned to its own programming. Since Los Angeles is the capital of content production (see the following case study of the entertainment industry), some technology firms are locating close to the entertainment industry, though content alone cannot explain these firms' presence in the region.[5] Silicon Beach today boasts close to 800 tech start-ups, 50 accelerators and incubators, and 59 venture capital funds. In 2013 the Venice firm Snapchat became the focus of several friendly offers from major firms such as Facebook and was sold in 2014 for $16 billion.

Thus, even if we take all three of Greater Los Angeles's tech clusters together, the region still has not developed a technology sector that decisively improves the economic standing of the region. As noted earlier, the Bay Area is half the size of Greater Los Angeles, but has five and a half times the venture capital financing for new start-ups, or about ten times the density. The top ten zip codes of venture capital investment in the United States in 2012 were in the San Francisco Bay Area ($8.195 billion), followed by Boston ($2.153 billion), New York ($1.953 billion), and Southern California ($1.668 billion). Silicon Beach, in other words, is a small hill in the mountain ranges of the high-technology landscape of the United States (Kolko, 2002).

A Tale of IT in Two Regions: Conservative Transposition Versus the Emergence of New Organizational Forms

The origins and success of Silicon Valley have now been the subject of vigorous academic and public debate since Saxenian's pioneering work (Saxenian, 1983). Klepper (2009) has made a provocative argument that Silicon Valley is more like Detroit than we are accustomed to thinking. Silicon Valley, in his view, is "a chip off the old Detroit bloc," because both areas expanded through spin-off from older firms to newer ones, in a dynamic chain of reactions. This contrasts to the argument of economic sociologists such as Powell and colleagues (Powell et al., 2012; Powell and Sandholtz, 2012), to the effect that Bay Area success has been due to its invention of new organizational forms at every point where major technological and market opportunities arose. In another perspective, popular folklore is dominated by "great man" theories of Silicon Valley's rise (or what we have called "robust action"): heroic and transformative strategies by individual entrepreneurs such as Jobs or civic and academic actors such as Terman. And finally, there is a persistent trope in popular and academic accounts that attributes the Valley's creation to the Pentagon's picking of the region and its firms as winners.

This comparative examination of high technology in two regions allows us to shed light on this debate. The high-tech sector in Greater Los Angeles has been weaker than its northern counterpart in all ways except its dependence on federal government procurement: less spin-off, fewer new organizational forms, weaker internal labor mobility, weaker connections of scientists to businesspeople, and fewer robust actors. Los Angeles's early participation in creation of the Internet never developed into a regional cluster in part due to being too early: the Internet matured and its commercialization rode on the intermediate steps of software and servers, and by the time HTML came around, a huge pool of technologists and venture capitalists and students in the Bay Area were ready to spring on it.

All of the forces cited in the debate over Silicon Valley's origins are indeed relevant, but the decisive catalyst was the emergence of new organizational forms and types of actors in the Bay Area and the organizational inertia in Greater Los Angeles. Skills existed in both, but the transposition in the Bay Area was stronger, and more recombination into new practices occurred there than in Los Angeles.

The story of a more recent technology industry, the biotechnology sector, sharply confirms this analysis, as we shall now see.

Biotechnology: The Bay Area Invents a New Form of Capitalism

Biotechnology refers to the use of cellular and genetic manipulation to generate new products and organisms. While biotechnology is largely applied within health and medical industries, its products have application well beyond these fields, most notably in the creation of agricultural products. The biotechnology industry is research-driven, with roots in academic departments in molecular biology, cellular biology, virology, and biochemical engineering. The R&D process is time consuming, and it is risky and expensive to bring a new drug to market. In addition to lengthy research, a biotechnology product must go through a series of tests and clinical trials before it can be marketed, often lasting between five and twelve years (Casper, 2009; Kenney, 1986; Powell et al., 2012). This means that many start-up companies operate at losses for a considerable period of time before they might turn a profit, if companies make it that far at all (Dibner, 1999). These two traits have carved out special niches for both universities, the primary home for basic scientific research, and venture capitalists, who invest in start-up products.

If we were to travel back in time to 1980, a keen observer might have predicted that Los Angeles would emerge as one of the leading global centers in the biotechnology industry. In the 1980s, Los Angeles housed premier research institutions and was home to what is still today one of the largest biotech companies in the world, Amgen, located in Thousand Oaks in the Los Angeles suburbs. The region was also home to the early scientific breakthroughs that led to the birth of the biotechnology industry. Yet thirty years later, San Francisco is home to more than seven times the number of biotech firms that can currently be found in Los Angeles, and the Bay Area dwarfs Los Angeles in terms of both the number of patents created and venture capital investment (Casper, 2009).

Two First Movers: The Origins of Biotech in Los Angeles and San Francisco

In the early phases of the industry, both the Bay Area and Southern California were home to important breakthroughs in biotechnology. In 1976, two Los Angeles–based scientists, Art Riggs and Keiichi Itakura, who worked for the City of Hope hospital in Hollywood, were the first to demonstrate that strands of DNA could be created synthetically (Casper, 2009). At the same time, research at the University of California, San Francisco by Herbert Cohen, and at Stanford University by Stanley Boyer, led to the granting of the Cohen-Boyer patent for recombinant DNA in 1980. This involved Cohen's work on isolating and cloning genes and reinserting them into other cells, and Boyer's work on isolating enzymes that could be used to cut strings of DNA.

A further significant discovery occurred in 1985 when Fu Kun Lin of Amgen sequenced and cloned erythropoietin, a hormone that produces red blood cells. This discovery led to the creation of Epogen, a drug that increases red blood cell levels in the human body, an important discovery for both anemia and chemotherapy treatments, and Neupogen, a drug that enhances the circulation of white blood cells. Furthermore, in 1986, Leroy Hood, Michal Hunkapiller, and Lloyd Smith, all at Caltech, invented the automatic gene sequencer. The industries in each region were boosted, at an early stage, by the emergence of flagship firms: Genentech in the Bay Area and Amgen in

Southern California. Genentech, created in 1976, was the first biotech IPO in 1980. Robert Swanson, a venture capitalist, and Herbert Boyer, a professor at UCSF, created the firm in 1976. The firm has been at the source of major scientific discoveries, such as the synthesis of insulin. In the 1970s, it was not easy to persuade scientists to leave well-paid, tenure-track positions for the private sector. To sidestep this problem, a new organizational form was created where university professors would be employed on scientific advisory boards of corporations, where they would be advisors, recruiters of trained personnel, and sources of information in the field. The labs of some scientists doubled as research space for fledgling companies, giving rise to a new type of "amphibious" scientist (Powell et al., 2012). Since traditional industrial investors, such as large corporations, were initially wary of investing in biotech companies, venture capital firms stepped in. Universities and venture capitalists combined to create a new organizational form, what Powell and colleagues (2012) refer to as the science-based company or what Kenney (1986) first labeled the "university-industrial" complex and "science-based capitalism." Genentech exemplified this hybrid structure. Its young scientists were encouraged to publish their work in academic journals. Taking their cue from the IT industry, Genentech's senior managers have spawned twenty-three biotech firms in the San Francisco Bay Area. This mobility between start-up firms creates strong networks of biotechnologists in the Bay Area. Of the inventors in each region, 2,700, or 56 percent, in the Bay Area have worked together in a firm at some point, but in Greater Los Angeles, a mere 56, or 2 percent, of all patenting biotechnology scientists have done so (Casper, 2009).

Amgen, too, emerged from academia, but it followed an entirely different path from that of Genentech. Amgen was the brainchild of a Silicon Valley venture capitalist, Bill Bowes, who wanted to create a biotech firm with an all-star scientific advisory board. Bowes asked a Stanford geneticist, Robert Schimke, to assemble the board. Schimke declined the invitation but recommended Winston Salser, a molecular biologist at UCLA. Salser in turn chose Thousand Oaks in which to locate Amgen, using the rationale that it was roughly equidistant to Caltech, UCLA, and UC Santa Barbara, campuses from which the advisory board was heavily drawn (Powell et al., 2012). The location is significant: the firm was located in a suburb that is distant from both academia and any supporting network of investors or other technology-based firms.

In 1983, with the company running out of cash, it made an IPO. To ensure that the company did not go the way of other biotech firms at that time, which were run by academics, a management team was imported to run Amgen from Chicago-based Abbott Industries. George Rathman, a former employee of 3M, became the firm's CEO. A large part of Amgen's early success is attributed to the fact that it had managers experienced in how to run corporations, rather than inexperienced academics. The management team was indeed successful in raising capital and marketing its discoveries. Around a third of all biotech patents in Greater Los Angeles are held by Amgen, and the company has a reputation for having a stable workforce, where senior managers have chosen to stay and pursue careers within the firm. This traditional corporate model, however, has another effect: Amgen has spawned only five spin-off companies.

Genentech, by contrast, became a model of a new form of science-based capitalism, launching a process of expanding regional networks and agglomeration processes—another complex organizational ecology for the Bay Area (Casper, 2007, 2012). Over the period 1976–2005, 214 biotechnology firms were created in the Bay Area, compared to 55 in Greater Los Angeles. Sixty-four of the firms in San Francisco achieved IPO status, compared to only 3 in Los Angeles. Large differences persist in the level of patenting in the two regions. By the year 2000, 4,500 Bay Area inventors had filed 9,913 patents. In Los Angeles, 1,500 inventors had filed 4,182 patents. Over the period 1970–2000, UC San Francisco filed close to 500 biotechnology-related patents and both Stanford and UC Berkeley filed over 300 each. In Los Angeles, by contrast, the best performer was UCLA, which filed around 200 patents, followed by Caltech, which filed around 150. UC Irvine and the University of Southern California each filed around 100. By many standard measures of research output, Caltech is considered the top technology university in the world. But Caltech did not even create a technology transfer office until 1995. UCLA's computer science department was in on the creation of the Internet, but patenting and firm creation by UCLA professors in science and engineering—even when controlled for discipline and size of university—is well below that of UC Berkeley and Stanford (Casper, 2009). Between 1976 and 2005, Bay Area biotech firms received $8.33 billion from venture capitalists. Los Angeles firms received $551 million over this period. Also over this period, Bay Area firms raised $2.9 billion from IPOs; Southern California firms raised just $54 million.

Why are the two regions' universities and firms so different in how they participate in the New Economy? Casper (2009) argues that it is not due to interregional differences in scientific capacity or inventiveness, but because the regional organizational environments are different. The Bay Area has more demand for entrepreneurial innovation. In the Bay Area, there is a vibrant set of relational networks—"invisible colleges" of investors, entrepreneurs, and scientists—that link academic scientists to the entrepreneurial milieu. They respond to that demand (Lazega, 2001).

Greater Los Angeles has no equivalent to the invisible college of managers of biotech firms who have worked together at one point or another. The absence of these networks results in brain and entrepreneurship drain northward to the Bay Area or southward to San Diego. In the words of the founders of Launchpad LA, a privately operated business incubator created in Santa Monica in 2009, the incubator emerged "from our frustration with seeing LA companies receive funding from Northern California VCs and then choose to relocate their teams." Similarly, the founders of Momentum Biosciences, another privately operated incubator in Culver City (on the west side of Los Angeles), write that "born out of the frustration of LA-based inventions moving to the more established biotech hubs of San Francisco and San Diego, UCLA and Caltech faculty banded together to create a local home for entrepreneurial academics and their new ideas."

The emergence of biotechnology is something like a natural experiment for the organizational capacities and relational infrastructure of the two regions. Both regions had early breakthrough inventions from cutting-edge R&D. Both regions had early, first-mover firms. From there, however, these first-mover firms began to reflect the different characteristics of their respective regional economies, and this led to radically different outcomes. Unlike IT, where there is an important—though, as we have argued, not determining—role for the sudden collapse of aerospace/defense in the weak uptake of high-level IT development in Los Angeles in the 1990s, biotech illustrates that even with very good initial endowments and breakthroughs, the problem in Greater Los Angeles is the persistence of old-fashioned organizational practices and a weak relational infrastructure. The story of biotechnology also confirms the legacy of isolation of Los Angeles's universities from the world of commercialization.

Hooray for Hollywood

Southern California is the world leader in producing entertainment—cinema, television, and music. Los Angeles is also the leading U.S. region as an international transport hub for goods, with the largest port-logistics complex in North America. Why have these Los Angeles success stories not enabled Greater Los Angeles to keep up with Bay Area incomes? We can begin with Hollywood.

The industries that produce filmed entertainment, including television and cinema, as well as recorded music and animation, are known collectively as the "entertainment industry." Hollywood is a neighborhood of the City of Los Angeles (northwest of downtown Los Angeles), where the industry had its initial geographical center in the early twentieth century. Today, the entertainment industry is located throughout Los Angeles County, principally in the neighborhoods of Hollywood, West Hollywood, Beverly Hills, Century City, West Los Angeles, Culver City, Universal City, Burbank, North Hollywood, and Van Nuys, but "Hollywood" is also commonly used as a moniker for the entertainment industry.[6] In addition to entertainment, Los Angeles is, along with New York, a major center for an extended "creative arts" sector of the economy, involving fashion, artists, art galleries, furniture design, architecture, and decoration, and is developing a world-class museum and art conservation sector (Currid, 2006; Currid-Halkett, 2007; Molotch, 2002). In a complex synergy with their entertainment industries, New York and Los Angeles are probably the most important generators of pop or "street" culture in the Western world, with images of Los Angeles omnipresent in advertising, music videos, and youth culture everywhere.

Los Angeles's share of the nation's employment in motion pictures increased from 48.8 percent in 1990 to 58.7 percent in 2006. Los Angeles's share of employment in distribution is 24 percent of the national total, 46 percent for postproduction, 30 percent in recording, and 47 percent in services to entertainment. In the broader creative arts sector, Los Angeles County's share of national employment rose from 11.7 percent to 15.6 percent between 1990 and 2006, and 26.4 percent of the wages in the U.S. national creative arts sector are paid out in Los Angeles County alone, compared to Los Angeles's national share of all wages at 3.7 percent (Bureau of Labor Statistics, 2014). The sector accounts for a hefty 10 percent share of Los Angeles County wages, up from 6.7 percent in 1990. In motion pictures and video, Los Angeles County receives 73 percent of the national wage bill, 47.9 percent in distribution, 51 percent in postproduction, 70.6 percent in "other postproduction services," and 38.8 percent for managers (and 53 percent of their total earnings). This is one of the most clustered industries in the world, and Los Angeles County is its core location.

Hollywood's entertainment industries exhibit all the features of success that we described earlier for information technology and biotechnology in the Bay Area. From the 1920s until the late 1940s, Hollywood organized the world's most efficient and powerful production system for filmed entertainment, known as the "studio system." The studio system applied mass production methods to moviemaking. Studios were large vertically integrated firms that produced large numbers of films, using in-house crews, equipment, and stars under long-term employment contracts. The image to have of Hollywood in those days is of everyone from electricians and carpenters to stars showing up at eight a.m., Monday to Friday, to work on getting the product out (Storper and Christopherson, 1987). Films were generated as slightly tweaked varieties on one another, using motifs and themes that were then reused by in-house staff writers for the stars that were on hand, under long-term contract. The mass production system was made possible because studios owned the retail end of the business: movie theaters. In most U.S. cities, a single studio would own most of the local theaters, essentially creating a geographically fragmented set of local monopolies, ensuring audiences for the owner studio's films and excluding the others.

Hollywood: A New Economy Before Its Time

All of this began to unravel in the late 1940s. In 1948 the U.S. Supreme Court issued its *Paramount* decision, which required studios to divest themselves of movie theater chains. This effectively broke up the local monopoly of distribution for the major studios and made the industry much more competitive. The 1950s, in turn, threatened the cinema industry with competition from television. Then again, in 1970, financial syndication rules forced the three commercial television networks to purchase outside programming rather than produce content in-house.

From the 1950s onward, Hollywood responded to these technological and market changes by becoming a flexibly networked, project-based industry, thus foreshadowing the organizational ecology of Silicon Valley. Studios reduced their employment dramatically and many independent supplier firms arose, while many of the industry's workers became free agents, and the product became more and more innovative (blockbuster films, television, differentiated market segments, new filming technologies and aesthetic modes) (Christopherson and Storper, 1988; Scott, A. 2005).

Much motion picture filming moved outside Los Angeles because of the invention of lighter, handheld equipment and a growing taste for more realistic environments. It was also attracted by growing subsidies offered by states and cities in the United States and around the world (Elmer and Gasher, 2005). In spite of this decline in its share of filming, Los Angeles has strengthened its share of the industry's employment and wages. Pre- and postproduction remain overwhelmingly concentrated in Hollywood, and the key skilled "above the line" personnel for a film are also overwhelmingly sourced from Greater Los Angeles. The recent rise of a new "golden age" of television has created a major new source of employment in Hollywood, accompanied by the concentration of the "semi-independent" film industry sector. The production of content—from writing to dealmaking to execution—remains clustered in Los Angeles (A. Scott, 1999, 2002, 2004).

Hollywood's cluster has flourished by reacting to external challenges by generating new types of products, that is, innovation. It has embedded its production work in new organizational forms and drawn on its strong networks of creative people, firms, and dealmakers to do so. In the organizational revolution of Hollywood from the 1950s onward that we described earlier, Hollywood became a new economy before its time.

As in any innovative cluster, Hollywood has had its ups and downs, and it is the subject of ongoing struggles over incentives and creative control, between unions, studios, telecommunications companies, and now the IT sector (Hill, 2004; Littleton, 2007; Christopherson, 2006). But as Steve Dodd, the chairman and CEO of the Motion Picture Association of America, argued after the most recent protracted strike by the Writers' Guild of America: "Time and again, artists and technicians have worked with innovators and entrepreneurs to embrace new technology, reinvent our business model, and reinvigorate our industry" (AMPTP, 2011).

Yet in spite of the unprecedented level of clustering of Hollywood and its ongoing process of self-reinvention, entertainment is not a big enough industry in Los Angeles to maintain the region's per capita income rank. In Table 3.2, we calculated Hollywood's employment as 2.5 percent of the Greater Los Angeles region in 2010. An alternative method of calculation used by the U.S. Bureau of Labor Statistics gives much higher total employment in entertainment by including more independent contractors or part-time project workers. In this view it accounts for between 3.9 and 5.2 percent of Los Angeles County employment. Hollywood is a high-wage industry compared

to the county as a whole. Indeed, average wages in the entertainment industry are 75 percent higher than the county-wide average for all industries and
34.9 percent in the extended creative arts sector. In Table 3.3 we reported average wages for entertainment in Greater Los Angeles as $69,000 annually, but
once again, Los Angeles County is the high-wage core of the industry and it
has more of the high-wage occupations than the rest of Greater Los Angeles
(e.g., producers and directors earn $130,000 on average, writers $116,000, and
film and video editors $98,000). Average hourly wages in Los Angeles County
were $25.30 in 2010, compared to $42.11 for entertainment, and Los Angeles
wages in entertainment were 58 percent higher than the national average for
the industry (Dolfman et al., 2007).

In light of these high wages, coupled to extremely high concentration in
the region, it is therefore tempting to think of entertainment in Los Angeles
in the same way we think of IT for the Bay Area: as a motor of its prosperity
and economic development. This is undoubtedly true to some extent, if the
hard-to-measure spillover effects of Hollywood on the arts, design, finance,
and the regional consumer market are taken fully into account. Nonetheless,
there is only so much weight that entertainment and the arts can carry on
their shoulders. Its wages are high for Los Angeles but are still 30 to 50 percent
below those reported for IT occupations in the Bay Area (see Table 3.3). This
explains why Hollywood's expansion and continued global leadership has not
been sufficient to maintain Los Angeles's per capita income rank.

It has become common to claim that the so-called creative arts sectors
are the keys to city prosperity today (Markusen and Schrock, 2006; Otis College of Art and Design, 2013). No other region is as spectacularly successful
in creative arts as Los Angeles. If the arts cannot lift Los Angeles's fortunes,
they can at best make a modest contribution to regional incomes anywhere.
Creative arts are not a big enough part of the twenty-first-century developed
economy to make a big region generally prosperous.[7]

A Paradoxical Success: The Los Angeles Port and Logistics Industry

Over the past three decades, Greater Los Angeles has become a globally leading trade and transshipment center. Los Angeles International Airport is one
of the biggest cargo airports in the world, and the region has a maritime port
complex on San Pedro Bay that is the biggest container handling port in the

United States and one of the top five in the world. The port we refer to here consists of two side-by-side deep-water maritime transport hubs, one owned by the City of Los Angeles and the other by the City of Long Beach. When accounting for the economic impacts or measuring their size or performance, they should be considered together.[8]

Until the 1990s, total shipping industry employment in Los Angeles was comparable to that of the Bay Area, with its ports of Oakland and San Francisco, as illustrated in Figure 5.1. The Los Angeles region subsequently became the third port region (after the ports of South Louisiana and Houston) in total tonnage handled (U.S. Department of Transportation, 2011), and first in total container traffic. Moreover, both California port complexes are employment-intensive compared to the Louisiana and Texas ports, because there is more handling for automobiles and containers than there is for bulk commodities, as in Houston and New Orleans (Merk, 2013). In 1970 the share of total regional employment in the logistics industry in the two regions was small and comparable in the two regions; from the late 1980s the share in Los Angeles began to grow, and by 2006 the Greater Los Angeles logistics industry represented 2.3 percent of total regional employment, more than double the employment share of the Bay Area logistics industry.

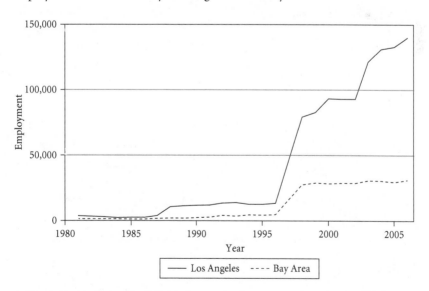

FIGURE 5.1 Trade and logistics industry employment, Los Angeles and the Bay Area, 1980–2006
SOURCE: Authors' calculations using *County Business Patterns data.*

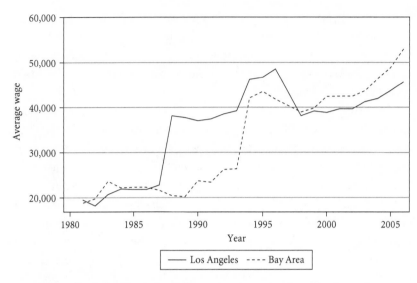

FIGURE 5.2 Trade and logistics industry average wage, Los Angeles and the Bay Area, 1980–2006
SOURCE: Authors' calculations using *County Business Patterns data.*

Wages in the two regions roughly track one another over the long run, though wages in the much smaller Bay Area industry overtook those of Los Angeles from the mid-1990s onward (Figure 5.2).

A Successful Regional Strategy

The logistics industry in Los Angeles has grown and its success is due to deliberate regional action. The San Francisco and Oakland ports in the Bay Area enjoy the advantage of a natural enclosed bay, whereas the ports of Los Angeles and Long Beach have an open bay on the ocean, requiring the creation of an artificial deep-water harbor; however, Los Angeles is closer to the rest of the United States than the Bay Area, and goods can be shipped across the continent without having to cross the Sierra Nevada mountain range, in contrast to goods offloaded in Bay Area ports.

The Port of Oakland was the first port in the United States to handle containerized freight, in 1956. Los Angeles County overtook the Bay Area through deliberate public policy. The twin ports in San Pedro entered the container age beginning in the 1960s by investing in state-of-the-art facilities. They completed dredging of the main channel to 45 feet by 1983, opened the Intermodal Container Transfer Facility in 1986, and dredged Pier 300/400 from 1994 to 2000 while the Port of Long Beach opened its megaterminal at Pier T.

Most importantly, in 1981, the ports of Los Angeles and Long Beach recognized that the key bottleneck to expansion of their container traffic would be the congestion around the ports as trucks took goods from ships to downtown Los Angeles, where the goods are loaded onto the continental rail freight system or transboarded to warehousing and dispatching facilities further inland. The two ports then approached the California Department of Transportation to seek funding for reducing congestion. This in turn required the State of California to designate the Southern California Association of Governments (SCAG) as a metropolitan planning organization, thus qualifying it for state transportation funds. With this achieved, SCAG created a Port Community Advisory Committee that convened many different actors to seek a solution to the congestion between the ports and the continental railheads in downtown Los Angeles. The committee involved an impressive range of actors: the two ports, local elected officials from cities and counties, the U.S. Navy, the U.S. Army Corps of Engineers, the railroads (privately owned in the United States), the trucking industry and the Los Angeles County Transportation Commission. These agencies came up with the idea of constructing a dedicated high-speed rail link between the ports and the continental railheads in downtown Los Angeles, known as the Alameda Corridor. The Alameda Corridor Transportation Authority (ACTA) was founded in 1989, as a joint powers authority of the port owners (the cities of Los Angeles and Long Beach), with a governing board of fourteen members, including the six municipalities through which the corridor passes. The project began construction in 1997 and was completed, on time and on budget, in 2002 at a cost of $2.4 billion (Cambridge Systematics, 2009). Concerted and effective public action at a regional scale for more than half a century has made Los Angeles into a great port city (Erie, 2004).

The Economic Effects of Becoming a Leading Port City

Table 5.2 shows that wages in most of the occupations for the industry are at or below the regional average.

The successful growth of the port-logistics industry in Greater Los Angeles has, paradoxically, contributed to the region's declining per capita income

TABLE 5.2 Share of employment and wages by trade and logistics subsectors, Los Angeles, 2006

Logistics subsectors	Share (%)	Employees	Average wage ($)
Freight (trucking, air, and sea)	41	57,828	41,124
Warehousing/storage/packing	29	40,191	39,363
Consulting and navigation services	18	24,752	49,216
Port operations and cargo handling	12	17,173	70,248

SOURCE: Authors' calculations using *County Business Patterns* data.

ranking. As the executive director of SCAG notes, "The logistics industry is not the industry that creates high-paying jobs. The high-paying jobs are not here" (Ikhrata, 2011). The relatively low wages in transportation and logistics are accounted for by two factors. First, workers in the large-firm (shipping company) sector are mostly recruited from low-wage countries, and their ships call at the California ports. The onshore labor in the port-logistics sector, essentially in container handling and unpacking, is subject to increasing pressures from automation, and in any case requires only moderate educational credentials. The trucking segment is where most of the employment is generated: taking the containers from the port to warehouses in inland Los Angeles or directly to the railheads for the continental rail freight system. The trucking and offloading segment has been restructured in recent years. Trucking is now outsourced to small independent operators, with 80 to 90 percent of establishments employing between 1 and 20 employees. These small firms almost always employ immigrant labor and are less unionized than in the past, when the powerful Teamsters Union represented workers in large trucking firms (Bonacich and Wilson, 2008). The large logistics companies and shippers negotiate with small owner-operators, who in turn compress wages.

Economic benefits of a huge port-logistics complex are, of course, not limited to direct wages (Haezendonck, 2001). Most of the economic benefits of the transport sector are not regional; cheaper shipping makes it possible to provide consumers everywhere with cheaper imports or a wider variety of goods, as well as to allow domestic industries to incorporate lower-priced foreign inputs. More locally, ports can stimulate related activity in the region. Port-related industries consist of services necessary to maritime trade (port-required industries), firms attracted to the region because of the presence of a port (port-attracted industries), and firms that have expanded markets by exporting through the port (port-induced industries) (Yochum and Agarwal, 1987). Port-required industries include transportation services and port services (such as terminal operations, stevedoring, and towage). Port-attracted industries are either firms that export commodities or firms that import products or raw materials (e.g., refineries, steel factories). "Port-induced industries" is a more fluid category. For example, there are functional links between port activity and firms in maritime services, such as ship finance, maritime insurance, maritime law, and maritime consultancy. But the location of firms in these sectors more closely follows the global cities hierarchy than the geography of port cities, as indicated, for example, by relatively strong positions of nonport cities such as Paris and Madrid (Jacobs, DuCruet, et al., 2010; Jacobs, Koster, et al., 2011). London, a city where most port activity has disappeared over the last decades, has a leading cluster in advanced maritime services. Greater Los Angeles ranks low among port cities in maritime services, reflecting its latecomer status and the persistence of lock-in advantages to older port cities (Verhetsel and Sel, 2009). Los Angeles also has a low level of patent intensity in the shipping industry. Though it is second-ranked in absolute terms among U.S. cities in patenting related to shipping (with 2.1 percent of the U.S. total, just behind Houston, with about 3.9 percent), the Bay Area, with a port complex one fourth the size of Los Angeles's, accounted for 2.0 percent of patents (Merk, 2013: 29).

Neither the San Francisco Bay Area nor Greater Los Angeles can be said to be specialized in air transportation, unlike metropolitan regions such as Atlanta or Dallas. Though they have large airports, they have location quotients for air transport (NAICS) that are about 1 (compared to, say, Dallas, which has a quotient of over 3). Los Angeles is the United States' fifth largest air freight forwarding center, and the fourteenth in the world by tonnage. About half this cargo arrives in the holds of passenger airplanes. The U.S. Bureau of Labor Statistics does not release detailed data on about employment and wages in the air cargo sector, but given the tonnages, we can surmise that Los Angeles is specialized in the air cargo part of the air transportation sector (Button et al., 1999). Estimating direct and indirect wage effects of this sector are equally difficult because of data suppression, but surveys of key occupations in the air freight sector give an average annual wage in Los Angeles of $63,000, compared to the countywide average wage of about $49,000 (Mercury Corporation, 2014). Therefore, the air freight subsector of the air transportation industry probably offers a positive contribution to Los Angeles's per capita income position. But since it is a small part of the region's economy, which is in turn not specialized in air transportation more generally, it is unlikely to have much of an overall positive effect.

Logistics: The Southland's Pyrrhic Victory

Los Angeles's business and political leaders anticipated the growth of the trade and logistics industry and actively created the infrastructure and technology for capturing the flow of goods from across the United States to and from the Pacific Rim. These investments required a high level of coordination among public agencies at local, regional, state, and national scales. By 2006, the region had built an industry with over 130,000 workers, equivalent to the size of the entertainment industry. But Los Angeles leaders focused their energies on developing a medium- to low-wage industry, which contributes to the region's slide down the per capita income rankings (with the exception of the small air cargo subsector). Chapter 7 shows in detail how attention to developing the port has crowded out political and policy attention to tasks that would have led to a high road to economic development in the Greater Los Angeles region. The crowding out started in the 1980s, when regional leadership exaggerated the port's potential benefits for the regional standard of living, confusing quantitative growth for the quality of employment. It continued in the early 1990s when vast policymaking energies were devoted to the Alameda Corridor project as every other attempt to respond to Los Angeles's industrial woes and social crises were met with failure.

And it continues today. The negative externalities from the port—in the form of pollution, land use effects, and traffic congestion—command considerable policy attention. Los Angeles is a leader in certain air pollution abatement measures related to its port activity. These efforts are laudable because they are leading to environmental improvement and some efforts at neighborhood improvement in the port area (indeed, Los Angeles is considered to be a world-leading innovator in these areas). But they consume a large amount of the limited policy attention that any region's leadership can devote to development. Paradoxically, because the Bay Area has a much smaller port industry with consequently much lower negative environmental externalities from its ports, its leadership has more attention to devote to other tasks. In an even more cruel paradox, because the port industry's trucking segment has become a major source of new and unstable forms of employment (temporary contracts, subcontracting, and so on), it contributes negative economic externalities to the Los Angeles region that also take up policy attention, a problem that requires less attention of Bay Area leaders. The "losing" region is in many ways the winner: the exact definition of a Pyrrhic victory.

The Key Role of Organizational Change

In popular accounts of the two regions' fates, the Bay Area's successes are almost always attributed exclusively to its extraordinary labor pool and ecology of innovative firms, as well as the deliberate vision of its heroic actors such as Steve Jobs and Fred Terman. These contributed a great deal to the region's success, but there were also a lot of lucky breaks and unintentional outcomes. The opposite is done with typical accounts of Los Angeles's fate: a lot of bad luck and externally generated shocks from Washington (aerospace) and Mexico (immigration) left the region reeling. The detailed case studies in this chapter show that just as San Francisco's success is not entirely due to good fundamentals, Los Angeles's slide is not solely due to bad luck.

There were many turning points when the history that occurred could have gone different ways. We specifically identified the following critical turning points:

- Harry Chandler and Douglas in financing aviation in Southern California
- The civic leadership, in concert with academic leadership, that created and located RAND in Los Angeles
- The "tinkering" of Litton and Hewlett, in the 1930s and 1940s, in the radio communications industry in the Bay Area, then providing high-end boutique services to aviation and aerospace in the 1950s and 1960s
- The failure of the proposal to create SRI in Los Angeles, and its success in the Bay Area in 1946
- The emergence of the concurrent engineering system in Southern California aerospace in 1955
- Hollywood's creation of a new project-based organizational structure in the 1950s and 1960s
- Fairchild's break from defense-related semiconductors in the late 1960s

- Steve Jobs's inspiration from *The Whole Earth Catalog* and "beautiful" IT applications in the early 1980s
- Los Angeles's Alameda Corridor Project in the 1980s and 1990s
- Amgen's go-it-alone strategy in biotechnology in the 2000s
- Genentech's science-based capitalism in biotechnology

The responses to turning points that are described in this chapter—the capture of good first-mover advantages in the Bay Area IT industry and the unsuccessful adjustments from aerospace to IT in Los Angeles, the more favorable nurturing of biotech in the Bay Area compared to Los Angeles, the limited regional spillovers from Hollywood, and the capturing of elite attention by the port industry in Greater Los Angeles—are what need to be explained in order to account for the radical divergence of the two regional economies. Thus, in interpreting the rich vein of qualitative information we have presented in this chapter, it is important to avoid the tendency to confuse what happened with why it occurred. Economic development occurs not just as a deterministic outcome of discrete factors and causes, but from how resources and events were combined into roads taken or not taken (Alchian, 1950; Dosi et al., 1988; Dosi, 1982; Nelson and Winter, 1973, 1982). This is why we have examined the main tradable sectors of these two regional economies by going back to the starting points for main tradable sectors and then examined how things unfolded. Changes in specialization of these two regions were generated by the ways their existing resources and practices were mobilized to shape responses to challenges and opportunities and the priorities of leaders. The following chapters go into these forces in detail.

6 Economic Development Policies

Their Role in Economic Divergence

POLITICIANS DECLARE THAT THEY ARE COMMITTED TO economic development (ED), and this is nowhere more so than at the local level. In the United States, cities devote between $7 and $16 per year per resident to the budgets of their economic development agencies (about $3 billion to $6 billion). But this is the tip of the iceberg of expenditures, as the United States offers at least $20 billion per year in tax incentives for local business attraction in the United States, and even more for local workforce development (Bartik, 2012). In addition to these local policies, the U.S. federal government is heavily involved in economic development policy, much of it implemented at local and regional scale. In 2004, the Federal Reserve Bank of Kansas estimated that the federal government had over 180 programs that could be described as having an economic development objective (Drabenstott, 2005). In the State of California, there is an Employment Development Department and the governor has an office of Business and Economic Development.

In contrast to this picture, our interviewees and a large scholarly literature are quite skeptical about the notion that deliberate formal policies at the local or regional level could have significantly shaped the divergence in development and incomes between the Bay Area and Greater Los Angeles. They are especially skeptical about measures commonly included under the rubric of "business climate" (Kolko et al., 2013). Michael Woo, a former member of the

Los Angeles City Council who was educated as a city planner, states that "successful government initiatives are secondary or tertiary factors, not as direct for example, as interaction between entrepreneurs or the encouragement of inventors and other innovators" (Woo, 2009). Mark Pisano, long-term director of the Southern California Association of Governments, told us, "when I look at the Bay Area. . . . I would be hard pressed to go to a city council and say now what did the city council do to create Silicon Valley" (Pisano, 2009). And again, Michael Woo commented,

> [I]n terms of non-educational institutions such as city government, county government, I don't think that [they] play much of a role in regional economic development in either the Bay Area or Southern California. . . . I don't think there is much government impact on the entertainment industry in Southern California. . . . and I don't think that local government had much to do with the development or education of the workforce or encouragement of cooperation between entrepreneurs and corporate entities in Silicon Valley. (Woo, 2009)

Sean Randolph of the Bay Area Council pointed out that key economic development actions occur outside government through a private industry leadership group—the Bay Area Council—that convenes leaders in the region to align policy priorities (Randolph, 2009).

In assessing the evidence, there are three possibilities: (a) formal ED policies contributed importantly to divergence because they were different; (b) they did not contribute to divergence, because they were similar; or (c) they did not contribute to divergence even though they were significantly different. Complicating matters, it is possible that even though policies did not have a significant effect on divergence, they nonetheless did have positive or negative effects on economic development; this refers to a counterfactual world where, had such policies not been carried out, the regions would today be richer or poorer in absolute terms, though the gap between them would still be what it is today. Most of the scholarly evidence on policies is about this latter issue rather than income divergence (cf. Blakely and Bradshaw, 2002; World Bank, 2002). We will therefore have to carefully parcel out that literature.

This chapter is another detective story. We will search for clues about ED policies and their effects, and then connect dots.

"It Wasn't Our Fault": National Policies and External Shocks to Regions

Many of the formal ED policies that might affect regional economic development are not local and regional. National governments have broad powers for affecting the economic development of their subnational regions. National states have sovereign powers over trade, immigration, and monetary policy and are also able to apply fiscal policy to stimulate growth in their territory as well as extensive powers to regulate wages and labor practices. All of these policies have differential regional effects, because each type of firm and industry reacts in a specific way to the policies according to its labor needs, sensitivity to trade, and underlying growth potential. Moreover, national policies, especially those relating to transportation infrastructure, can affect the distribution of economic activity within the country. National R&D policies, which include the location of nationally funded major facilities (such as military bases and research laboratories) can also affect regional development.

National public procurement policies that favor and disfavor certain industries will visit their effects according to the uneven economic geography of those industries. Many of these policies are implemented by agencies that do not have the term *economic development* in their title. As described in the previous chapter, Los Angeles was the center of the U.S. aerospace industry in the 1970s. A good share of this private sector industry's output is commissioned by and sold to the U.S. federal government in the form of military equipment. Federal government procurement contributed mightily to the growth of the aerospace complex in Greater Los Angeles until the late 1980s; then it reversed course, inducing consolidation of the industry, downsizing many weapons programs, and relocating much of the work to other states, in accordance with the political deals worked out in Washington. This external shock to the Los Angeles economy was greater than any such shock experienced in the period under examination by the San Francisco Bay Area. It corresponds to a period in which regional incomes diverged sharply, the 1990s.

How big was this policy-based shock to Los Angeles per capita income in the 1990s? We showed in Chapter 3 that per capita income in Greater Los Angeles was about 2.4 percent lower in 2000 than it would have been without the loss of aerospace jobs and their multiplier effects during the 1990s, about one eighth of the actual gap that opened up in per capita income.

Federal government policies and the restructuring of aerospace therefore played an important role, but by no means the dominant role in Los Angeles's slide down the ranks of American city-regions.

Identifying Local and Regional ED Policies: A Difficult Challenge

It is a daunting challenge to get a handle on what has been done in the name of ED policy in the two regions under consideration. Local and regional economic development policies and measures are carried out by a dizzying variety of governmental jurisdictions agencies, aided by innumerable private-sector subcontractors and NGO grantees. There are also many different kinds of policies and measures that go under the rubric of "economic development." Sweeping claims about benefits are made by politicians, who like to confuse any employment change with "net jobs created," and all enrollees in training programs as "workers trained." These figures exaggerate benefits, underestimate direct costs and indirect opportunity costs, and do not account for the counterintuitive but powerful indirect effects of policies (Flyvbjerg et al., 2003; Flyvbjerg, 1998). More often than not, local planners and administrators, as well as some community or interest groups, go along with the fictions that are propagated about local ED policies and especially about construction projects (Flyvbjerg, 2005).

Reese and Rosenfeld (2004) document the major types of local and regional economic development policies used in the United States, based on a survey carried out between 1994 and 2001. These include regulatory policies (streamlined permitting processes for business location, imposing employment requirements, requiring training or linkages, growth management, zoning of land use, and special development zones such as enterprise zones); infrastructure investments including arts and cultural facilities, transport, and downtown developments; and land use policies (including site development, zoning, and industrial parks). The most important policies concern business attraction, assistance, and retention, including tax incentives, business incubators, and various kinds of underwriting or subsidies for labor training, as well as for leaseback of land and public investment in specific new infrastructure (especially for sports stadiums or major new land development for siting new businesses). Surprisingly, there exists no reliable database on the nature, extent, or costs of these measures for U.S. states, counties, cities, and special districts.

Political scientists catalog the actions of the U.S. Congress in terms of the policy problems they address. The assembled data indicate the "policy agendas" of the legislative branch (Jones and Baumgartner, 2005). Such a task would be onerous for a metropolitan region because it contains many executive and legislative bodies (counties and cities). Specifically, Greater Los Angeles consists of five counties and 184 municipal governments, and the San Francisco Bay Area is composed of ten counties and 105 municipal governments. Cities and counties have legislative branches, respectively city councils and boards of supervisors. Executive functions generally involve a mayor, for cities, and a county administrator, who in turn directly supervise a wide variety of administrative agencies. In 2005, a report prepared for the Los Angeles city controller identified seven separate departments that played a direct role in economic development action for the city: the Community Development Department, the Community Development Agency, the Department of Water and Power's Economic Development Group, the Harbor Department, the Housing Authority, the Los Angeles International Airport, and the Mayor's Office for Economic Development (Cosio et al., 2005).

In addition to this, cities and counties may occasionally set up line agencies that are not directly supervised by their executive branches but that may have strong impacts on economic development. These can include publicly owned utilities, such as the Los Angeles Department of Water and Power, the Metropolitan Water District of Southern California, or the East Bay Municipal Utility District in the Bay Area. They sometimes include special authorities for owning and operating ports, airports, and transit systems. In each of our regions, special authorities construct, own, and operate some regional rail transit systems (Bay Area Rapid Transit, Metropolitan Transportation Agency of Southern California), while the principal airports are owned and operated directly by cities, as are the eponymous ports of Los Angeles and Long Beach. Cities and counties are important, therefore, but not necessarily the only important centers of policy implementation. All told, there are more than seven thousand local government entities in California.

Our research team attempted to construct an inventory of ED policies in Los Angeles and the Bay Area, coding measures according to policy agendas, following the methodology developed by Jones and Baumgartner (2005). We discovered that the economic development departments of the major cities in Greater Los Angeles and the Bay Area do not keep historical records of their actions. We also discovered that city council legislative agendas do not use clear and consistent labeling for what they consider to be "economic development," sometimes being overly restrictive (not labeling something that might affect development) and often—for political marketing purposes—labeling actions that are irrelevant or trivial as economic development. It is therefore nearly impossible, at the current state of the art, to precisely identify the public policies of cities and counties that are devoted to economic development.

The fact that such an expensive area of public policy cannot be reliably documented and its effects evaluated is worrying. In what follows, we infer from the evidence gathered from less direct sources. We concentrate on several types of policy: job creation through workforce development (labor supply policy); tax policy, enterprise zones, and cluster policies, intended to develop businesses and hence shape labor demand; and megaprojects that supposedly affect aggregate regional activity levels. Then we turn to analysis of overall regional public spending patterns to determine whether there are overall differences in public spending priority that might affect job creation or labor force development.

Labor Supply: Workforce Development Policies

Bartik (2012: 547) argues that "we should define as 'local economic development policies' all the policies that seek to affect the quality and the quantity of local demand or supply of labor, *and thereby increase local per capita earnings.*" Concretely, policies cannot be defined as successful if they merely cause the number of jobs to increase, raise the size of the workforce, or even increase its skills. For example, job creation could lower per capita income if new jobs have lower wages than the existing pool. By the same token, local per capita income can rise with a shrinking population. Most local ED policy has a stated purpose of generating local employment. A measure that increases the *number* of local jobs does have long-term effects on local employment *rates*, but not as straightforwardly as politicians typically claim. About four fifths of increases in demand are met by in-migration and one fifth through increases in local employment-to-population ratios. A 1 percent local labor demand increase provides a long-run boost in employment of *residents* of 0.2 percent. Since about half the population is active in the labor market, a 1 percent increase in local labor demand has a total effect on earnings per capita of about 0.4 percent (Bartik, 2012; Partridge and Rickman, 2006). Moreover, this effect differs between economic development clubs. Moretti (2010) demonstrates that local employment multipliers are of five jobs to each one created in high-technology industries, compared to just two in the old manufacturing sectors. Since high-technology industries locate more in high-cost (mostly coastal) U.S. cities, and low-tech more in the South and the intermountain West, policies that raise total employment will have very different effects in the two clubs. The Sun Belt cities have more in-migration for a given increase in employment than coastal cities (Partridge and Rickman, 2006). Inversely, increases in labor demand in the coastal high-wage club will be met more by increases in employment-to-population than in Southern cities.[1]

Another type of local ED policy attempts to raise local labor participation through education, matching of people to jobs, and job training (Hollenbeck and Huang, 2006). There is considerable, rigorous evidence of success in this type of policy, which when it is well designed and executed can create jobs (Bartik and Erickcek, 2010). Its relationship to per capita income, however, is not so clear. About 50 percent of people who are subjects of such policies will remain, over the long run, in the metro area of their early childhood, and about 60 percent in their childhood state. Much lower percentages will remain in their neighborhood, and thus, research is quite clear that policies to increase or improve quality of labor supply are ineffective as "community" or "neighborhood" development policies and much better as regional development policies.

About half those who are trained will stay in the region. A third of them, on average, take jobs from existing members of the workforce, a phenomenon known as "displacement" (Bartik, 2005). This means that if the population is *successfully* trained, about 35 percent will both stay in the region and raise the region's employment rate. There may be additional positive effects, which we identified in Chapter 4 as regional wage spillovers. Such spillovers from increasing the quantity of jobs or skills of labor raise local demand generally (hence tightening the labor market for nontradable goods and services), and may help firms in the region raise their productivity across the board by substituting more skilled workers into their production processes. But we are at present unable to precisely measure such positive spillovers (Moretti, 2004, 2012; Dickens et al., 2006).

The policies with the most positive effect on local incomes are those that develop the local labor supply for particular *sectors* (Bartik, 2012: 558); they are the workforce development branch of cluster policies, also known as targeted workforce development (Holzer et al., 1992). Policies such as manufacturing extension and customized job training have a ratio of net present value of increased local earnings to the cost of the policy in the range of about 30, whereas nontargeted business tax reductions have a ratio of 0.5 (that is, they have more cost than value), and even the best-designed (industry-targeted) business tax incentives have a multiple of just 3. In U.S. and California workforce policy, however, such industry-targeted programs are quite recent, and they are small (Clagett, 2006). For example, the Regional Industry Cluster(s) of Opportunity II (RICO) initiative encourages regional networks of economic and workforce development practitioners and industry to form industry sector partnerships, which are in turn supposed to develop regional strategies to support and advance targeted industry clusters. The principal measure, as of this writing, is a mere $1.5 million program for workforce development in the electric vehicle industry.

There is a very large, decentralized and complex system of providers of workforce training in California. Most of them do not train for particular economic sectors but for particular types of people. The Workforce Accelerator Fund targets long-term-unemployed, returning veterans; individuals with disabilities; low-income workers; disconnected youth; and ex-prisoners. Such programs are in turn implemented by a wide range of government agencies and NGOs. The names are suggestive: Los Angeles Job Corps, Los Angeles Workforce Investment Board, Los Angeles County Workforce Development Division, Bay Area Workforce Funding Collaborative, Orange County Workforce Investment Board, Orange County Community Investment Division.[2] The system is therefore not oriented to targeted-industry workforce development, which is what scholarly research finds to be the most promising form of workforce training. Given the system's lack of focus, extreme complexity, and high number of moving parts, it has a low level of accountability and a high level of waste (Henken, 2014).

What about regional programs to train the workforces for their key industries? Historically, the role of local government in training Hollywood's workforce has been weak; instead, the universities in Greater Los Angeles developed film and television schools that became national magnets for prospective industry workers. More importantly, Hollywood has always drawn its workforce from around the country and the world, with most skills acquired through experience. This also was the case for Silicon Valley. In the 1950s and 1960s, when the industry began to emerge, most Bay Area universities did not even have computer science programs (Scott and Storper, 1987). Some of them had electrical engineering faculties that were related to the communications and radio guidance industries. The key workforces of the principal tradable specialization industries of the two regions were not created through deliberate workforce development strategies, and formal training mostly emerged as a consequence of the development of the cluster, not as an independent cause.

Labor Demand: Tax and Land Use Policy to Attract Firms

Business attraction policies encourage firms to locate in a certain place. Southern states, from the 1920s, have actively used such policies to foster their industrialization, including tax exemptions, subsidized financing, marketing strategies, and publicly funded site and infrastructure improvements, to lure out-of-state firms within their borders (Bartik, 1991, 2005; Donahue, 1997; Eisinger, 1988). Most of the funds spent by local governments on economic development is channeled into such firm recruitment programs (Markusen and Glasmeier, 2008). The State of Michigan, for instance, was still spending three quarters of its economic development funds on industrial recruitment at the turn of the century (Bartik, 2005).

Business tax competition is a principal element in ED policies of states in the United States (Bartik, 2003; Fisher and Peters, 1998). It is thought by many politicians to be an effective way of attracting businesses that are prone to relocate.[3] Porter, Rivkin, and Kanter (2013) show, however, that tax rates (both business and personal income tax rates) are less important to relocating firms than are underlying wage rates and that firms that are sensitive to such tax rates are virtually all in the narrow segment of the economy that is highly mobile, that is, routine manufacturing (Funderburg et al., 2013). They note that high-tax states such as California attract different types of employment—generally higher-wage and skill—than low-tax states.

Local economic development policy in California has become oriented to attracting firms, but generally not firms that compose the tradable core functions of a regional economy (Neiman et al., 2000). Instead, cities use local land use policy to attract businesses that generate sales tax revenue, mostly in the retail sector. The reason that California local governments are so oriented to generating sales taxes is that an elector-voted law (Proposition 13, in 1979) restricts local governments from raising property tax rates. This law has been very effective. To confirm this, we calculated local property tax rates and the local part of the sales tax rate in all the counties of the two regions for the last two decades. The Bay Area regional average ranges from 1.07 percent in the 1990s to 1.13 percent in 2011–2012; in Greater Los Angeles the figures are 1.06 percent to 1.11 percent, very close to Proposition 13's target of 1 percent.

As a means to increase their revenues, California local governments began favoring retail developments that would generate sales tax revenues, since these taxes are not capped at 1 percent by Proposition 13 (Chapman, 1998; Barbour, 2007; Neiman et al., 2000). In 2009, the Public Policy Institute of California surveyed municipal economic development departments in 88 cities in Southern California and 53 cities in the Bay Area (Neiman and Krimm, 2009). Of the 258 city departments surveyed, 63 percent identified increasing the local tax base as a very important objective, while only 18 percent indicated that they considered reducing unemployment to be very important. Only 8 percent of cities indicated that incubating and nurturing new businesses was their most important economic development priority. There were no major differences in the responses of cities in the Bay Area and Los Angeles to the survey. The policy agendas of California cities are not very concerned with job creation.

In principle, local governments could raise property tax revenues through promoting greater density, but in California this is typically limited to downtown areas, because of opposition from existing residents to more density. Dense urban redevelopment in downtown areas was promoted by a statewide urban redevelopment program that was terminated in 2011. Intensive urban land use, as in downtown redevelopment, does not have much relationship to the IT, biotechnology, entertainment, and logistics industries; it could assist development of financial and producer services industries (as in the case of New York). Downtown redevelopment in San Francisco and Los Angeles probably has had some effect on keeping the finance industry, but neither metropolitan region is specialized in finance, in contrast to New York and Chicago. And a good deal of Los Angeles's finance industry is not in downtown Los Angeles, but scattered in Century City, downtown Beverly Hills, Woodland Hills, and Irvine.

Surveys show that large (multilocational) firms rarely identify local property taxes as a consideration in their location choices. This is because firms that are preoccupied by property taxes in the first place are generally in land-intensive activities and consider only locations with low land prices; any firm that is considering locating somewhere such as the core of the Bay Area or Los

Angeles is locating there for access to labor quality, markets, information, and supply chains. Such firms are more concerned with labor costs, labor skills, access to transportation networks, and energy availability and costs (Area Development Online, 2009). Large-scale differences in specialization due to land prices are much more likely to operate between regions whose overall range of land prices is significantly lower (such as Fresno, Phoenix, or Las Vegas) and expensive regions such as the Bay Area and Los Angeles. This is the economic development club phenomenon we identified in Chapter 2.

Is it possible that the higher absolute level of property taxes per average unit of land in the Bay Area, a natural consequence of higher average land prices in Bay Area, has somehow been indirectly responsible for the Bay Area's success? Recall that in Chapters 1 and 4, we discussed economic theories that argue that high land prices "select" for higher-skilled individuals, which in turn shape the specialization of the economy. In those chapters, we argued that causality runs in the other direction. Greater Los Angeles is, indeed, more fundamentally land abundant than the Bay Area (because of the absence of a bay in the middle of it). But between 1982 and 1997, the Bay Area and Southern California expanded their built-up areas by exactly the same proportion (27.6 percent) (Fulton et al., 2001), and this is consistent with the evidence presented that average regional land use regulation is not appreciably different, in spite of the Bay Area's environmentalist reputation.

All in all, it is hard to detect significant influence of tax and land use policy in shaping income divergence between the Bay Area and Los Angeles.

Labor Demand: Geographically Targeted Business Attraction

Special employment zones, generally known as enterprise zones in American parlance (but also called empowerment zones in the 1990s or New Markets Tax Credit [NMTC] in the 2000s) emerged as an economic development tool in the 1980s in the United States and in other countries (Rubin and Wilder, 1989). Such zones generally provide for lower taxes and fees, certain rebates of taxes, and streamlined regulations for business that locate in a designated area (Elvery, 2009; Freedman, 2012; Peters and Fisher, 2002). They are justified by the claim that they will unleash an entrepreneurial wave that will engender job growth and reduce poverty for local residents of economically poorly performing communities. These policies combine features that are

"place based" (administered to a specific geographical area) and others that
are "people-based" (administered to individuals, who are potentially mobile)
(Barca et al., 2012).

California's enterprise zone program was created in 1986 and ended in
2013. It was the state's single largest economic development program, offering
tax credits and other incentives to businesses to locate within one of the state's
42 zones. Nine enterprise zones were created in Greater Los Angeles and four
in the Bay Area. In 2009, there were roughly 700,000 people employed within
the enterprise zones in Los Angeles and 500,000 people employed in the zones
on the Bay Area. In a thorough study of the state's enterprise zones, analyzing the period 1992–2004, Neumark and Kolko (2010) found that, on average,
enterprise zones had no impact on local firm creation or job growth when
compared to the performance of control groups outside the zones.

It is possible that because labor is mobile and skills created in the zones
can be transferred to other industries or neighborhoods, the ensemble of
such neighborhood-based policies could have positive impacts on the *regional*
economy as a whole. One study found mild evidence of such spillover effects (Hanson and Rohlin, 2013), but the bulk of studies that compare larger
samples of enterprise zones finds no positive regional employment or income
effects (Boarnet and Bogart, 1996; Neumark and Kolko, 2010; Papke, 1994; Peters and Fisher, 2002). One study found that the 1990s federal empowerment
zones (of which one was in Greater Los Angeles) increased employment by
some 15 percent over the baseline, but that the effect was less due to the empowerment zone itself and more due to complementary federal grants to increase public services in those areas, an effect due to classical federal stimulus
rather than business tax incentives (Busso et al., 2010). In any event, *high-wage*
employment was not generated in enterprise zones. We can thus safely rule
out enterprise zone–type local development policies as significant to the interregional divergence at hand.

Labor Demand: Cluster Policies

Another approach to economic development consists of trying to develop
particular, desirable industries in the regional economy. Some states of the
United States use industry-specific business tax incentives, as in abatements
for "green industry" or export-oriented industry. Studies have found that
these targeted tax incentives are more effective than reductions in general

business tax rates (Bartik and Erickcek, 2010). During the period under examination, however, California did not extensively use such credits.

The most famous version of industry-targeted development policies in recent years is the fashion for developing "clusters." There has been a global policy fashion for attempting to become the next Silicon Valley, with great energy devoted to attempting to reverse engineer what are thought to be the components of its ecosystem. Cluster policies have many different mechanisms they attempt to use: incentives for firms to locate, development of the labor force for a particular sector, supporting the R&D and innovation system that is thought to stimulate entrepreneurship and firm formation in a particular area, and stimulating demand for the products of a targeted industry through public procurement and private tax credits. A significant empirical academic literature argues that cluster policies have been ineffective in stimulating employment in general or geographically concentrating it (Duranton, 2010, 2011; Nathan and Overman, 2013; Martin et al., 2011; cf. Bresnahan and Gambardella, 2004). Another literature concludes that such policies have generally failed at raising the local level of innovation (Falck et al., 2010).

Economic geographers have long held that first-mover clusters emerged where breakthrough innovations take place, as in the case of Fairchild's better chip or Douglas's better airplane (Scott and Storper, 1987). They are increasingly supported by economists in this point of view (Chatterji et al., 2013; Kerr, 2010). There is no large-scale evidence that cluster policies have determined the specific locations of these breakthrough innovations or industry-building entrepreneurs (Storper, 2013).

Other authors hold that existing cluster policies have had limited success because they focused too much on "hard" factors (firm subsidies) and not enough on the development of the "softer" elements of successful clusters, such as new forms of organization, networks of entrepreneurs, and forward-looking world views (Storper and Salais, 1997; Rodríguez-Pose and Storper, 2005; Rodríguez-Pose, 2013); in this view, clusters emerge not only where there are breakthrough innovations, but also where the organizational conditions for those innovations can be applied and developed.

The Los Angeles aerospace cluster emerged as a result of a breakthrough innovation in the 1920s (the DC-3), and federal funding subsequently strengthened the cluster from the 1940s onward. In the 1990s, when the cluster suffered an external shock from decline in federal spending and restructuring of aerospace companies, Los Angeles undertook a number of geographically targeted business development programs. The woes of the region were inten-sified by social strife as well. In 1992, an African American named Rodney King was photographed while being beaten by Los Angeles police, and the acquittal of the policemen involved led to a major civil disturbance in the city, which caused significant property damage and loss of life.

In response to the shock of the Rodney King riots and to growing poverty and low-income population, an ad hoc organization known as Rebuild LA was formed at the behest of the Los Angeles mayor's office and the Los Angeles city council. Its board of directors was composed of the major civic and cor-porate leaders of Los Angeles, who pledged substantial financial contributions to support its research and implementation activities. Rebuild LA stressed the development of industrial clusters, similar to SCAG's strategy of the same pe-riod. Rebuild LA folded in 1994, a mere two years after inception, and was widely considered to be a failure. As Kevin Starr stated in 2004 in an interview with the *Financial Times*, "the great and good of Los Angeles strove and failed to engineer the recovery through a many-headed 'rebuild LA' commission" (Parkes, 2004: 13). Peter Ueberroth, who co-chaired the commission, quit "in frustration when corporations were too slow to commit to jobs in inner-city neighborhoods" (Kasindorf, 2003: 3A). Michael Woo considers the Rebuild LA experience typical, observing that "there is a long history of carcasses of abandoned strategic development efforts" in Los Angeles (Woo, 2009).

The Hollywood cluster has also been the object of significant policy atten-tion. There are innumerable policies providing tax breaks for location shoot-ing and various ways to smooth the regulatory issues faced by studios that want to shoot on location in California or Greater Los Angeles. These un-doubtedly have reduced the amount of location shooting that might have left the region and the state. But over the study period, Los Angeles's share of loca-tion shooting has continued to decline, even though its share of the industry's wage bill and total employment has continued to rise, and these two trends go back to the 1980s (Christopherson and Storper, 1988). When we speak of the Hollywood cluster, we are not referring to location shooting, but due to geographical concentration of the businesses, organized into a highly flexible, networked organizational ecology, and to the regional labor pool that sources most of the highly paid labor on films shot on location outside the region.

Were cluster policies responsible for the emergence of IT in the Bay Area in the 1970s or, more recently, for the Bay Area's lead in biotechnology? Silicon Valley benefited from significant federal research funds (as did Greater Los

Angeles in its semiconductor and computer industries). The key events that sealed Silicon Valley's leadership were breakthrough innovations (Fairchild); robust actors (Terman, Shockley); and the beginnings of its spin-off and labor mobility practices, beginning with the Shockley "massacre" described in Chapter 5. None of these was the result of cluster policy.

Subsequently, problem-solving organizations and coalitions emerged to support the growth of the IT cluster. Among these were Joint Venture Silicon Valley and the Bay Area Council Economic Forum. Though they did not establish Silicon Valley, they may have helped sustain the divergence it set into motion. Chapter 7 will show that Bay Area research institutions and local governments have responded more actively to policy support for the biotechnology industry, notably in capturing the State of California's QB3 initiative, which is the biomedical consortium of the Berkeley, Davis, and Santa Cruz campuses of the University of California. They created a site at Mission Bay in San Francisco, designed to enhance synergies in their research in biology, medicine, and complex biological systems, and to have strong relationships to the private sector and the venture capital world of the Bay Area. These policies build on the existing organizational ecology of the Bay Area that we described in Chapter 5. The absence of such concerted action in Los Angeles will likely lead to further divergence between the two regions.

More recently, the U.S. federal government, following the international policy movement, has established a new focus on promoting high-growth entrepreneurship in clusters, mostly by reorganizing existing programs administered by the Department of Commerce's Economic Development Administration. Its future effects on other potential clusters and regional development processes remain to be determined.

Geographically Targeted Stimulus: Megaprojects

Major metropolitan regions have always been the favored locations for large-scale development projects such as sports stadiums, convention centers, concert halls, and museums. These projects are flashy and therefore tempting for both public officials and private philanthropists. During the period under study, such projects in Los Angeles included the Walt Disney Concert Hall, the Getty Center, the Museum of Contemporary Art, the Staples Center and the associated L.A. Live entertainment development, and the expansion of the Los Angeles County Museum of Art. In the San Francisco area, the Embarcadero was rebuilt following the region's major earthquake of 1989. Other Bay Area megaprojects include the Louise M. Davies Symphony Hall, the Museum of Modern Art, the Pac Bell Stadium, the Moscone Center/Yerba Buena redevelopment, the California Institute of Science and the de Young Museum, the rebuilt Palace of the Legion of Honor, and the Jewish Museum. There are megaprojects in San Jose, such as the 49ers stadium in Santa Clara, just as Orange County built its major performing arts centers and several civic centers during the same period. In this, the two regions were not exceptional; throughout the United States, the 1990s and early 2000s were one of the biggest project-building eras in history, especially for culture facilities. Over the period 1990–1999, for example, $21.7 billion was spent by U.S. cities subsidizing sports stadiums, and nineteen stadiums were built, compared to eight in the previous decade, leading some observers to claim that a competitive "bread and circus" race to build convention centers and sports stadiums had gripped the nation's cities (Eisinger, 2000; Siegfried and Zimbalist, 2000). In terms of the total volume of investment in such projects, San Francisco and Los Angeles come just after New York City (Woronkowicz et al., 2012).

Scholarship on the economic effects of megaprojects centers on the opportunity costs of investing in them and on their ability to create employment or raise the potential level of output of the regional economy (Baade and Sanderson, 1997). The economic development effects of such projects in terms of employment or output, as well as their associated opportunity costs, have largely been assessed unfavorably (Noll and Zimbalist, 1997). Moreover, the claims used to justify megaprojects frequently display "optimism bias" (exaggerate benefits) and "strategic misrepresentation" (lying) (Flyvbjerg et al., 2003).

Jobs at convention centers and sports stadiums are primarily low-paid service-sector positions. A professional sports team employs around 70–100 people in its front office. On game days, the club can hire anywhere between 1,000 and 1,500 additional people. Most of these game-day workers are ushers, parking attendants, or concession and retail workers. These jobs are often part time, low-skilled, and low wage in nature, and they frequently lack benefits such as health insurance. Baade and Sanderson (1997) examined the employment effects of a publicly subsidized stadium for the Milwaukee Brewers, which was constructed in 1994. While the sports players for this franchise did well financially, the grounds crew received pay of between $4.85 and $6.56 an hour, without benefits. Ushers were compensated at a rate of between $4.50 and $6.38 an hour. Almost all ushers and grounds crew worked on a part-time basis. Moreover, sports facilities and convention centers are unused most of the time. In the case of football stadiums, for example, an NFL team is guaranteed to play a maximum of thirteen home games per season. Should a team make the playoffs it could potentially play an additional three games at home. But of the 32 teams in the NFL, only 12 of them can make the playoffs in a given season. The same profile is true of employment at convention centers, and their multiplier effects are low as well.

There are opportunity costs of the use of public funds to support stadium or convention center construction. If such facilities are located in dense and growing urban areas, the land will not be available for other uses, though this concern is less valid for a declining or low-density urban area. The second concern is universal: public subsidies given to such facilities could have been put to better use. In February 2011, proposals for a new football stadium in downtown Los Angeles were unveiled. While the bulk of the construction funds would come from the sale of the naming rights of the stadium, the City of Los Angeles would still contribute to the project somewhere in the region of $350 million through a municipal bond—this in a city with a persistent long-term budget deficit with resulting pressure on its credit rating. The city council approved the $1.2 billion project in September 2012, via a unanimous 12–0 vote, even though there was no NFL team in Los Angeles, and approved an accompanying $315 million upgrade of the nearby Los Angeles Convention Center. The council explicitly justified these actions through the lens of their effects on economic development. Thus, city councilman Paul Koretz called the plan "the economic development project of our generation" (*Los Angeles Times*, 2012).

While there is significant land with low-density uses in and around downtown Los Angeles, it is generally speaking a high-land-cost area, with significant increases in density anticipated. Likewise, recent stadium construction near downtown San Francisco may have negative impacts on the housing market there, crowding out housing construction and pushing up housing prices. One can also legitimately ask whether the amount of attention given to megaprojects crowds out the attention the political class could have alternatively devoted to implementing policies with more direct effects on economic development, such as the targeted workforce development discussed earlier.

Convention center megaprojects are usually justified via export-base theory, which holds that they are tradable sectors that leverage multiplier effects in the regional economy. Thus, proponents argue that they attract visitors from outside the region, and as a result raise the baseline level of regional economic activity (Euchner and McGovern, 2003). To generate new economic growth within a regional economy, such megaprojects must raise the region's level of nonresident visitors from what it would be in the absence of the project, which in turn will depend on the level and composition of the business events that occur in a region's convention centers. Las Vegas and Orlando are the two most specialized in convention activity in the United States, just as Paris is internationally. Along these lines, Las Vegas has a location quotient of 16.67 for convention organizing; Washington, D.C., 2.64; Greater Los Angeles, 1.34; and the Bay Area, 0.96 (Bureau of Labor Statistics, 2014). Neither of the regions is strongly specialized in this sector and if they were, the average wages associated with direct employment in this sector would be below their regional averages. The two regions are big tourism destinations because they are big regions, but neither is specialized in tourism as are Miami, Orlando, and Las Vegas. In any event, there is no evidence to suggest that either region had significantly different job development or income effects—positive or negative—from megaprojects.

Infrastructure-Driven Regional Industrial Policy: The Port-Logistics Industry

One of the most common myths about infrastructure, from roads to ports to airports, is: "build it and they will come." This leads to a particular temptation for public policy to build it. Much infrastructure is publicly owned or built with public funds, because it is subject to a variety of well-known market failures (it requires a lot of land or very long-term financing, or it must ensure coverage to both profitable and unprofitable operations, some of which are in the interest of universal service). Infrastructure obviously underpins any regional economy's productivity, by affecting the cost and time of the movement of goods and people, and hence the basic plumbing of any regional economic system.

Yet there is no positive correlation between overall levels of investment in infrastructure and regional economic development. When economic development policy consists primarily of building physical infrastructure, most such regions do not experience growth in employment or income (Crescenzi and Rodríguez-Pose, 2012). This does not imply that infrastructure provision is irrelevant to economic development, but rather that infrastructure is not an independent cause of economic development. It must instead be built in a way that closely tracks underlying demand for it. A further complication is that sometimes new interregional infrastructure attracts activity to outlying areas, but sometimes it has the opposite effect of sucking activity back to established centers.

A different case may be made for infrastructure that is dedicated to specific tradable sectors in the economy, such as air freight or maritime transport. As we demonstrated in Chapter 5, Greater Los Angeles developed its regional economic specialization in the port-logistics sector and moved well ahead of the Bay Area by improving the infrastructure for that sector. Without public investments and regulation of land use for the necessary infrastructure, the strengthening of Los Angeles's specialization as an international trade hub would not have occurred. It is probably the clearest link we can find where deliberate public policy has shaped specialization in the period under consideration.

There are other examples of government-led specialization strategies that are principally based on infrastructure outside the transportation field. North Carolina developed a second-mover high-technology cluster, in Research Triangle Park (RTP), by developing—as the name implies—a large-scale industrial park to attract high-technology firms. It combined this with workforce development and tax incentives for business. RTP is not a market-driven type of agglomeration as is Silicon Valley but rather a business park for R&D and some production activities by major technology firms; there are many examples like it across the world, such as Sophia-Antipolis near Nice, France, or the Japanese national Science Cities policy. Infrastructure development in this case, however, does not build the kinds of innovation-based, high-wage, world-class clusters like Silicon Valley (Wallsten, 2004).

Policy Agendas as Revealed by Public Spending Patterns

As we noted earlier, it is next to impossible to generate an accurate overall inventory of the economic development policies of cities and regions. We therefore turn to other means in order to shed further light on the policy capacities and priorities of our two regions. One way to do so is to compare their levels and patterns of public expenditures. Public spending might conceivably have shaped specialization, either directly by influencing the conditions for entrepreneurship and innovation, or indirectly by influencing the skills of the workforce. Getting from the available data to these specific issues will require considerable interpretation.

Bay Area governments (cities and counties combined) have consistently spent more per resident than their southern counterparts since 1991.[4] Over the period 1991–2000, Bay Area governments spent $31,425 per resident on public services, whereas governments in metropolitan Los Angeles spent $27,115. Even after the dot-com bubble burst in the year 2000, governments in the Bay Area spent a combined $35,722 per resident, compared to $28,212 in Los Angeles. To a great extent, this is a reflection of the fact that the Bay Area has higher per capita income than the Southland. Data pertaining to regional GDP are available since 2001. Over the period 2001–2007, total public spending in Los Angeles represented 11 percent of the region's economy, compared to 10 percent in the Bay Area. There is no evidence, then, that Bay Area residents have an aggregate preference for a more active public sector than Los Angeles, but at a similar rate of local and regional taxation, the Bay Area has more in absolute terms to spend.

Table 6.1 shows the composition of expenditures of all cities in the two regions, divided into eight broad categories. There are some sharp differences between the two regions. Bay Area cities spend considerably more on transportation and health care as a share of their total budget than the Los Angeles region's cities. On a per capita basis, the Bay Area outspends Greater Los Angeles in every major category except public utilities (Table 6.2). The starkest differences are in culture and leisure, health, legislative and management support, and transportation. Greater Los Angeles's higher level of utilities spending is probably due to the existence of the major public utility systems of the City of Los Angeles (Los Angeles Department of Water and Power), which provide electrical power services that are privately produced in the Bay Area; we therefore cannot interpret this difference as a difference of priorities.

The difference can be corrected by removing public utilities from the picture. When this is done, over the period 1991–2000, Bay Area cities spent $19,814 per resident on all categories other than public utilities, compared to $12,284 in Greater Los Angeles. The same figures for the period 2001–2010 are $22,530 for the Bay Area, compared to $13,766 in metropolitan Los Angeles.

Transportation is the largest spending category in the Bay Area, which spends twice the amount per resident on this category that Los Angeles does.

TABLE 6.1 Municipal spending patterns in the Bay Area and Los Angeles

	1991–2000		2001–2010	
	Bay Area	Metro Los Angeles	Bay Area	Metro Los Angeles
SPENDING BY JURISDICTION				
City	$135,000,000,000 (72%)	$241,000,000,000 (62%)	$176,000,000,000 (70%)	$303,000,000,000 (66%)
County	61,513,061,835 (28%)	153,029,507,510 (38%)	75,459,826,039 (30%)	158,928,283,228 (34%)
Total	**216,513,061,835**	**394,029,507,510**	**251,459,826,039**	**461,928,283,228**
Per capita	31,425	27,115	35,722	28,212
COMPOSITION OF SPENDING, ALL CATEGORIES				
All community development	11%	9%	7%	8%
All culture and leisure	9%	8%	8%	8%
All health categories	18%	10%	19%	7%
All legislative/ management/ support	10%	7%	12%	9%
All other expenditures	1%	1%	0%	2%
All public safety	22%	26%	22%	25%
All public utility	8%	26%	10%	26%
All transportation	22%	15%	22%	16%

TABLE 6.2 Per capita municipal expenditures in the Bay Area and Los Angeles

	1991–2000		2001–2007	
Category	Bay Area ($)	Metro Los Angeles ($)	Bay Area ($)	Metro Los Angeles ($)
All community development	2,335	1,473	1,690	1,545
All culture and leisure	1,871	1,197	2,102	1,386
All health	3,854	1,507	4,773	1,368
All legislative/management/ support	2,063	1,149	1,694	1,722
All other expenditures	184	198	6	134
All public safety	4,733	4,218	5,412	4,587
All public utility	1,775	4,301	2,472	4,739
All transportation	4,686	2,512	5,583	2,974
Total expenditure	**21,589**	**16,585**	**25,002**	**18,505**

TABLE 6.3 Transportation expenditures in the Bay Area and Los Angeles

	1991–2000		2001–2010	
Transportation category	Bay Area (%)	Metro Los Angeles (%)	Bay Area (%)	Metro Los Angeles (%)
Streets, highways, and storm drains	31.0	43.9	25.9	43.71
Street trees and landscaping	2.4	5.5	2.1	5.5
Parking facilities	3.7	2.4	4.1	2.2
Public transit	20.8	9.6	20.5	8.9
Airports	34.1	18.1	37.5	22.7
Ports and harbors	7.4	20.0	9.1	16.8
Other	0.5	0.4	0.5	0.5

Some of this could be due to differences in natural geography (the bay as an obstacle), but the Los Angeles region also has considerable natural obstacles in the form of mountain ranges; we therefore doubt that the entire difference is due to geography. Table 6.3 suggests that some of the difference is driven by different policy preferences or agendas: the Bay Area share spent on public transit and airports is twice that of Los Angeles. This seems to be consistent with popular perceptions and observable policy differences in the two regions. In many parts of Greater Los Angeles, most notably Orange County and the Inland Empire, road building takes priority over other forms of transportation.

Bay Area cities spent twice the share of Greater Los Angeles cities over the period 1991–2000 on health care and well over twice the share over the period 2001–2010 (Tables 6.2 and 6.3). Bay Area municipal expenditures on health care might in turn be skewed by inclusion of the County of San Francisco expenditures under the City of San Francisco accounts. Counties provide basic services to unincorporated areas, which are not under the administration of city governments. They also provide certain services that are mandated by, and generally funded by, state and federal governments, for both incorporated and unincorporated areas such as welfare, the criminal justice system, and health care. If we combine the amounts spent by the two regions on health care across city and county governments, we see a real preference for greater public health care expenditure in the Bay Area. Bay Area cities and counties combined spent 18.1 percent of their total budgets on health care over the period 1991–2000 and 17.3 percent over the period 2001–2010. In Los Angeles, the share was 12.2 percent and 11.8 percent, respectively, with sharp per capita differences as well.

Differences persist when we examine total county and city expenditures on transportation as well. Bay Area cities spent around 22 percent of their budgets on transportation, compared to 15 percent in Greater Los Angeles. This is not entirely due to the combined City and County of San Francisco, because all Bay Area governments combined allocate 16 percent of their total budgets to transportation in the period 1991–2000, compared to 9.7 percent in Greater Los Angeles, with the corresponding figures of 15.3 percent and 9.9 percent in 2001–2010. The interregional differences are thus real, and not due to the existence of a combined city and county government in San Francisco.

County spending patterns have smaller, but still significant, differences across the two metropolitan regions. As previously noted, counties have much less autonomy than municipal governments in terms of how they raise and spend money. County budgets are itemized into 30 categories. Over the period 1991–2000, across these 30 categories, there were only two in which the proportion of the funds spent across the regions differed by more than 2.5 percentage points: welfare and police protection. This was also true for the period 2001–2010. In the first of these periods, Bay Area counties spent 22 percent of their budgets on welfare, compared to 29 percent by their southern counterparts, while they spent 15.9 percent of their budget on welfare, compared to 24.5 percent in the Southland over the period 2001–2010. On police protection, Bay Area counties spent 4.7 percent of their budgets over the period 1991–2000, compared to 8.2 percent in metropolitan Los Angeles. In the same category, Bay Area counties spent 6 percent of their budgets over the period 2001–2007 compared to 10.1 percent in Greater Los Angeles.

Public expenditure priorities indicate important differences in policy agendas between the two regions, with the Bay Area conforming more to the image of a socially liberal, pro-state agenda than Los Angeles, more oriented to infrastructure for private use and to a less expansive provision of public goods. The generally higher per capita *levels* in the Bay Area are due to higher income levels in that region, which—at a constant overall expenditure level— give rise to a significant difference. In other words, they could be an outcome of the divergent development we analyze in this book, in what is known in the local development literature as the "widening fiscal capacities" phenomenon due to uneven economic development (Moretti, 2012). But there are also different expenditure *patterns*. Do they respond to different objective realities? Or do they reflect different regional priorities?

We believe the latter is the case. Chapter 7 will show that there are broader and more time-consistent "liberal" political majorities in the Bay Area than in Greater Los Angeles. Such majorities are more favorable to public goods generally and to certain types of them. This notion is known in social science as a constructivist approach to human action: the role of beliefs and worldviews on priorities, and not just objective circumstances, which is known as a structural approach. Let us provide one illustration here. In 2010, FBI data on crime by region show the Bay Area to be ranked 39th in overall crime levels (43.40 per 100,000 inhabitants), while greater Los Angeles was ranked 112th (11.40), with the numbers in parentheses indicating the difference from the national crime rate. Even a low-wage area of the Greater Los Angeles region, such as Riverside–San Bernardino, was ranked 121st (9.24), similar to San Mateo County (124th, 8.34) while all the high-wage areas of both regions (Orange County, Ventura County, Santa Clara) were similarly low. There were no significant differences in regional crime levels in the 1980s, though—as throughout the United States—the levels were higher back then (Federal Bureau of Investigation, 2012). And yet, Southern California spends more on public safety than the Bay Area.

The two regions had somewhat different agendas, policies, and beliefs about economic development. How much did these different agendas affect specialization? We do not have the data to answer this question with certainty. Did higher Bay Area expenditure shares on public goods, health, and education make the region more alluring to the kind of people who were key to its success in the New Economy, whether as workers, inventors, or entrepreneurs? We return to these questions in Chapter 9.

Conclusion: Assessing the Regional Effects of Local Economic Development Policies

Once again, we have identified many clues and it is time to connect the dots.

Local governments carry out a wide range of tasks that they label "economic development," but there is considerable reason to be skeptical about the application of this label to most of what they do; the label is generally abused, as we saw earlier. The measures localities do implement mostly concern local land use—using incentives to attract commercial facilities, helping with land clearance or consolidation and planning permits, and occasionally using public funds to leverage private investment in key facilities or sectors. In other words, they do urban and regional planning. Along these lines, cities can use their physical planning and redevelopment powers to make specific neighborhoods or business districts more attractive. Providing such amenities undoubtedly affects the *intra*regional allocation of economic activity and may improve subregional quality of life (Kemeny and Storper, 2012). But since the regional economy is a regionwide system of people and jobs, using local urban planning to shape the location of activities *within* the region has no direct relationship to its overall (that is, regionwide) level of employment or income.

What are the combined regional effects of all these local policies? Imagine a hypothetical baseline world, where neither region's cities had engaged in the policies discussed in this chapter. In such a case there would have been less use of land use regulation to attract sales and property tax revenue; less urban megaproject construction; fewer or smaller convention centers and sports stadiums; fewer place-based community development efforts, such as workforce training; less firm recruitment; less construction of regional rail transit and other public transportation systems; less improvement of ports and airports; and so on. Regional population levels would be different from what they now are in this hypothetical world of "no local development policies." Developing intraregional transportation infrastructure (highways, transit) is critical to shaping the elasticity of the labor supply, because without such policies, it is much more difficult for people to get to work, which, in the language of economics, "reduces the effective supply of labor." In a mirror image of this, transportation improvements increase the effective housing supply. Together, they allow efficient expansion of the regional economy.

In the period under consideration, the two regions had different transportation spending levels and priorities, with Los Angeles emerging as the latecomer to fixed rail transit compared to the Bay Area, and also as the nation's innovator in improving its bus system, especially in Los Angeles. These policies probably were essential to the two regions' ability to expand housing and employment. Both regions are at the top of U.S. metropolitan areas in traffic congestion, with Los Angeles in first place and San Francisco second, and thus transportation infrastructure has probably not impeded one more than the other in its ability to match people with jobs. This is evidenced by the fact that both regions doubled their populations and housing stocks and extended their geographical reach into formerly remote peripheral regions

(Inland Empire and Orange County in Los Angeles, and Central Valley and southern Santa Clara County in San Francisco). The fact that their per capita incomes diverged so much in spite of all this physical expansion demonstrates that urban and regional planning policies were not the significant factor in shaping their income differences. In the absence of such policies, though population levels would certainly have been lower (because businesses and people would have turned away from the regions). Per capita income is another matter. Incomes might actually have been higher in both with more restriction of development, by making population growth more selective in favor of the skilled. In any event, the income divergence is not principally due to them.

Policies that are most effective in shaping per capita income and that have the highest ratio of overall benefit (net present value) compared to cost are all in the area of sectorally targeted worker training. Most place-based employment policies such as enterprise zones are ineffective or even have negative overall impacts on development because of their insufficient targeting to specific industries (Bartik, 2012). A few of these policies were announced in crisis-racked Los Angeles County in the 1990s, but they were implemented at best halfheartedly and usually abandoned. Direct cluster policies were not implemented in the period that lead up to the interregional divergence, namely, the 1950s through the 1970s. It is difficult to find any powerful relationship of formal cluster policies to the establishment of the entertainment, aviation-aerospace, IT, or biotechnology clusters; by contrast, the port-logistics complex of Greater Los Angeles is directly a consequence of formal governmental policies to develop infrastructure. That approach, of course, cannot be transferred to high-wage New Economy industries. On balance, the standard policies used for business retention or stimulation—tax incentives, tax competition, and megaproject investments—did not differ between the two regions enough to have caused their income divergence.

But now consider another counterfactual possibility: that some of the resources devoted to the policies they did follow had instead been devoted to the policies that the economic development literature suggests work best at raising per capita income, which are industry-targeted workforce policies and other measures that specifically stimulate high-wage, high-skill sectors (about which we say more in Chapter 9). What if Greater Los Angeles had had the knowledge and foresight in the 1980s to implement sectorally targeted workforce development programs, more incentives for its researchers in emerging industries to link to entrepreneurs, creating new forms of finance for New

Economy industries? Would Los Angeles have entered the New Economy more successfully with these active cluster policies and hence avoided or reduced its per capita income gap to the Bay Area? The policies that were followed had costs in terms of using up limited political attention and material resources. The same could be said for the Bay Area. Though the Bay Area has had an impressive economic performance, we cannot know if it maximized its potential performance until we lift the veil of obscurity that lies over local and regional economic development policies. For this to happen, local and regional governments, along with the federal government, will have to develop clearer categories for economic development measures and report them in an honest and consistent manner.

7 Beliefs and Worldviews in Economic Development

To Which Club Do We Belong?

NOBEL PRIZE-WINNING ECONOMIST DOUGLASS NORTH argues that "the dominant beliefs—those of political and economic entrepreneurs in a position to make policies—over time result in the accretion of an elaborate structure of institutions that determine economic and political performance" (North, 2005: 2). As North put it in his Nobel Prize lecture:

> Belief structures get transformed into societal and economic structures by institutions—both formal rules and informal norms of behavior. The relationship between mental models and institutions is an intimate one. Mental models are the internal representations that individual cognitive systems create to interpret the environment; institutions are the external (to the mind) mechanisms individuals create to structure and order the environment. There is no guarantee that the beliefs and institutions that evolve through time will produce economic growth. Learning then is an incremental process filtered by the culture of a society which determines the perceived pay-offs, but there is no guarantee that the cumulative past experience of a society will necessarily fit them to solve new problems. Societies that get "stuck" embody belief systems and institutions that fail to confront and solve new problems of societal complexity. (North, 1993)

In the first part of this chapter we examine the beliefs (worldviews) of leadership groups in the Bay Area and Greater Los Angeles about their economic futures. In the remainder of the chapter, we trace the extent to which each region's public and private actors developed and institutionalized capacities to do things together, which we call regionalist behaviors.

What Club Are We In? Old Economy, New Economy

The economy has clubs of regions and nations that differ by orders of magnitude in their underlying cost structures, productivity levels, and income. Each club thus has its own set of possibilities and constraints for how it can respond to challenges and opportunities. Low-income regions generally cannot specialize in high-wage, high-skill activities (their productivity is mismatched to these activities). For all city-regions, successful further development requires a deft combination of playing to the club the city belongs to, and at the same time gradually nudging one's mix of activities, labor force, and institutions into another club or, if already in the top club, staying at its cutting edge through innovation in order to remain there. When this occurs, the economy can be said to take a high road; when it does not carry out these tasks and its income position slips, it is taking a low road (Cooke, 1995). It is therefore essential that the key economic actors of a region understand what club they are in. This allows them to align their expectations and strategy to the requirements of staying in that club, if they are at the top, or moving up if they are not yet there.

Los Angeles and the Bay Area were both members of the very-high-income club in 1970, and both remain members of the very-high-cost club of regions, because of their combination of high land, housing, and consumer prices. Since 1970, they have lost manufacturing to other clubs of regions, whether to medium-income regions of the United States or low-income regions in the developing world. But leaders in the two regions did not react to these changes in the same way. Los Angeles's leaders generated a low-road narrative for themselves, while Bay Area leadership coalesced around a high-road vision for their region.

These discourses and narratives can be found in reports produced by the regional councils of government (the Southern California Association of Governments [SCAG] and the Association of Bay Area Governments [ABAG]), and a host of other business-civic leadership organizations in Greater Los Angeles and the San Francisco Bay Area.[1] In documenting what certain leadership groups believed and how they saw the world, our purpose is not to determine the veracity of such discourses; rather, their narratives and discourses are raw material, evidence of how they perceived problems and opportunities during the several decades under examination.

There are some similarities in such discourses, because SCAG and ABAG have similar mandates to identify regionwide needs for transportation and housing. They are essentially regional talk shops. The principal inputs to these bodies are local governments. As SCAG and ABAG devoted a great deal of their efforts to their principal mandate, regional physical planning and management, they had to consider regional economic futures. In addition to these councils of government, business leadership groups had contrasting visions. We will see this in how the Los Angeles Economic Roundtable and the Los Angeles Chamber of Commerce generated very different narratives from those of the Bay Area Council and Joint Venture Silicon Valley.

As far back as the mid-1980s, ABAG called attention to the Bay Area's "[l]ocational advantages, outstanding educational facilities, [and] a labor force market skilled in the occupations of the future" (ABAG, 1985: 29).[2] A typical ABAG declaration from that period is this one: "[i]nsufficient housing production and transportation capacity could alter the competitive position of the region" (ABAG, 1985: 29). Nongovernmental regional business-civic organizations in the Bay Area focused more on the regional economy; thus, of 51 Bay Area Council Economic Institute reports published since 1999, 33 refer to the Bay Area knowledge economy, innovation, and/or productivity in their title.[3] Examples of such titles include "The Bay Area: Winning in the New Global Economy" (1999), "The Innovation Economy: Protecting the Talent Edge" (2006), "Bay Area Innovation Network Roundtable: Identifying Emerging Patterns of the Next Wave of Innovation" (2007), and "Innovation and Investment: Building Tomorrow's Economy in the Bay Area" (2012). Throughout these reports, one finds concern with human capital and technology clusters, productivity growth, shareholder return growth, growth of private companies, the Bay Area venture capital industry, the number of Fortune 500 corporate headquarters in the region, the presence of world-class academic and research facilities, measures of innovation, and resilience in the face of economic restructuring.

In 2012, the Bay Area Council Economic Institute summed up the perspective they held throughout this period:

> The region's ability to conceive, research, develop and commercialize new technologies and business models is based on an interconnected innovation system

composed of a diverse set of institutions and actors that are linked by networks and share distinct cultural perspectives on how value is created. Together, these components and processes constitute an innovation value chain that—because innovation is dynamic and often non-linear—can also be described as an innovation cloud. This system has proven resilient, reinventing and repurposing itself through multiple crises and economic cycles. (Bay Area Council Economic institute, 2012a: 1)

A similarly consistent focus on the knowledge economy can be found in 36 Joint Venture Silicon Valley (JVSV) reports published since its creation in 1993, with a further emphasis on the resilience of the regional economy and the capacity of the region to collaborate in response to its challenges, especially coming from the first wave of chip plants leaving the Valley (Saxenian, 1983; Khanna, 1997).[4] Joint Venture's vision was "to build a community collaborating to compete globally."

The Bay Area leadership was also lucid about the implications of globalization for a high-wage, high-cost economy:

[M]ost early-stage, low-volume and high-end production is likely to remain in advanced economies, so long as their research and innovation capabilities are differentiated and superior. Similarly, production of goods that involves sensitive intellectual property, or that requires a high level of adaptability to respond to fast-changing demand and customer service needs, will be located close to local markets, often in higher-cost locations such as California. Thus, the global manufacturing footprint of the future, even for a single company, likely will involve a mix of locations, with "basic," high-volume production offshore and "customized" production maintained domestically. (Bay Area Economic Forum, 2005)

In contrast to the Bay Area leadership, SCAG vacillated on whether to pursue a high-wage, high-skill economy as a regional goal. To its credit, SCAG recognized the rise of the new knowledge economy as far back as the early 1980s, attributing the loss of manufacturing in Los Angeles to

[t]he rise of the knowledge economy. . . . Understanding the character of these transformations may lead to innovative regional policy formulation as regards industrial change (such as policies for research and development, investment patterns, education and retraining programs for the labor force in the region). (SCAG, 1984: 11)

But this type of statement was the exception for SCAG. Throughout the 1980s SCAG produced mostly bland technical statements about the "ongoing transition taking place, as typified by the following statement: "The key task for policy is "[m]atching labor-supply and qualifications with employment demand." (SCAG, 1984: 16).

The early 1990s brought a recession to the U.S. economy, which was more severe in Greater Los Angeles than in the country as a whole. The real estate sector in Los Angeles, hit by the end of a national real estate cycle in 1989, suffered bigger and longer declines in value than in Northern California. The woes of the region were intensified by social strife, as well. In 1992, the "Rodney King riots" occurred. In this atmosphere of crisis, SCAG focused briefly on the New Economy. In its first regional comprehensive plan (RCP) in 1993, SCAG declared that "[t]he fundamental economic goal of regional planning must be to improve the welfare or standard of living of those who work and reside there . . . the objective measure that comes nearest is real personal income" (SCAG, 1993: 2.4). Therefore, "[i]ncome targets for 2010 should be expressed in terms of growth rates of real income between 1990 and 2010" (SCAG, 1993: 2.4). To achieve improvement in income growth, SCAG called for ambitious cluster-based development in apparel, entertainment, tourism, environmental technology, aerospace and defense, foreign trade services, advanced transport systems, environmental technologies, and biomedical equipment. Echoing this, the Los Angeles Economic Roundtable declared,

> An industrial development strategy could help salvage aerospace's capital investment and the economic productivity of its skilled workforce by improving prospects for retaining current industries. It could also help spark a new, dynamic growth trajectory for the region's economy. (Los Angeles Economic Roundtable, 1992)[5]

SCAG also emphasized the importance of addressing the needs of the most economically vulnerable populations:

> Public, private and non-profit organizations must understand and flexibly respond to different communities and to the varying needs of their residents. To develop inter-group harmony, existing organizations must work to build dialogue at the community level and create forums where local issues may be addressed. (SCAG, 1993).

But these concerns were to be a flash in the pan. From the numerous clusters identified in SCAG's 1993 RCP, foreign trade services (i.e., the port-logistics complex) was the only one to retain leadership attention by the end of the decade. As Hassan Ikhrata, SCAG's executive director since 2008, put it, "just after the aerospace [decline], the logistics industry became a major contributor to economic activity; the ports, airports, warehousing, et cetera. So the region adjusted pretty well in kind of reinventing itself with industries" (Ikhrata, 2011). This is what we referred to in the previous chapter as excessive attention to the port-logistics industry having the effect of crowding out attention to the New Economy.

In place of a New Economy agenda, regional leaders turned to developing low-wage sectors, such as light manufacturing. They believed that Los Angeles County could leverage its existing manufacturing skill base to generate regional growth in this way. To support cost-sensitive manufacturing, SCAG's 2001 *State of the Region* report stressed the need to reduce business costs. Los Angeles County should "unlock political barriers to redevelopment of its underutilized land" (SCAG, 2001: 33). In their view, Los Angeles could thus be more welcoming to "[m]iddle and working class manufacturing or wholesale sectors." Such support would reduce their relocation "to places like Riverside-San Bernardino or Eastern Orange counties" (SCAG, 2002: 29). In essence, then, Los Angeles County leaders believed that they could still compete directly with low-wage, low-land-cost interior regions, even though those areas are in a different development club. Even though no measures could have reduced Los Angeles's land costs to the point where they could attract land-intensive manufacturing back into the city, SCAG's perspective influenced Los Angeles city policy.

> In response to the exodus of industrial jobs out of Los Angeles and specifically out of Downtown Los Angeles, the mayor called for changes in land use to discourage or prohibit the conversion of industrially zoned land to residential or other nonindustrial uses. This was part of Mayor Villaraigosa's industrial jobs strategy. (Woo, 2009)

Woo himself understood the weakness of SCAG's reasoning and voted against restricting the conversion of industrial land:

> As a planning commissioner, even though I am sympathetic to the role of maintaining industrial jobs, I thought that very little of this had to do with

zoning, that there are other factors such as wage levels which had a lot more to do with where industrial jobs are located than the zoning of downtown property. (Woo, 2009).

SCAG's continued emphasis on traditional manufacturing was echoed by the Los Angeles Economic Development Council/Kyser Center for Economic Research, in their 2011 report titled *Manufacturing: Still a Force in Southern California*: "[I]f we want to attract manufacturing firms to the region, we need to have sufficient industrial land available and for neighbors bordering industrial zones to understand the importance of manufacturing to the local economy" (LAEDC and Kyser Center, 2011). In other words, at a time when the share of manufacturing in the United States and every other advanced economy was declining rapidly, metropolitan Los Angeles's leadership believed they could retain it and that it would have a positive effect on the region's income level.

SCAG's explanation for the region's decline in per capita income was not the structural transformation of the regional demand for labor, through technological change and the relocation of routine manufacturing, but rather the regional supply of labor. The 1980s and 1990s, as discussed in Chapter 4, were the peak of Latin American immigration to Los Angeles. At the same time, the economic downturn of the 1990s contributed to domestic outmigration. "While 81 percent of the domestic out migrants completed at least a high school education, only 46 percent of the recent immigrants were able to achieve the same" (SCAG, 2002: 3). This demographic shift, argued SCAG, was driven by "an unprecedented large flow of net domestic outmigration due to the recession and the sustaining flow of foreign immigration" (SCAG, 2002: 3). SCAG slipped into fatalism: "Look, this is a market economy. No entity, not private or public, could ever dream that they themselves can sort this. So I think the market adjusted itself [to the aerospace decline] more than anything else" (Ikhrata, 2011). SCAG actually compared the Los Angeles region to Texas, which is in a different development club from Los Angeles:

Companies are leaving Southern California, California in general, because I think it's a well-known fact that companies, big corporations, have to contend with more regulation than, say, Texas. I'm not saying that is all that bad, to a certain limit California is attractive because it's trying to do the right thing and it's progressive, but on the other hand if you're a company with 100 employees

and you're gonna pay a zillion dollars just to get started, and it's cheaper somewhere else, you go somewhere else (Ikhrata, 2011).

The Los Angeles Economic Roundtable had a more nuanced analysis than
SCAG but ultimately showed considerable ambivalence. Of its 32 reports, 8
were published in the 1990s and 23 in the 2000s.[6] Six of the eight reports published in the 1990s were focused on defense conversion to high-wage commercially focused industries or other knowledge-based industrial clusters in
the region. But by the 2000s their attention turned to homelessness, poverty,
unemployment, affordable housing, inequality, and the environment, with
only 3 of the 23 reports focusing on high-wage cluster development such as
green tech and tourism.

In sharp contrast to Los Angeles, since the 1980s Bay Area elites have consistently perceived their regional economy as a new knowledge economy,
stressing technology, innovation, and skills. No matter what the central
purpose of the reports we analyzed—from economic recovery to housing,
transportation, and the environment—the Bay Area leadership consistently
perceived theirs as a knowledge economy. The Bay Area leadership narrative
exhibited a nuanced and multifaceted understanding of the New Economy,
including human capital and industrial clusters, as well as socio-institutional
and relational networks, seen as keys to innovation and resilience. Los Angeles leadership persisted in believing that they could turn back the clock and
become cheaper, and by traveling this low road they could hence compete
with Texas, Alabama, and Mexico. They did some of this in the name of social justice, calling for jobs for low-skill workers. But these noble intentions
emerged from belief structures about economic development that were anti-
quated and inappropriate to the high-cost club of regions to which Greater
Los Angeles belongs by virtue of its size and density and the irreversibly high
land, labor, and consumer prices that this status brings with it.

Learning to Act Regionally

Neither metropolitan region has a single regional development agency with
powers to coordinate regional development policies. Nevertheless, many
regionally important projects are carried out either by the biggest cities in
the region or by special-purpose agencies created by political coalitions
among the cities and counties. By regional projects and initiatives, we mean

specifically projects of a regional scale, with major impacts or spillover effects; such projects include certain types of hard infrastructure or regionwide regulation (such as air or water, coastal management, or open space set-asides). These projects and initiatives are of interest here because they serve as trace elements of what North (2005) defines as the "social learning" part of institution building. In what follows, we are less interested in the regional projects themselves than what they reveal about regional coordination capacities, political cultures, and the process of learning that each region has undergone.[7]

1900–1950: Los Angeles and San Francisco Build Regional Infrastructure

Both regions were rapid developers from the late nineteenth to mid-twentieth centuries (Brechin, 2006; Erie, 1992; Fogelson, 1993). During these early development phases, both regions implemented ambitious regional-scale infrastructure projects. For example, in the early 1900s, both San Francisco and Los Angeles developed infrastructure to import water from inland California to the semi-arid coastal zones they occupy: the Los Angeles Aqueduct from Owens Valley and the Hetch Hetchy aqueduct and reservoir in Yosemite National Park. In the first half of the twentieth century, both the Bay Area and Los Angeles also built extensive rail transit systems. Los Angeles was serviced by two rail systems: the Yellow Cars, a system of streetcars in central Los Angeles, and the Red Cars, a regional electric railway system connecting Los Angeles, Orange, Ventura, San Bernardino, and Riverside Counties. In the Bay Area the Key System linked the entire East Bay and connected to San Francisco by ferry, while San Francisco consolidated its streetcar system into the San Francisco Municipal Railway. In addition to rail networks, both regions engaged in large-scale construction of roads and highways, catalyzed by the California Highway Act of 1916, the Federal Highway Act of 1925, the Breed Act of 1933, and the Collier-Burns Act of 1944. These state and federal projects were accompanied by extensive city street construction in both regions.

Both regions also developed regional strategies for reducing air pollution. Smog attacks in Los Angeles became increasingly common in the first half of the twentieth century, with a severe such attack in 1903 mistaken for an eclipse of the sun by Los Angeles residents (Air Quality Management District, 1997). Between 1939 and 1943 visibility deteriorated substantially because of expanding industrial activity. The Los Angeles County Board of Supervisors responded in

1943 by appointing a Smoke and Fumes Commission in 1945—the first in the
United States. They banned the emission of dense smoke and formed the office
of Director of Air Pollution Control. But only the City of Los Angeles adopted
the recommended smoke regulations, with 45 other cities taking little or no action. The supervisors responded with legislation establishing a countywide air
pollution control district in 1947, over fierce opposition from the Los Angeles
Chamber of Commerce and oil companies, immediately requiring all major
industries to seek air pollution permits. By 1950 Orange County had formed
its own Air Pollution District (APD), with Riverside and San Bernardino following suit in 1957. The four APDs merged twenty years later to form the South
Coast Air Quality Management District (SCAQMD) in 1977.

In the north, Santa Clara County set up its own Air Pollution Control
District in the late 1940s, followed by a regionalization process as in Southern
California, with the creation of the Bay Area Air Pollution Control District in
1955, the first regionwide district in the nation (Bay Area Air Quality Management District, 2011). The air district initially included the counties of Contra
Costa, Marin, San Francisco, and Santa Clara. Napa, Solano, and Sonoma
initially were included as "inactive members," becoming full members in 1971.

The pre-1950s period also saw the construction of the ports of Los Angeles
and Long Beach, the port of San Francisco, and major airports in both regions. The two regions thus carried out the main tasks of region building. But
there was one significant difference. The Bay Area's natural geography, with a
bay in the middle of the region, encouraged different communities and political jurisdictions to seek common engineering and institutional solutions to
costly cross-bay crossings, because they involve economies of scale and high
sunk costs (thus, difficult to change).

San Francisco Bay acts as a natural spur to intergovernmental coordination, since it is ringed by many counties and cities; it is impossible to connect
these areas merely by connecting decentralized local arterial infrastructure.
The connections require major engineering projects with strong irreversibili-
ties and economies of scale, and cost-sharing and joint governance among the
jurisdictions. The Greater Los Angeles region does not have such a unifying
geographic feature to encourage agreement on the part of multiple regional
interests and jurisdictions. Michael Woo sums up this difference:

> I wouldn't dismiss the importance of geography in terms of not just the dis-
> tance, but in terms of [a] geographic feature like the large body of water that

such a high percentage of the population sees or drives by or [is somehow] influenced by, but here there is nothing like that that can galvanize people to do something in the same way the fight to save the bay led to the creation of BCDC [Bay Conservation and Development Commission]. . . . There is no single dominant geographic symbol that galvanizes people here [in Southern California] the way that, for example, the Bay galvanizes people in the Bay Area. (Woo, 2009)

The main bridge projects—the Bay Bridge, linking San Francisco and Oakland/the East Bay, and the Golden Gate Bridge—both required establishing multicounty authorities to build and operate them. There were no equivalent region-spanning, special-purpose agencies in Greater Los Angeles. Many of the region's infrastructure needs were simply provided by the big "imperial" player in the region, the City of Los Angeles. Yet, as Albert Hirschman observed in his classical work on development projects, it is sometimes the case that having obstacles (such as a bay and fragmented decision-making structures) turns out to be an advantage, by encouraging the development of routines of cooperation that subsequently turn out to be useful for other purposes (Hirschman, 1967). We will now see this in the case of the politics of regional rail mass transit.

The Great Divergence in Learning and Institution Building

The social learning of regional leaders diverged sharply beginning in the 1950s. The divergence can be seen in several different policy areas: the politics of regional public transit systems; saving San Francisco Bay from infill; and preserving regional open space. Even though both regions had constructed local and regional transit systems, as the regions matured these systems were challenged by the automobile. By the 1940s, Los Angeles was embroiled in a debate about what to do with its Red Car system (Pacific Electric Company). The system connected downtown Los Angeles with the other main urban centers in Greater Los Angeles, but growth of these other cities was changing the population distribution and mobility patterns of the region. The citizens' Rapid Rail Movement advocated upgrading Pacific Electric's interurban rail links, with the goal of connecting downtown Los Angeles with the growing cities. But the newer urban centers perceived such a plan as "an effort to encroach upon and colonize their hinterlands" (Adler, 1991). In the meantime the popularity of the automobile was reducing ridership. Both the interurban system and the local electric streetcar company owned by Los Angeles Railway had suffered operating losses since 1932; investment declined and the system fell into disrepair. In this context, the Automobile Club of Southern California proposed the construction of an extensive network of intraregional freeways that would link the region's cities. The Los Angeles city council sponsored a study in 1945 that supported both freeways and rail networks in the median strips of the freeways, as well as upgrading the Red Car system, believing that the latter would favor downtown Los Angeles as a location for the headquarters of large companies.

The council appointed the Los Angeles Chamber of Commerce's Metropolitan Traffic and Transit Committee (MTCC), which in turn formed the Rapid Action Transit Group (RTAG). RTAG sponsored a transit district enabling bill and unveiled their $310 million regional transportation proposal, "Rail Rapid Transit—Now!" to an audience of eight hundred business, civic, and political leaders in 1948. The rail portion of the project was opposed by the Los Angeles County division of the League of California Cities. The Long Beach city council unanimously opposed the project, with Councilman Ramsey claiming that local shoppers would travel to Los Angeles "to buy a spool of thread if this high-speed rail line should be operated" (Pomona *Progress-Bulletin*, January 27, 1949; cited by Adler, 1987: 158). The mayor of Claremont opposed the project, claiming that citizens "have no faith in Los Angeles," and the Manhattan Beach mayor echoed this perception of Los Angeles claiming a "growing resentment" by people in surrounding cities. An editorial in the Santa Monica *Evening Outlook* wrote that the project was "designed to save the Downtown shopping district and at a terrific cost to all taxpayers. No real economic need for it exists beyond the need of downtown Los Angeles merchants to reverse a twenty-five year old trend" (Santa Monica *Evening Outlook*, April 18, 1949; cited by Adler, 1987: 158). Opposition to the district bill was even voiced from neighborhoods within Los Angeles that saw themselves as rivals to downtown. The Los Angeles Realty Board, based in the Wilshire District, called the project "socialistic" and bound to require taxpayer subsidies in perpetuity, due to Los Angeles's low density at the time. In this environment, even the Los Angeles city council, with the most to gain from the project, voted 8:6 against it.

The Bay Area faced similar challenges but dealt with them very differently. World War II and the postwar boom in population had greatly increased congestion and accidents on the Bay Bridge. Two studies were commissioned to find a solution. The Joint Army-Navy Board (JANB) recommended the short-term solution of building an alternative rail crossing between Alameda County south of Oakland and southern San Francisco, and a long-term solution of a trans-bay underwater tube connecting rail transit lines on both sides of the bay. This was the first mention of the Bay Area Rapid Transit (BART) concept (Adler, 1987: 162). The California Department of Public Works released their recommendation a few days after the JANB report, proposing a rail crossing a mere three hundred feet north of the Bay Bridge.

Pitted against each other were downtown Oakland leaders and land developers in central Contra Costa County (in support of the parallel crossing north of the Bay Bridge), versus the Peninsula counties of San Mateo and Santa Clara and southern Alameda, in support of the southern crossing. San Francisco initially supported the southern crossing to reduce downtown congestion and to divert transcontinental rail terminals to South San Francisco, which at the time terminated in Oakland. But the railroads opposed this idea, and, as a consequence, the San Francisco business community switched its allegiance to the northern crossing, while at the same time launching a movement for a regionwide rail rapid transit system.

Like their counterparts in secondary cities in the Los Angeles region (such as Long Beach), Oakland leaders opposed the regionwide rapid rail system proposed by San Francisco.

> Oakland, together with several of the smaller East Bay cities, saw the San Francisco transit initiative as another effort to defend the historic pattern of regional domination, and geared themselves for resistance. (Adler, 1987: 164)

San Francisco sponsored a transit district enabling bill, just as the Los Angeles Chamber of Commerce had done with RTAG. The divergence between the Los Angeles and San Francisco rapid transit movements was set in motion when the Los Angeles Chamber of Commerce dropped support for a rail system, while San Francisco business leaders regrouped and succeeded in gaining passage of a state law forming the Bay Area Rapid Transit Commission (BARTC) in 1951. Both BARTC and the Los Angeles Metropolitan Transit Authority (LAMTA) approached the state legislature for funding for regional transportation need assessments in 1953, but BARTC's request was granted and LAMTA's was rejected. "At this point the two movements radically diverged" (Adler, 1987: 165).

The rift between San Francisco and Oakland was resolved by a study titled *Regional Rapid Transit* (RRT) conducted by the construction firm Parsons, Brinckerhoff, Hall, and MacDonald. They recommended an underwater tube along the existing trans-bay corridor with East Bay transit lines to converge in a downtown Oakland hub, consequently aligning the interests of downtown Oakland with those of downtown San Francisco. This came at the price of a new rift with the southern Bay Area counties of San Mateo and Santa Clara, which preferred a southern crossing. An additional hurdle to be overcome was the long-standing East Bay plan to create the Alameda–Contra Costa Transit District (ACCTD) for buses, to replace the Key System. ACCTD proponents did not perceive the East Bay transit system and the regional transit system as mutually exclusive but rather emphasized the importance of East Bay independence and autonomy. San Francisco had its own municipal railway, which did not stand in the way of a regional transit system, as they saw it. San Francisco civic leader Cyril Magnin proposed a special committee composed of both San Francisco and East Bay members, which agreed to support a regional transit system, with San Francisco in turn agreeing to accept the creation of the ACCTD. The different areas overcame their rivalries, with the help of strong civic leaders, to secure outside resources. Business interests were more strongly committed to regional interests, especially as compared to downtown Los Angeles leaders, who could not get their own city council to support rail, and who allowed accusations to flourish that equated public transit to socialism.

Political Geography and Regional Governance

Political geography is perhaps the most important difference in influencing the learning to be regional. The Bay Area is composed of ten counties (as of the 2010 census), and there are several counties with populations in the 2 million range, creating a rivalry of equals. Greater Los Angeles, at more than twice the size, has only five counties and one of them, Los Angeles County, has a population greater than that of the entire Bay Area. The Bay Area's more fragmented political geography turned out to be fortuitous. San Mateo County withdrew from BARTD (the Bay Area Rapid Transit District, the successor to BARTC) in 1962, followed by Marin County, rendering unfeasible a Golden Gate crossing. Outlying Contra Costa County interests tried to build on this momentum by attempting to pull Contra Costa County out of BARTD but failed in part thanks to BARTD support by residential developer interests who had long wanted trans-bay rail as a way to move prospective suburbanites to employers in downtown Oakland and San Francisco. Having stepped back from the brink of collapse, a "much smaller BART system than the one envisioned in the RRT limped on to the 1962 ballot, where a very heavy pro-BART vote in San Francisco, linked to the freeway revolt, barely edged it over the top" (Adler, 1987: 170). Thus, when opposition to BART emerged in Santa Clara, Marin, and San Mateo Counties, it was possible to reconfigure the project and allow a scaled-down version of it to be approved by only three counties.

Los Angeles's political geography made this type of outcome impossible in the Southland. Los Angeles County is the United States' biggest, and it accounts for 60 percent of its region's population, for which there is no equivalent county in the Bay Area. Measures must be approved by countywide majorities in what is a very internally heterogeneous jurisdiction, and this makes approval hard to obtain. A counterfactual scenario can illustrate this point. Had Los Angeles County been divided into, say, four counties of equal size, its outlying areas would have been able to take themselves out of a regional transit project; they would have been to Los Angeles what Marin, San Mateo, and Santa Clara Counties were to the Bay Area BART vote. By contrast, if the urban core of Los Angeles, from downtown Los Angeles to Santa Monica, and possibly including some of the industrial belt running south and east of downtown Los Angeles, had been in, say, two densely populated high-employment counties, they would have been something like the equivalent of San Francisco and Alameda Counties in the Bay Area. They would have been able to consider a scaled-down project and would have been more likely to approve it. This scaled-down project, like BART up north, could initially have been built without service to less dense outlying areas.

In all the historical events described here, neither region built coalitions easily, and this remains true today. Sean Randolph, president of the Bay Area Council Economic Institute, says that fragmentation makes it "very, very difficult to get direction or consensus or any kind of joint action or planning at the metropolitan level with all these jurisdictions typically riding in different directions" (Randolph, 2009). But a combination of stronger civic leadership, different natural geography, and different political geography all helped the

Bay Area act regionally. In turn, each time the Bay Area managed to act regionally, its cities and civic leaders reinforced their capacities for so doing in the future.

Alesina and Spolaore (2003) propose a formal model of this phenomenon. Large jurisdictions have the advantage of being able to undertake projects with high economies of scale, but they face the challenge of finding majorities in support of them, given that their size is likely to group together a population composed of groups with more diverse preferences. Smaller jurisdictions (such as small countries) have the advantage of being more internally homogeneous, so decisions involve less conflict and lower political transaction costs. But their small size is a disadvantage when projects have a large minimal optimal size. When they want to carry out bigger projects, they need to form coalitions with other jurisdictions. Viewed through this theoretical lens, the Bay Area had several medium-sized counties and cities with majority preferences in favor of BART, but Los Angeles had none. The Bay Area attempted a regionwide coalition and failed but was able to unite enough smaller jurisdictions to achieve the minimal scale required to make BART feasible. Such preferences were diluted to below-majority thresholds in Greater Los Angeles within bigger, more internally heterogeneous counties, especially Los Angeles County.

Natural Geography and Regional Governance: Saving the Bay in the 1960s

In addition to its role in promoting regional rail transit, the natural geography of the Bay Area encouraged learning to solve other regionwide problems. In 1959, the U.S. Army Corps of Engineers published a study showing that San Francisco Bay was being filled in for urbanization at a rate that would almost eliminate it within 100 years. In response to this, a citizens group known as the Save San Francisco Bay Association was set up in 1960, led by three East Bay women, among whom was the spouse of the president of the University of California system. Save the Bay grew to have thousands of members in a short period of time and began a campaign to convince the public that the problem of filling the bay was a regional one (Berke, 1983: 490). The Institute of Government Studies at UC Berkeley responded by publishing a more extensive report in 1963 titled "The Future of San Francisco Bay" (M. Scott, 1963). Save the Bay organized a legislative campaign, culminating in Senate Bill 14, which set up the San Francisco Bay Study Commission, composed of nine board members representing each of the nine Bay Area counties. The 1965 report to the legislature recommended creating a San Francisco Bay Conservation and Development Commission (BCDC). The California legislature enacted the McAteer-Petris Act in 1965, giving BCDC power to approve or reject developer or city proposals to fill in the bay. Since then, bay fill has diminished substantially, even registering a small net gain in the size of the bay by 2012 through tidal marsh restoration. Public shoreline access has increased from 4 miles in 1969 to 200 miles today (Save San Francisco Bay Association, 2012). BCDC was effectively the first coastal zone management agency in the United States.

The Save the Bay movement was an important social learning experience in the Bay Area. In the words of Dorothy Ward Erskine, the founder of People for Open Space:

> Fighting these battles you begin to develop a sense of team with different new people willing to join. And the effect upon the individual in doing this is really extraordinary. . . . People completely change under the effort to do these things. (cited in Walker, 2008: 187)

The save-the-bay movement is not unique in the Bay Area. The Bay Area is the principal source of twentieth-century American environmentalism. The Sierra Club was created in San Francisco in 1892, in reaction to San Francisco's construction of a dam that flooded and destroyed part of what is now Yosemite National Park for its municipal water supply. The Sierra Club is today the largest conservation organization in the United States. The U.S. environmental movement emanating from the Bay Area lobbied for creation of the National Park Service in the 1910s and the establishment of the country's largest state park system in the 1920s. The Save the Redwoods League and national wilderness protection movements both emerged in the Bay Area in the 1930s.

By the 1950s, these conservation movements turned their attention increasingly to their home region. California's suburbs were expanding rapidly into the agricultural fringe of the Bay Area in the 1950s. The Bay Area environmental movement responded by advocating the region's first greenbelt conservation law in 1955 in Santa Clara. They subsequently pushed for the statewide California Land Conservation Act of 1965 (the Williamson Act), which offered agriculturists tax relief in return for not converting their land to urban use. This saved the Napa Valley—the heart of the California wine country—from urbanization in the 1960s and 1970s.

Between the 1950s and 1970s the Bay Area environmental movement focused on urban containment and the creation of a regional greenbelt. This movement can be traced back to three groups. Telesis, a group of planning students from UC Berkeley in the 1930s, "mounted an influential exhibit called 'Space for Living' in 1939 that awakened San Franciscans to modern planning and architecture and to the idea of an urban greenbelt" (Walker, 2008:192). A second group came out of the Bureau of Public Administration at UC Berkeley, which was "steeped in the Progressive tradition of municipal reform and had long been an incubator of regionalism and good government" (Walker, 2008: 192); a third group was a group of critical intellectuals composed of scientists, reformers, and journalists who were critical of the environmental impacts of rapid population growth and development. These groups first promoted regional government and although they failed to obtain it, their ideas motivated the creation of ABAG. By 1958 a rare alliance in American politics emerged, consisting of modernist city planners, environmentalists, and urban reformers, in the form of Citizens for Regional Recreation and Parks. Their third conference on open space led directly to the Quimby Act of 1965, giving local governments the right to require developers to dedicate space for parks or open space, or to charge for park acquisition. In the 1970s attention turned to growth control. Cities from across the Bay Area began setting limits to growth by limiting the number of housing units, sewage hookups, timing controls, urban-service limit lines, green lines, city limits, placing large swaths of land in agricultural reserves, and supporting stricter regulations on industrial location.

Chapters 1 and 4 presented evidence that the Bay Area and Los Angeles have similar levels of land use regulation and that both readily added housing stock and population in the period under examination. The Bay Area's stronger open space movement did not stop the Bay Area from growing, but by establishing greenbelts throughout the metropolitan area, it caused growth to leapfrog over them. This is similar to what occurred in London (Cheshire, 2013; Cheshire et al., 2013). It helps explain why the Bay Area today has lower average density than Greater Los Angeles and similar traffic problems, though it has the appearance of more demarcated and compact local communities with high housing cost peaks. The Bay Area reshaped growth but did not stop it.

As Walker observes in his historical analysis, "The Bay Area environmental story bears witness to the importance of the elite in land conservation and nature protection" (Walker, 2008: 37). Bay Area regionalist networks involve a diversity of participants, Including citizen coalitions, intellectuals and academics, scientists, business leaders, political elites, environmentalists, planners, lawyers, journalists, and private foundations. The social learning associated with the region's long history of environmental activism thus cuts across social, geopolitical, and economic boundaries.

The Alameda Corridor: Learning How Not to Act Regionally in Greater Los Angeles

As noted in Chapter 6, the Alameda Corridor is a 20-mile rail cargo express-way between the two San Pedro Bay ports and downtown Los Angeles, whose construction is a successful case of regional industrial policy, in the sense of a policy that strengthened a regional economic specialization. It was not successful in raising per capita personal income in Greater Los Angeles, however, because of the low wage structure of the port and logistics industries. But the project did require substantial interagency cooperation and a strong political coalition. In this sense, we can consider the Alameda Corridor project as a possible example of learning to act regionally, in the way that building and managing the Bay Area's bridges, saving San Francisco Bay from infill, and creating the Bay Area greenbelt were instances of learning to act regionally, in spite of different and often conflicting local interests, in that region.

The Alameda Corridor project was completed in just 21 years from concept to beginning of operations and within its projected budget, a rare occurrence for any major public works project (Flyvbjerg, 2005). However, the project did not involve what could be termed an experience of learning to act regionally in the sense that we define it in this chapter. The Alameda Corridor project passes through eight cities. Its governing board (ACTA) initially included representatives from all the cities, in addition to two privately owned railroads, the ports, and the county transportation authority. However, "the large size of the governing board led to repeated disagreements and disruption of meetings. ACTA could not make any significant decisions, and the project was more or less stalled" (Agarwal et al., 2004: 2). The midcorridor cities

> remained concerned about the local effects of construction activity, increased rail traffic and other negative impacts on residents and businesses adjacent to the Corridor. They persisted with these concerns, arguing that while the ben-

efits of the project were widely dispersed regionally and even nationally, its external costs and adverse impacts were highly concentrated in the areas through which the corridor passed. (Agarwal et al., 2004: 13).

The two San Pedro Bay Ports reacted to the position of the midcorridor cities by cutting them out. In 1995, they amended ACTA's joint powers agreement, thus transferring the finances of the project to a newly created finance committee consisting of the ports and the county transportation agency, "essentially voting the six mid-corridor cities out of power" (Agarwal et al., 2004: 14). The midcorridor cities sued over this exclusion but lost. The governing board of ACTA was reduced from sixteen members to only seven, permanently excluding these cities. The new governing board consists only of representatives from the two ports, the cities of Long Beach and Los Angeles (owners of the ports) and the county transportation commission.

The new ACTA still had to contend with the land use powers of the cities, which had to give construction permits for the project. So ACTA divided them to conquer them, negotiating with them separately and proposing significant mitigation funds to these mostly poor cities, then icing the cake with economic development measures designed to assuage angry working-class constituencies. While some community and labor groups were successfully co-opted, many remained angry.

Most of the lower benefits and higher costs are concentrated in the midcorridor communities that were excluded from decision making. Even though the Alameda Corridor project was successful in reducing transit times from the ports to downtown Los Angeles from two to six hours to only 45 minutes, and it has been able to bear its costs through revenues, the initial project forecasts of economic benefits to Greater Los Angeles, especially to the corridor cities that were cut out of decision making, were highly unrealistic (Erie, 2004). In this respect, the project was typical of the tactics used to justify megaprojects around the world (Flyvbjerg et al., 2003).

In terms of governance and social learning, the Alameda Corridor Project is another example of what Mark Pisano, the former director of SCAG, calls the "big dog" behavior in the Greater Los Angeles region, where the big cities build infrastructure by dominating weaker localities or simply annexing territory and building and owning it themselves (Pisano, 2009). The Alameda Corridor experience is another example of how, in Greater Los Angeles, special districts and big cities do not learn to act regionally. The major public entities in the Bay Area and Los Angeles have thus learned to make regionally important decisions differently from one another.

The New Social Mobilization in Los Angeles

In the late 1980s and 1990s, evidence of a change in regionalist capabilities could be seen in Los Angeles. Following decades of failure to reach consensus on regional transportation priorities, regional business and political leaders began to realize that deadlock was resulting in the region's failure to obtain federal funds. In 1980 Proposition A was put forward by the Los Angeles County Transportation Commission to fund the completion of the four-pronged transportation plan of the late 1970s. This plan included the Red Line (an underground metro line), the Blue Line (a surface light rail to Long Beach), express buses in carpool lanes, and ride sharing. The carefully marketed proposition to raise a half-cent sales tax was approved in 1980, unlike the six previous attempts, "and Los Angeles was finally able to mobilize for the construction of a rail transit system" (Wachs, 1996: 138). Even though these measures occurred within Los Angeles County, it is a very large and diverse jurisdiction compared to the smaller Bay Area counties. In this sense, its growing consensus about public transit can be considered regional. In 1990, Los Angeles voters doubled the local transit sales tax, and the transit plan grew to include Metrolink, the suburban commuter rail service linking all the Greater Los Angeles counties. Thus,

> [f]rom being unable to reach consensus on a single rail project prior to 1970, the Los Angeles region has again turned transportation politics on its head and is now pursuing the most vigorous transit capital investment program of any metropolitan area in the country, perhaps in the world. (Wachs, 1996: 138)

A fabric of community-based organizations also began to be woven together in Los Angeles in the 1980s. Some scholars see this as an emerging shift toward progressivism and greater regionalism (Pastor et al., 2009; Soja, 2010). From the early twentieth century until the early 1980s, Los Angeles's conservative business elites had exerted a firm hold on city politics and successfully subdued progressive and labor movements (Brodkin, 2007, 2009). Economic restructuring in the 1970s and 1980s brought a wave of mergers, acquisitions, and closures of many Fortune 500 firms whose headquarters were based in Los Angeles and whose leaders had constituted "the oligarchy of the downtown business interests" (Montgomery, 2011). Seizing this emerging power vacuum, several business groups and social movements began to organize in the region.

These movements have many different objectives. Homeowner and neighborhood associations have become more active in Greater Los Angeles. Some are traditional NIMBY movements attempting to preserve low density, with little concern for distributional issues, and they can be hostile to developers for this reason. They are not necessarily regionalist or progressive, as in the powerful coalition of homeowner associations and businesses in the San Fernando Valley that forced a vote on their unsuccessful attempt to secede from the City of Los Angeles in 2002 (Purcell, 2002). On the other side can be found "a network of progressive labor unions, community organizations, and environmental groups" (Dreier et al., 2001). The two most prominent and widely recognized coalition-building organizations in Los Angeles were the Los Angeles Alliance for a New Economy (LAANE) and Strategic Actions for a Just Economy (SAJE), two organizations with strong links to union locals in Los Angeles (Haas, 2009). The rise of community and labor movements has some parallels to the earlier and more intense rise of community activism in the Bay Area. Instead of environmentalism as the key uniting feature of these movements, however, in Los Angeles County it is social justice issues. In the context of manufacturing decline and a rise in low-wage employment in the 1980s, union membership grew in Greater Los Angeles at a time when unionization rates were declining in the United States (Milkman, 2006; Soja, 2010: 127). Unions were important in the election of Tom Bradley as mayor of Los Angeles in the 1980s and have since consolidated their role in Los Angeles city politics (Regalado, 1991). This was in no small part due to the unionization of immigrants, many of them working in service industries and the public sector. Los Angeles now has public-sector unionization rates just below those of the Bay Area and slightly higher private-sector unionization. By 2001–2002, the overall gap in union density between the two regions had narrowed to less than half a percentage point: 16.9 percent for the Bay Area and 16.5 percent for Los Angeles (Laslett, 2008). Therefore, argues labor historian John Laslett:

> This difference is the basic reason for the superior degree of political influence possessed by the labor movement in Los Angeles . . . it is this factor, more than any other, which has enabled the LA unions to catch up with their counterparts in San Francisco. (Laslett, 2008: 8).

Some of the powerful Los Angeles unions join in coalitions with community groups on public policy issues in Greater Los Angeles, as is the case in the Bay Area (Purcell, 2002; Frank and Wong, 2004). For example, in 1989, a Bus Riders Union was organized by the Labor/Community Strategy Center, and it organized a successful campaign to redirect transit expenditures from rail to buses, arguing that a greater benefit for the low-waged would be achieved with this type of transit mix. Another campaign, known as Justice for Janitors, called public attention to low wages for building maintenance workers hired by private companies under subcontract to major building owners. Since many such buildings are government-owned, the campaign was able to persuade local government to revise the contracts. A similar logic operated in the so-called living-wage campaign: unions and community activists succeeded in getting local governments to enforce higher minimum wages for direct public employees and industries with fixed locations (such as hotels), in return for building permits. The Alameda Corridor Jobs Coalition took advantage of public debate over the building of the Alameda Corridor rail link between the ports and the main railroad switchyards in central Los Angeles to attach wage conditions and secure promises for workforce training. The Figueroa Corridor Coalition for Economic Justice mobilized around the proposed developments along a 2.5-mile boulevard between USC and Los Angeles's downtown convention center to secure various conditions desired by the local neighborhoods. The LAX Coalition for Economic, Environmental and Social Justice successfully negotiated a Community Benefits Agreement in November 2004 with the Los Angeles World Airports that included workforce training, wage, employee benefit, and local hiring quotas.

These coalitions are described by Manuel Pastor as "thick coalitions," in the sense that they represent long-term repeated interactions (Pastor, 2010: 253) and draw support from historically fragmented labor, environmental, and community-based groups (Montgomery, 2011; Pastor et al., 2009; Brodkin, 2007, 2009). Hurd, Milkman and Turner (2003: 107) argue that such coalition building has been central to the revitalization of the American labor movement, spearheaded by large labor unions and local activist networks "typically led by 'bridge builders' with interests, contacts and backgrounds that extend beyond the labor movement."

Yet Los Angeles remains far behind the Bay Area in the strength of its overall social mobilization or civic activism sector. This can be seen by comparing the nonprofit organizations devoted to this kind of civic activism in the two regions. Organizations in the nonprofit sector are classified into more than 30 types by the United States Internal Revenue Code (the U.S. tax laws), because nonprofit organizations are mostly exempt from income taxes. "Public charities" (Internal Revenue Code section 501[c][3]) represented almost 60 percent of all registered nonprofit organizations, 60 percent of total nonprofit assets, and 70 percent of total nonprofit revenues in the United States in 2010. These charities include arts, education, environment, health care, and human services organizations, among other types of organizations to which donors can make tax-deductible donations (Blackwood et al., 2012). "Other" 501(c) organizations represented about a third (32 percent) of all nonprofit organizations in the United States in 2012 (NCCS, 2012). This sector is predominantly composed of 501(c)(4) social welfare organizations such as large managed health plans; a mix of advocacy groups and civic clubs; labor unions and farm bureaus; business leagues; and social and recreational clubs. These two categories account for over 90 percent of all registered nonprofit organizations.

Data to compare these two comes from the National Center for Charitable Statistics (NCCS), which draws on IRS Form 990, which all nonprofits with revenues above $50,000 are required to submit.[8] Between 1989 and 2004, per capita revenues in the Bay Area's public charities were consistently around twice as high as those in Los Angeles. Los Angeles's per capita revenues in "Other 501(c) organizations" was only 60 percent of those in the Bay Area. These overall relative differences are also reflected in the number of nonprofit organizations, suggesting that revenue differences are not likely to be a function of a few very large organizations in a given region.

Table 7.1 presents per capita revenues for nonprofits engaged in environmental work and labor union and housing advocacy. The Bay Area's environmental sector is nearly nine times as large as Los Angeles in per capita revenues. The Bay Area in 2004 had a third more environmental organizations (163 versus 123) and has five organizations with revenues greater than

TABLE 7.1 Revenues per capita for social mobilization activities, 2004

	Environmental advocacy ($)	Labor union advocacy ($)	Housing advocacy ($)
Greater Los Angeles	5	54	13
Bay Area	44	100	26

SOURCE: Authors' calculations using National Center for Charitable Statistics 501(c)(3) public charities data.

$10 million, including one with revenues greater than $100 million (Trust for Public Land). In Los Angeles, only two organizations had revenues greater than $10 million; none earned more than $12 million. Per capita revenues of labor organizations in the Bay Area are twice as large as those in Greater Los Angeles in 2004, 1995, and 2000. In terms of housing advocacy, both regions have numerous well-known community benefit organizations (CBOs). However, these organizations in the Bay Area have twice the revenues per capita of those in Greater Los Angeles.

Hence, notwithstanding significant recent growth, the social mobilization sector is smaller in Los Angeles than in the Bay Area. The learning process may have begun, but it has a long way to go to catch up with its northern neighbor.

Regionalism: United or Divided Regional Identity

Another indicator of the capacity to act regionally is indirect: the extent to which the regions have large and consistent political majorities. If a region has a strong and consistent political complexion, it is much more likely that consensus on policies can be achieved across different interest groups and areas.

In what follows, we report the results of research on this issue. First, we look at how the residents in the different counties within our regions voted in presidential and congressional elections since 1970. This gives us a sense of the unity or fragmentation of the regions about basic political orientations. Second, we look at how residents within the two regions have voted on ballot measures relating to economic governance. We make no judgments about whether a liberal (left-leaning) region may be more conducive to economic growth than a conservative (right-leaning) region, but rather concentrate on the extent to which the two regions are internally unified or divided.

Figures 7.1 and 7.2 display how most residents within the counties within our regions have voted in presidential elections since 1972. Recall that the Bay Area is composed of ten counties, while there are five counties in Greater Los Angeles. In both regions, there is a shift from the majority of counties preferring the Republican candidate until the 1980s to the majority favoring the Democratic candidate in 2008. This change is stronger in the Bay Area, where the majority of residents in every county voted for the Democratic candidate since 1992. Since Ronald Reagan's reelection in 1984, only in Napa County in 1988 has a majority of residents voted for the Republican candidate.

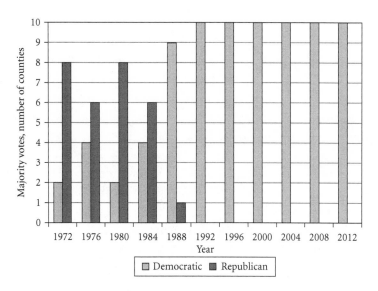

FIGURE 7.1 Bay Area presidential vote by county, 1972–2012

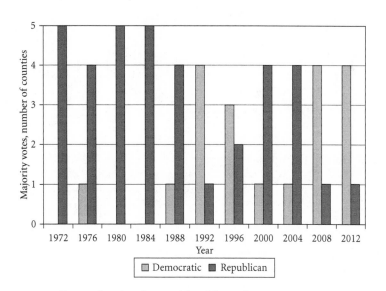

FIGURE 7.2 Greater Los Angeles presidential vote by county, 1972–2012

For the last five elections, Bay Area counties have been unanimous in their support for Democratic candidates. In Greater Los Angeles, by contrast, political preferences remain more divided, though they have started to converge with the Bay Area. As in the Bay Area, the majorities in most of Greater Los Angeles's counties favored Republican candidates into the 1980s.

In the five elections from 1972 to 1988, only in Los Angeles County did the majority of residents vote for the Democratic Party candidate; this happened in 1976 and 1988. Since 1992, in contrast to the Bay Area, in Greater Los Angeles preference for the two parties has swung back and forth. In 2012, Orange County voted for the Republican presidential candidate, and majorities for the Democratic incumbent were narrow in San Bernardino and Riverside; Los Angeles County resembled the Bay Area, voting very strongly to reelect Democrat Barack Obama. Max Neiman of the Public Policy Institute of California contrasts the political complexion of the two regions:

> So the way in which the two regions are organized I think it is really important; certainly the Bay Area I think speaks with a more unified and clear voice partly . . . you can explain it by being down the road from Sacramento, but it is more uniform and unified on political grounds, I mean, you know, it is heavily Democrat until you get into the Central Valley and Sacramento Valley areas so you don't have the kind of political splits that you get in Southern California . . . inland Southern California has become more diverse and more competitive politically but still, you know, is still heavily Republican in comparison to LA County. (Neiman, 2009)

Bill Vardoulis, mayor of Irvine in the 1970s and former president of the Irvine Chamber of Commerce, highlights the effects of these differences:

> If you really laid the cards on the table, Northern California counties [are] almost exclusively, heavily Democratic. . . . Here in Southern California, other than LA County, you know Riverside, Orange, [and] San Diego Counties are very heavily Republican. (Vardoulis, 2009)

The composition of congressional delegations from the two regions provides a more finely grained picture of political preferences than presidential elections. Since 1970, the Democratic Party has had a majority of seats in the Bay Area delegation, but this has become almost unanimous since 2000 (Figures 7.3 and 7.4).

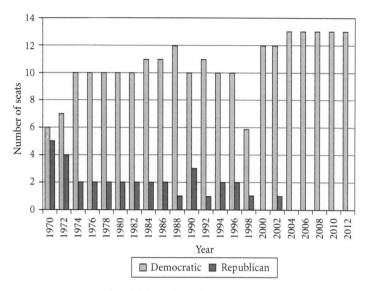

FIGURE 7.3 Congressional delegations, Bay Area, 1970–2012

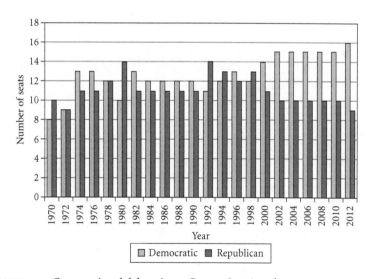

FIGURE 7.4 Congressional delegations, Greater Los Angeles, 1970–2012

Greater Los Angeles once again continues to be less politically homogeneous than the Bay Area, in spite of a steady increase in the Democratic Party's share, largely due to the increasingly democratic delegation from Los Angeles County.

We can also see political consensus and priorities by examining the outcomes of direct democracy. Since 1911, it has been possible in California for proposed legislation to be submitted directly to a popular vote (known as an initiative measure). A initiative is be placed on the ballot via a petition that is signed by a number of registered voters equal to either 5 percent or 8percent of the number of people who voted at the last gubernatorial election, depending on whether the proposition revises a California statute or is an amendment to the state's constitution. The state legislature may also submit a proposed statute or constitutional amendment directly to the voters.

The California secretary of state classifies the content of propositions into 20 different categories, covering a range of issues including bond issues, campaign reform, the judicial system, law and order, and election and political campaign rules. We selected a sample of ballot measures relating to economic policy and regional governance: bond authorization, fiscal policy, government regulation and agency formation, social and welfare aid, pensions, and taxation.[9] In total, there were 27 measures in these areas over the period 1990–2008. If we consider cases in which 80 percent of the counties in the regions voted the same way on a ballot (which would mean an 8–2 majority in the Bay Area and a 4–1 majority in Los Angeles), then in 25 of the 27 elections, Bay Area counties reached this majority threshold on a decision, compared to 21 in Los Angeles. In other words, in 6 of the 27 ballots considered, Greater Los Angeles counties were divided 2–3 on whether a measure should be approved or not.

There were also differences in the nature of the consensus, where it existed:

- Bonds for commuter rail (Prop. 116, 1990: Los Angeles rejected)
- Limits on local taxes (Prop. 226, 1990: Los Angeles approved)
- Bonds for the development of parks and historic sites (Prop. 180, 1994: Los Angeles rejected, Bay Area was divided)
- Campaign contribution and spending limits (Prop. 89, 2006: Los Angeles rejected)
- Increase in personal income tax for schools (Prop. 217, 1996: Los Angeles rejected)

- Taxes on cigarettes to fund childhood development (Prop. 86, 2006: Los Angeles rejected)
- Private-sector outsourcing of public works projects (Prop. 35, 2000: Los Angeles approved)
- Bonds for high speed rail (Prop. 1A, 2008: Los Angeles rejected)

Most of these differences are typical left-right divides, with the Bay Area more consistently expressing faith in activist government and raising government revenues than Los Angeles. These results can be thought of in relation to the analysis of city and county budgets in Chapter 6, where we identified differences in public spending priorities that do not mirror differences in objective circumstances. The urban core of Los Angeles County has a political complexion similar to that of the San Francisco–Alameda County part of the Bay Area, but Greater Los Angeles has more areas, in inland Los Angeles County, the South Bay, Orange County, and the desert counties, that are conservative in ways that no longer have any equivalent in the San Francisco Bay Area. Greater Los Angeles thus has a more fragmented and less consensual political culture than the Bay Area.

Conclusion: Beliefs, Worldviews, Politics, and Learning

Bay Area leadership has had a more focused and time-consistent perception of its regional economy as a new knowledge economy. Greater Los Angeles's leadership beliefs and worldviews have been inconsistent over time, with fleeting conceptions of the New Economy subsequently crowded out by the perception of Greater Los Angeles mainly as a gateway to international trade and logistics and specialized in manufacturing. Moreover, LA leadership's recognition of the knowledge economy in the 1980s and 1990s tended to be gestural, lacking an appreciation of the socio-institutional underpinnings of the New Economy, which were by contrast well appreciated by Bay Area business and civic leaders.

The differences persist. As late as 2011, the Los Angeles Economic Development Commission report on manufacturing blamed regional business costs for the region's problems.

> The State of California has comparatively high utility costs, strict air quality standards and AB 32 (California Global Warming Solutions Act) is coming. California and Los Angeles both have a difficult regulatory climate, which increases the cost of doing business here. (LAEDC and Kyser Center, 2011: 30).

This is a typical Old Economy way of thinking, implying that Greater Los Angeles could compete with lower-cost regions by being less aggressive about climate change or business regulation. But Los Angeles can never belong to the club of regions that can attract manufacturing back from cheaper regions of the United States or abroad; the cost differences between the Bay Area and Los Angeles and regions in other development clubs (such as the U.S. South or abroad) are structural, stemming from their history, size, and density. No level of tax abatement or realistic regulatory rollback could make them competitive in the activities that are central to the comparative advantage of these other clubs, in the same way that the United States can no longer compete with China for manufacturing many consumer goods.

Both regions were effective at region building in the late nineteenth and early twentieth centuries. But a great divergence in learning and building institutions for cooperation began in the 1950s. After thirty years as executive director of SCAG, Mark Pisano underscored this problem, and notably the way that Los Angeles County inspires competition and rejection by its neighbor counties:

> We are trying hard to catch up with respect to the business networking, but we have real impediments to doing that and the impediments, this is another interesting feature and that is they did not have excessively large institutions. When you have the city the size of LA ... when you take the size of our jurisdictions, it hurts, it breaks down, or you develop impediments to pulling people together. I mean, whenever you get big dogs in the room they will pick up the space and the little dogs are all pushed out of the way. Well, [in] the Bay Area you really didn't have any huge big dogs. I mean, you had San Francisco, who thought they were the big dog on the block, but population-wise they weren't and economic-wise they weren't. They had a lot of competitive organizations of equal size. I think that creates a better competitive and collaborative environment than having a huge, huge set of actors and [lots of] little people (Pisano, 2009).

The clues add up to a picture of two regions with widespread differences in how they confront regional problems and possibilities, in how they learn and what they learn.

8 Seeing the Landscape

The Relational Infrastructure of Regions

Why Study Relationships?

Societies and economies have many forms of order: markets, formal organizations, rules, informal routines, and human relationships. In social science, relationships can be captured in many ways, but two key aspects are networks of people and nongovernmental and nonmarket organizations. In economics, network membership can be valuable to members, enabling them to more easily carry out transactions, find information, secure employment, and gain access to capital and markets than can nonmembers (Granovetter, 2005). Powerful networks influence who become the key suppliers to emerging markets, through the way they filter access to the resources that allow entrepreneurship. As markets consolidate, the survivors—aided by their network connections—shape the markets for some period of time (Lazega, 2014). Networks are in tension with the disruption of structures that comes from innovation on the part of nonmembers, so they are not a mechanical determinant of economic outcomes. But networks also often absorb the innovators who then, once admitted to the existing club, strengthen their positions.

Networked interpersonal relationships are also found in many areas of political and economic life, including business leaders or elites, community-based organizations, philanthropists, and ethnic and professional groups (Breschi and Malerba, 2005; Casper, 2007; Whittington et al., 2009; Granovetter, 1985). Lazega (2014) calls our attention to the existence of "invisible colleges" in many areas of social and economic life, and not only in the obvious areas of elite dominance (such as Davos, Switzerland, the site of the annual meeting of the global business elite, organized by the World Economic Forum) (Rothkopf, 2008).

Networks can be especially important at times of change (Puga and Trefler, 2012). When a regional economy's firms are challenged to adapt to changing circumstances, or when its entrepreneurs are challenged to develop or capture promising new activities, they must be able to rapidly mobilize knowledge, labor, and talent and create organizations (firms, networks of firms, links to the labor market and to R&D) in order to generate new organizational ecologies in the region (Borgatti and Foster, 2003). Padgett (2012) calls this process the "transposition" of skills and organizational forms. The histories in Chapter 5 showed just how different the Bay Area and Los Angeles were in this regard from 1970 onward.

Networks and the invisible colleges they create are key determinants of how well labor, knowledge, skills, and inventors can lash up together to create this required newness. There has been considerable empirical research on invisible colleges at the scale of key tradable clusters of firms, such as Hollywood or Silicon Valley or the nascent biotechnology industry. It shows not only that these clusters operate through arm's-length market-based relations (buying and selling to one another), but that their key players have dense informal networks (Storper, 1995; Cooke and Morgan, 1998; Saxenian, 1994). There is little such empirical research at the scale of metropolitan regions, with the notable exception of Safford's (2009) comparative study of Youngstown and Allentown, Ohio. He shows that in Allentown, the business leaders of the region were deeply and broadly connected to one another, and that this enabled them to share visions of how to strategically guide the region away from declining manufacturing industries and into growing activities. The lack of such connected and overlapping networks in Youngstown stymied such a strategic reorientation and drew the economy deeper into decline.

In this chapter, we report an original statistical analysis of leadership networks in Greater Los Angeles and the Bay Area. To our knowledge, this is the first analysis of this type carried out for large metropolitan regions. The core evidence on corporate and civic networks is complemented with a number of other indicators of what we call the "relational infrastructure" of the two regions: business leadership organizations, levels of trust and "social capital," networks of innovators, and business-philanthropy relations. There were some small differences between the two regions in 1980, but since then a striking and increasing divergence of their relational infrastructures has developed.

Networks of Business Leaders

Sociologists principally measure business networks by examining when businesspeople serve as a member of a board of director of a firm other than the one in which they are chiefly involved (Barnes and Ritter, 2001). A board interlock exists when two or more corporations have at least one board member in common. For example, if a board member sits on the boards of two corporations, these two corporations are considered to be linked by their common director. Studies of these kinds of links conducted in the United States during the 1970s and early 1980s found that they revealed the existence of invisible colleges with shared worldviews (Pfeffer and Salancik, 1978); they also enhanced financial institutions' influence on corporate decision making (Kotz, 1978); provided the financial industry access to corporate and industry information (Mintz and Schwartz, 1985); and enhanced elite cohesion and political influence (Useem, 1984). More recent empirical research has found a clear relationship between board interlocks and "almost every important aspect of corporate governance, from executive compensation to strategies for takeovers and defending against takeovers" (Davis, 1996: 154). Through their experiences on other boards, interlocking directors provide a conduit for social influences that create an informational consensus for board decisions (Granovetter, 1985; Davis, 1996). This embeddedness has no normative value; under some circumstances it may facilitate coherent responses to common problems, while at other times it may result in groupthink that blocks creative problem solving.

The largest firms often set the agenda for how business will be conducted, and their board members are routinely seen as belonging to an elite stratum of the business world; much of the sociological research in this field has therefore focused on links among large firms (Davis et al., 2003). We therefore analyze board co-membership among the 60 to 70 largest corporations by revenue in each region in 1982, 1995 and 2010.[1] Across these three periods, we included 386 corporations with a total of 4,130 board members, an average of 64 corporations and 688 board members per region for each year. Information on these firms come from their annual responses to the U.S. Securities and

Exchange Commission's Form 10-K, required of all companies whose assets exceed $10 million and that have more than 500 owners of securities. 10-Ks include background and historical information on the firm, audited financial statements, executive pay, and organizational structure.[2]

There are three principal categories of formal network analysis: nodes, relations, and components. A node is the basic unit of network analysis; for us, the nodes are *firms*. Relations (which are also known as connections, ties, or links) between industries are said to exist when a director on the board of a company in one industry also sits on the board of another company in a *different* industry. More indirect relationships are called components of a network. If corporation A shares a board member with corporation B, and corporation B shares a board member with corporation C, then the three organizations are part of the same component. The largest component in a corporate network is therefore the one with the greatest number of firms that are directly or *indirectly* linked through board cross-memberships.[3]

Figure 8.1 shows that in 1982, the largest component of each region's corporate board network was similar in size, with around 60 percent of the region's largest firms connected to at least one other firm. However, over the subsequent three decades, the Bay Area maintained its relatively high degree of connectivity across its large firms, while the share of Los Angeles's largest

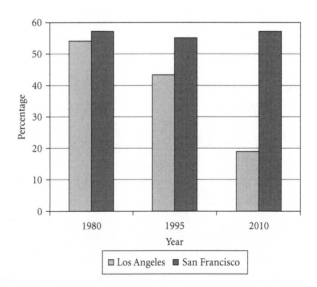

FIGURE 8.1 Percentage of sampled firms in the largest component

Part 1

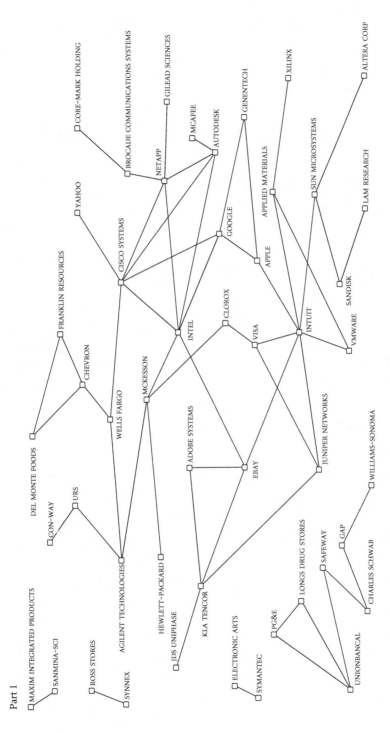

FIGURE 8.2 Board interlocks in the Bay Area and Greater Los Angeles, 2010

Part 2

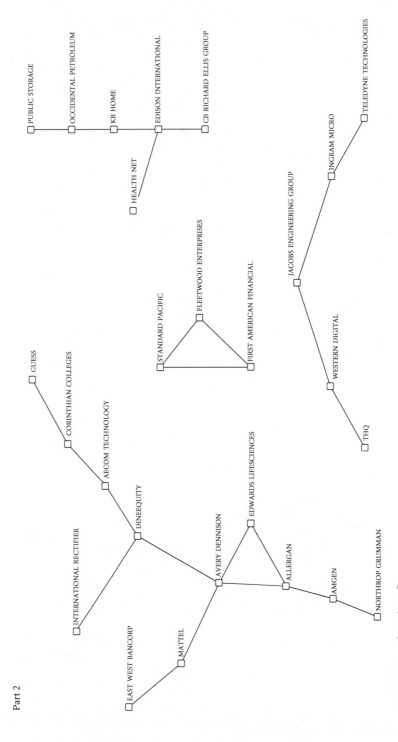

FIGURE 8.2 (continued)

component declined. By 2010 only 20 percent of Los Angeles's largest firms had interlocks. Figure 8.2 provides a graphical representation of the contrasting elite business networks in each region by 2010, with Los Angeles's network much more fragmented than that of the Bay Area.

The high level of relatedness of the Bay Area's business elites could simply reflect the region's deep specialization in technology activities, in the sense that it is more natural for leaders in the technology industries to sit on one another's board of directors. It stands to reason that Los Angeles's less specialized economy would have fewer such relationships. But this turns out not to be the explanation for the difference. To see this, we isolated the networks within the IT sector in 2010. Even within this narrow area of activity, where firms are working in the same type of markets, networks among the Bay Area's large information technology firms are considerably stronger than those in Los Angeles. In the Bay Area, for example, 13 of the 50 largest IT firms are in the largest component; in Los Angeles, only 4 of 50 are part of this component. Hence, the Bay Area's network structure is not purely a function of its greater specialization in IT, but reflects different propensities for connection within the business elites of each region.

Given Los Angeles's greater overall industrial diversification, we still expect it to have a wider range of industries represented in its board interlocks. Our sample of Greater Los Angeles's large firms is dispersed over a broader range of industrial sectors than those found in the Bay Area. For instance, in 2010, the three largest industries accounted for only 12 of the largest 50 firms in Greater Los Angeles, while in the Bay Area, the three top industries represents 37 of the largest 50 firms.

This difference affects networks in two ways. First, the two regions have different numbers of *cross-industry pairs*. A cross-industry pair exists when a directorate interlock connects two different industries (not just two different firms), as when a board member of an aerospace firm sits on the board of a communications firm. These are only counted once; if there are 20 aerospace firms that have board members who also appear on boards in the communications industry, this represents just a single cross-industry pair. Second, we consider differences in *number* of board interlocks that link firms in different industries, known formally as *cross-industry ties*. For instance, if three firms in communications are linked to one firm in aerospace, that would count as three cross-industry ties.[4]

TABLE 8.1 Cross-industry links

	Two-digit NAICS			
	Cross-industry pairs		Cross-industry ties	
	Los Angeles	Bay Area	Los Angeles	Bay Area
1982	65	57	94	86
1995	31	40	52	68
2010	22	30	27	52
	NAICS divisions			
	Cross-division pairs		Cross-division ties	
	Los Angeles	Bay Area	Los Angeles	Bay Area
1982	19	14	77	69
1995	13	11	41	52
2010	11	8	19	43

Table 8.1 confirms that in 1982 a similar number of cross-industry pairs existed in each region, and the cross-industry ties were also roughly comparable. By 2010, however, despite having a more specialized economy in a smaller number of industries, the Bay Area's elite business networks still span a wider range of sectors than the equivalent networks in Los Angeles, in addition to the fact that a larger number of its firms are interconnected across industries.

This result could conceal the fact that San Francisco's two-digit industries share a kind coherence or affinity, perhaps in terms of the technologies used, or their work styles. This is not especially plausible, because two-digit sectors are quite broad and hence inherently very different from one another: for instance, construction and utilities. Nonetheless, to the extent that such intersectoral affinity exists, this might lead elites to select each other when filling board positions. The counterfactual for this exercise is that corporate elites in the Bay Area may simply operate within a more highly interconnected social space. To help rule out bias arising from a latent interindustry affinity, we aggregate up to the level of industrial divisions, at which only 10 categories exist (compared to 24 two-digit NAICS sectors), with results shown in the lower panel of Table 8.1. The two regions have broadly similar numbers of industry division pairs, though Los Angeles has a somewhat higher number at each cross-section. In terms of cross-industry links, the Bay Area is considerably more interconnected in 1995 and 2010. Strikingly, Greater Los Angeles's business leadership has not just become less internally connected than the Bay Area's leadership; its broad industrial divisions have also become much less linked than they once were. Though there is a trend toward declining interconnection in both regions, in Los Angeles the decline is far steeper than in the Bay Area. The decline in cross-industry connections is expected in an increasingly specialized region such as the Bay Area but remains a mystery in Greater Los Angeles, which became less specialized.

In addition to measuring the *range* and *number* of cross-industry links, we can inquire into the *strength* of such ties, reflected in the average number of industry ties. We focus on sectors that have ten or more cross-industry ties, because the two regions had similar numbers with fewer than ten connections. In 1982, the average industry in each region had about six ties to other industries (Table 8.2). In those days, Los Angeles hosted several California and regional banks, including Security Pacific National Bank and Western Bancorp; meanwhile, the Bay Area was home to Wells Fargo and BankAmerica (later to become Bank of America). Board members in these firms were deeply involved civic leaders, and the same is true of electric, gas, and sanitary services, provided privately by PG&E in the Bay Area and Southern California Edison in Greater Los Angeles, in addition to the Los Angeles Department of Water and Power, a public utility. The analysis thus detects traditional corporate leadership networks of the early 1980s.

By 2010, in the Los Angeles network there was not a single industry with 10 or more ties to other industries; the maximum was just 5, and the mean industry ties declined to 1.5 (from 5.7 in 1980 and 3.7 in 1995). The Bay Area cross-industry network, however, maintained a mean of 5 ties and a maximum of 21 (for business services, closely followed by industrial machinery and equipment with 20 cross-industry ties, and electrical and electronic equipment and depository institutions with 10 cross-industry ties each). The main partner of the first three industries are the electronics industry and its associated sectors.

TABLE 8.2 Average number of cross-industry ties per industry

	1982		1995		2010	
	Los Angeles	Bay Area	Los Angeles	Bay Area	Los Angeles	Bay Area
Mean degree	5.7	5.7	3.7	5.2	1.5	5
Sum	94	86	52	68	27	52
Maximum	26	30	18	26	5	21

In other words, even though most of the Bay Area directors come from just a few industries, they still have more contact with directors in *other* industries than their peers in Los Angeles.

Finally, we consider the breadth of cross-industry linkages, with breadth defined as the total number of industries to which each industry is connected, rather than the number of connections (which are an indicator of strength, as in the previous section). To illustrate this point, business services in the Bay Area in 2010 have a total of 21 directorate interlocks to firms in other industries, but this does not indicate whether those ties are broad, as in to many other industries, or narrow, consisting of strong ties to one or a small number of other sectors. In 1980, Los Angeles's industries were linked to a broader range of sectors, with eleven industries tied to five or more industries, while the Bay Area had eight. By 1995, however, Los Angeles had only seven industries that were connected to five or more other industries, against eleven in the Bay Area. By 2010, Los Angeles had no industries connected to five or more other industries, and the Bay Area had four.

In sum, from comparable starting points in 1982, Los Angeles and Bay Area corporate elite networks have diverged over the study period. The strength of cross-industrial connections in the Bay Area is surprising, given its reputation as an industry town. Los Angeles's business leaders appear strikingly isolated from each other, both in relation to the region's own recent past and in comparison to its northern sibling.

Elite Civic Leadership Organizations

Leadership networks are also reflected in regional business leadership organizations. Chapter 7 showed that these business-civic organizations in Greater Los Angeles have had quite different beliefs about regional challenges and opportunities from those of the Bay Area. Having highlighted these differences, we now explore how well these organizations function as regional conveners. Mark Pisano contrasted the Los Angeles Chamber of Commerce with the Bay Area Council:

> When I first came here I went to the Los Angeles Chamber, which at that point in time was a five-county chamber, and said let's have a public and private co-ordination, and the Los Angeles chamber said we don't need the public sector and we really don't want to venture with you. You had a different attitude

between the Bay Area Council, which existed at that time and their regional organizations. . . . And I think to this date we still don't have the [equivalent of the] Bay Area Council down here. (Pisano, 2009)

Max Neiman, associate director and senior fellow at the Public Policy Institute of California, echoes this view:

So, there is a cohesiveness up here politically and institutionally that doesn't exist in Southern California. Southern California is much more decentralized politically. You don't have anything like really the Bay Area Council in Southern California. (Neiman, 2009)

Jim Lazarus of the Bay Area Council sees it this way: "The Bay Area Council calls us all together, so that we can say okay, we want these projects in the Bay Area or in Northern California, and now we are going to lobby as one" (Lazarus, 2009).

To investigate these impressions more systematically, we measure what is known technically as the "nBetweenness centrality" of the Bay Area Council and the Los Angeles Chamber of Commerce, in the networks of their respective regions. This statistic represents the degree to which an organization in a network lies on the shortest path between all pairs of firms in that network. If the nBetweenness score of a particular organization in a network is 15 percent, then this organization lies on 15 percent of the shortest paths between all pairs of organizations in that network. To make this more concrete, consider two Bay Area firms: Del Monte Foods and Genentech. If David West, the CEO (in 2013) of Del Monte, wants to find a mutual acquaintance at Genentech, the shortest path through the network of board interlocks is as follows: Del Monte Foods → Bay Area Council → San Francisco Chamber of Commerce → The Christensen Fund → Genentech. Hence, the Bay Area Council represents a link on the shortest chain that connects these two firms, suggesting that its members are likely to be involved in connecting these two firms.

The Bay Area Council lies on 18 percent of all the shortest paths between pairs of firms in the Bay Area network (Table 8.3). Meanwhile, the Los Angeles Chamber of Commerce lies on just 6 percent of the shortest paths. We broadened our examination to consider other business leadership organizations in each region, selecting organizations on the basis of those that received the largest number of media hits in LexisNexis. The Bay Area Council is the most central organization in either region. In addition, both the Silicon Valley

TABLE 8.3 nBetweenness of regional business leadership organizations and business leaders

Business leadership organization (BLO)	nBetweenness %
LOS ANGELES	
Los Angeles Chamber of Commerce	5.9
Los Angeles Economic Development Corporation	1.7
Valley Industry and Commerce Association	0.6
Orange County Business Council	0.0
CALSTART	0.0
BAY AREA	
Bay Area Council	18.0
Silicon Valley Manufacturing Leadership Group (SVMLG)	6.0
San Francisco Chamber of Commerce	5.8
Semiconductor Industry Association	5.0
Joint Venture Silicon Valley (JVSV)	0.0

Manufacturing Leadership Group and the San Francisco chamber of commerce are more central than any business leadership organization in Greater Los Angeles.

Broader Elite Civic Involvement: Philanthropic Networks

The United States has been characterized by a strong tradition of voluntary social engagement, as was remarked in the early nineteenth century by Tocqueville (1830 [2000]) in his classic work, *Democracy in America*. Today we would call this the strength of the "civil society," which refers to voluntary civic involvement by both elite and non-elite groups. Philanthropy is a form of elite civic involvement that covers a wide range of areas: social welfare, education, the arts, community development, health, cultural and arts institutions, youth issues, childhood development, higher education, and more. Private foundations are the key vehicle for philanthropy; these organizations are endowed by individuals, families, or corporations to make grants to public charities. Data from the National Center for Charitable Statistics (2012) show that private foundation assets in the Bay Area and Los Angeles were approximately the same size in 1989, but the Bay Area's foundations became more than twice as large on a per capita basis by 2008, most likely due to the immense wealth accumulation in the Bay Area high-tech community.

In 1989, by far the largest private foundation in either region was the J. Paul Getty Trust in Los Angeles, with over $4.3 billion total assets, equivalent to 41 percent of Greater Los Angeles's foundation assets. In 1994, the David and Lucile Packard Foundation, based in Los Altos in Santa Clara county, was the second foundation to break the $1 billion mark with total assets of $1.5 billion. The subsequent growth in total Bay Area private foundation assets was predominantly driven by the growth of the Packard and the William and Flora Hewlett Foundations, which together accounted for just under $16.5 billion in 2007, or 20 percent of Bay Area private foundation assets in 2007.

The network structure of the philanthropic community is reflected in the board interlocks of the 50 largest private foundations in the two regions. Links between private foundation trustees are generally rarer than those within the elite business community, with only minor differences across the two regions in each time period. But the picture for interlocks between large private foundations and corporations looks different. In 1982, about 50 percent of firms and private foundations were connected to at least one other organization in both regions (53 percent in Los Angeles and 51 percent in the Bay Area). By 2010, this declined to 40 percent of Los Angeles firms and private foundations, while it rose to 62 percent in the Bay Area.

This analysis of business and civic networks has some findings that confirm those of Safford (2009) but extends into new territory as well. As in Safford's cases, the more successful region has a more connected elite than the less successful one, and it has more centrally connected leadership organizations. We go beyond that to also analyze cross-industry relations in detail. This is necessary when considering very large economies such as Los Angeles and San Francisco. Their size makes it impossible that most industry leaders could belong to one or a small number of leadership organizations, as in Safford's case of two small cities. When we peer into the networks of different industries in the two regions, we find that networks differ in ways that are independent of the different levels of specialization of the two regions. A full map of the relevant networks in these two great city-regions would require much more data. But the results are starkly different enough to point to real differences in relatedness of business leaders in the two regions.

Networks of Innovators

Abundant Silicon Valley folklore refers to gathering points where new ideas were disseminated and people in different—often competing—firms, came together. The Wagon Wheel tavern in Menlo Park—where the early players in the IT industry would gather for drinks and networking—is the iconic such place. Considerable research shows that greater links among various parts of a region's innovation system, whether they are inventors, entrepreneurs, financiers, research universities, or established businesses, lead to greater economic vitality (Feldman, 2014; Breschi and Malerba, 2005; Almeida and Kogut, 1999; Gabe et al., 2009; Benner, 2003). In the high-technology industries in Los Angeles, there is no equivalent of the Wagon Wheel:

> So I think they [the Bay Area] got ahead of the curve with respect to the notion of networking systems that allowed for further dissemination of ideas, inventions to innovations . . . the Bay Area began to see the need for networks and networks operating within networks sooner than we did here. (Pisano, 2009)

Even in the heart of Los Angeles's New Economy, Orange County, there is a perception that the networking of innovators is incomplete:

> We have a higher per capita probably patent rate than other counties, but we don't have the management talent as much for those high-tech operations that the Bay Area has. They have a long bench of talent they can plug into particular opportunities, and we have some of that, but we have nowhere near what they have and so I think there's a whole lot of ecosystem that's developed up there . . . we are nowhere near there and it would be difficult to catch up, I think. (Walrod, 2009)

One way to determine whether the legend gives an accurate impression about networks in regional knowledge production is to examine patent citations (Jaffe, 1989; Audretsch and Feldman, 1996; Feldman and Audretsch, 1999). Each patent application includes a paper trail of citations to other patents that contributed to the development of the knowledge in the new patent. To the extent that such regional innovators cite one another's previous patents, rather than inventors in other regions, this could indicate that the region's inventors are closely interrelated—it could signal the effects of places like the Wagon Wheel at a systematic level, or of regional networks of innovators more generally (Laursen et al., 2011).

The citation of other regional inventors is measured in the form of the region's Net Local Citation Percentage (NLCP), as shown in Figure 8.3 (Sonn and Storper, 2008). A region's NLCP is greater than zero to the extent that its inventors cite past patents from their home region at a higher rate than would be expected if they cited them at the average rate that inventors in that industry cite each other regionally across all the metropolitan regions of the United States. Over time, an increasing NLCP indicates growth in the local knowledge referencing system. Inventors in both Greater Los Angeles and the Bay Area cited one another within their region above the national average, but from the 1980s onward, the Bay Area's inventors have relied increasingly on one another, with a large gap opening up in comparison to those in Los Angeles. The takeoff of regional citations in the Bay Area coincides with the income divergence between it and Los Angeles.

This evidence should be read with some caution. For one thing, many citations on a patent are included by U.S. Patent Office patent examiners rather than by the inventors themselves. Citations may thus reflect what a patent examiner believes to be the intellectual antecedents of a particular invention. Still, for most of the core activities of the New Economy, inventors in the Bay Area appear to rely on regionally sourced knowledge to a much greater extent

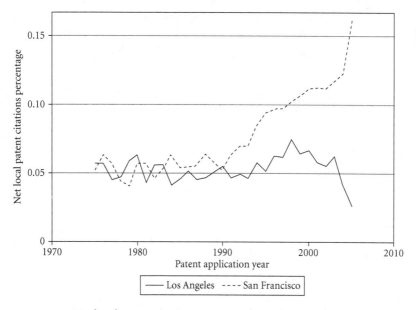

FIGURE 8.3 Net local patent citations, Los Angeles and the Bay Area, 1975–2007

than in Los Angeles, or that their inventions are more closely related to one another than in Los Angeles.

Casper (2012) analyzed networks between university-based inventors and entrepreneurs in the California biotechnology sector. As we noted in Chapter 5, though Greater Los Angeles started out with similar basic endowments of major research universities and federal funding, the region has translated its research into innovative economic activity at a much lower level than the Bay Area. UCLA, despite its large medical center, generated only 200 biotech patents between 1970 and the early 2000s; UC Berkeley, with no medical center, produced more than 300, and UCSF and Stanford together hold nearly 900. The Bay Area produced 250 patents that list the combination of a university researcher with a commercial assignee. Greater Los Angeles has just 75 of these patents. Adjusted for regional population, Los Angeles has one-sixth of these relationships as compared to the Bay Area.

Biotechnology spin-offs reflect the same interregional gap, with Bay Area and San Diego universities far more prolific than those in Los Angeles. Greater Los Angeles has a weaker web of entrepreneurs and companies to commercialize the results of its university science, and this deficit has become ingrained in the practices of the region's universities; in contrast, the Bay Area's strong web of companies in IT and biotech and related sectors nurtures a university culture with a high level of private-sector engagement. Casper (2009) notes that nearly 55 percent of Bay Area life sciences researchers were connected to one another through having worked together in a firm or research organization; in Greater Los Angeles this figure is a mere 2 percent. The same is true for managers and founders of biotechnology companies. In San Diego and the Bay Area, over 90 percent of senior managers and founders have been together in a company at some point in their career. Data for 2004 show, by contrast, that there is no recent history of senior managers leaving the two major Los Angeles biotech firms, Amgen and Allergan, to work in another Los Angeles–area biotechnology firm.

These differences have widened over time. Key figures in computing at UCLA, such as Henry Samueli, eschewed patenting. They did so because they reasoned that Berkeley and Stanford were so far ahead with chip patenting that they would focus in a different area, broadband circuits and systems, and they believed their expertise to be so unique that patenting was unnecessary. When Samueli subsequently founded Broadcom, they took the knowledge with them. Only much later on, with the failure of the market for broadband chips, did they go into patenting with verve (Lécuyer, 2006). Indeed, as pointed out by Kenney and Mowery (2014), even though the nascent West Coast computer industry was concentrated in Los Angeles after World War II, the electrical engineering and computer science department at UC Berkeley seized the opportunity of the California Digital Computer Project to plunge into the field in the 1950s. Subsequently the department engaged—over and over again—with industry, so that it became a center of top-level scientists accustomed to working on projects with breakthrough-to-market applications.

It is more difficult to assess networks of innovators in the entertainment industry because many of Hollywood's innovations (whether specific movie ideas, marketing techniques, or filming and editing techniques) are not patentable, though content can be copyrighted. By the same token, however, some of Silicon Valley's innovations, such as software products, are not patented, but copyrighted. The film industry's Hollywood watering holes from the 1930s and 1940s, such as the Brown Derby, Chasen's, or Nate 'n' Al's, were the Wagon Wheels of their day. Today, the gathering places for dealmakers in the entertainment industry are the Soho House and Cecconi's in West Hollywood, and the Polo Lounge and the Grill on the Alley in Beverly Hills. People test each other out and deals are made at these places through face-to-face contact (Storper and Venables, 2004).

But Hollywood's networking does not spill over very much to the rest of the region's economy. Hollywood leaders mostly do not identify themselves as an integral part of the region's civic leadership, as the following quote exemplifies:

> I remember in 1993 when I ran for mayor, after about a year of effort I had a meeting with Barry Diller, who was then the head of Fox Studios. I thought, well here is a famous corporate CEO, head of one of the powerful movie studios; it took me a year to get an appointment with him but I got it and then sat down with him and did the same thing I did with other business leaders, which was to settle down and ask him, what do you think are the three most important issues facing Southern California? And I was surprised; his answer was well, I don't know, you tell me. He basically said, I have a house in Malibu, I have this office here in Century City. I spend some time flying around to New York, but, you know, I don't actually focus that much on LA or Southern California. . . . Basically he had nothing to tell. . . . This may be a little bit of a

caricature, but in some ways it is not that much of a distortion ... especially in the entertainment industry, but also other business leaders in Southern California and their perspective on the world. (Woo, 2009)

The second constraint on networking between Hollywood and the rest of the Los Angeles economy is that there is a high level of unrelatedness between content-producing industries in Hollywood and technology-based industries (Rigby, 2012). The natural affinities of these industries have historically been weak. This may now be changing as content production increasingly relies on digital technologies, and technology-based companies move into content production and distribution. The effects of this new technology world on Los Angeles's business networks may therefore become more powerful in the years to come, but it is still at an early stage. New network relations that span Silicon Valley and Hollywood will come into being; however, it is not yet clear how much content procurement and management will be integrated geographically into Silicon Valley (as in the example of Netflix), or how much of it will be organizationally and geographically attached to Hollywood.

Divergent Quality of Entrepreneurship

Differences in economic growth rates across countries and regions have something to do with entrepreneurship, and there is therefore much scholarly research into the sources of entrepreneurship and its geography (Audretsch et al., 2012; Acs and Storey, 2004; Fritsch and Mueller, 2004; Audretsch and Keilbach, 2004; Bhide, 2000; Sutaria and Hicks, 2004; Rupasingha and Goetz, 2013). Since the work of Schumpeter (1934) and Kirzner (1979), the term *entrepreneur* has been used to define people who seek out and identify opportunities to reallocate resources and employ them in a manner that either improves the products of existing industries or creates products that become the bedrocks of new industries, or firms that have productivity-pushing products or processes that drive the overall rate of growth of the economy higher. All entrepreneurship is not equal. Some self-employment is just survival; much leads to firm creation in the local service sector. By contrast, entrepreneurship in key tradable sectors is different in its nature and growth process: what we can call "industry-building entrepreneurship" (IBE) (Feldman et al., 2005). Most entrepreneurship in both our regions is not of the IBE type (Acs et al., 2010). It takes place in the local service sector and shows up statistically as a

TABLE 8.4 Wages of the self-employed, 1970–2009

	1970 ($)	1980 ($)	1990 ($)	2000 ($)	2009 ($)
Greater Los Angeles	4,112	8,531	17,074	23,031	27,323
Bay Area	4,248	7,822	15,883	24,067	25,065

large component of the self-employed. Table 8.4 reveals that self-employed individuals in Los Angeles earn slightly more on average than their northern counterparts, but in both regions these figures are roughly equivalent to what the average Hispanic immigrant or high school graduate earns in Los Angeles (Table 4.12).

IBE is difficult to isolate statistically from entrepreneurship in general (Zhang, 2003). IBE is cyclical in relationship to the long-term growth of tradable industries (Armington and Acs, 2002). Over the period from 1989 to 2000, the Bay Area created around a fifth more firms per capita than Los Angeles. By the year 2000, this margin had narrowed, and by 2004, Los Angeles was creating more firms per resident than its northern counterpart, as the dot-com boom turned into a crash. From 1970 to the mid-1990s, average firm size in Greater Los Angeles was consistently greater than that in the Bay Area, reflecting the mature manufacturing firms and large aerospace firms that dominated the region's economy, compared to the early phases of the IT economy in the Bay Area, with the proliferation of start-ups there. By the mid-1990s, the Bay Area had generated a cohort of large IT firms, many of which grew from small start-ups to giants of twenty-first-century capitalism. As a result, average firm sizes converged between the two regions.

Underneath these cycles are differences in the role of IBE over time (Fritsch and Mueller, 2004). If the region is in that part of a development cycle where new firms are being created in industries with the potential to generate growth with high wages and high incomes, then average firm size will decline. Statistically, though, it is hard to break out this IBE from the broader category of self-employment. Thus, when Mark Zuckerberg created Facebook and moved it to the Bay Area, he was doing IBE, but he contributed to Bay Area firm formation statistics as much as a couple who might have started a dry-cleaning store that year.

Subsequently, either IBE may slow down, or the industry may consolidate, and this will be reflected statistically as an increase in average firm size. The Bay Area has recently been home to many firms that were formed and subsequently have grown to be Fortune 500 members, iconic names in the New Economy. This was true of Los Angeles in the heyday of the Hollywood studio system and then later in the formation of the modern aviation and aerospace sectors. Orange County has also hosted startups of many IBE IT and medical device manufacturing firms that are now large.

Casper (2009) argues that differences in entrepreneurial activity by regional scientific and technological innovators in Los Angeles and San Francisco are not due principally to differences in the supply of inventors, but rather that demand for using such scientific/engineering knowledge is currently much lower in Los Angeles than in the Bay Area, and this explains Los Angeles's lower rate of IBE in high technology. Scientists and engineers in the north have more entrepreneurs that demand their services.

One key to the process of matching potential industry-building entrepreneurs to the rest of the system is the existence of intermediaries. Contrasting the information technology sector in Orange County and the Bay Area, Feldman and Zoller (2012) find that the Bay Area has many more "dealmakers": agents who have deep connections to their regional economy through multiple roles as entrepreneurs, investors, and board members. While 2 percent of IT executives and board members in the Bay Area entrepreneurial economy had ties to four or more firms, generating enough to fill a football stadium, only 0.05 percent of actors in Orange County had similar connections. The presence of these regional dealmakers is strongly correlated with new firms because they act as information brokers between the R&D community, entrepreneurs, and markets. To the extent that differences in the presence of dealmakers spans beyond IT and biotech (admittedly an open question), it may help explain the differences in the quality and type of both patenting and IBE that have recently marked these two regions. Thus, the two regions do not display differences in their underlying entrepreneurial spirit. Rather, differences in specialization create differences in demand for IBE and in the conditions for industry-building entrepreneurs to succeed.

In this light, the period of high gap in the total quantity of entrepreneurship (the 1990s) was not an original cause of the existence of Silicon Valley. The Valley's development and the Bay Area's leadership in IT originated decades before the aggregate entrepreneurship gap opened up. The Bay Area's income gap with Greater Los Angeles has persisted even after the closing of the overall difference in firm formation, subsequent to the dot-com crash. In an earlier period, Los Angeles had an abundance of industry-building entrepreneurs in entertainment, aviation, and aerospace. Los Angeles will not close the gap with the Bay Area or a host of other cities by improving its overall rate of entrepreneurship, but only through a specific process of improving its economic specializations and, with that, the demand for IBE and the conditions for IBE success. We should therefore not mythologize Bay Area entrepreneurs as a unique source of Bay Area success; they were part of a complex process of creating new organizations within a broad ecological system.

Social Capital in the Bay Area and Los Angeles

The term *social capital* refers to "norms and networks that enable people to act collectively" (Woolcock and Narayan, 2000: 226; Bourdieu, 1986; Coleman, 1988; Putnam, 2001). Social capital is generally measured in two ways: one is group life (associations, which we examined in Chapter 7; see Table 7.1), and another is generalized trust, which refers to a common "set of moral values in such a way as to create regular expectations of regular and honest behavior" (Fukuyama, 1995: 153). Trust, in this sense, is an essential prerequisite for the formation of social networks that allows different tightly bonded groups (associations, communities of common interest, or primary social attachments such as ethnic groups) to be willing to deal with one another, to "bridge" and hence form coalitions around wider interests (Rodríguez-Pose and Storper, 2005).

In a pioneering empirical study, Knack and Keefer (1995) found that national economic growth is strongly associated with levels of trust, but not with associational membership. Further studies (Zak and Knack, 2001; Guiso et al., 2010) support these findings. Along these lines, Beugelsdijk and Van Schaik (2004) conclude that trust taken alone is not associated with growth across European regions. This is probably because some forms of trust can emerge from the tight bonding of traditional communities who act to restrict access by other groups and hence simply extract rents or try to perpetuate their narrow advantages. But when generalized social trust is coupled to a more dynamic institutional environment where many groups participate and there are bridges between the groups, then it seems to have a robust growth-enhancing impact (Farole et al., 2010; Crescenzi et al., 2013; Laursen et al., 2011).

Measuring social capital is a challenge, and it is especially so for the regional scale (Malecki, 2012). One common approach employs data on civic engagement—the degree to which individuals take an active role in the social, economic, and political development of their community—as a proxy for the stock of social capital. Other researchers use direct indicators of social or generalized trust. To capture civic engagement, we use data gathered by Rupasingha and Goetz (2008), who combine secondary public data at the county level on census mail-response rates, voter turnout in presidential elections, total not-for-profit organizations, the total number of associations per ten thousand residents, and other measures in 1990, 1997, and 2005. We then aggregate these to Combined Statistical Area values by weighting county-level values by population. We supplement the regionwide data with measures of social trust for Los Angeles and San Francisco Counties, gathered in 2000 as part of the *Social Capital Community Benchmark Survey.*

Table 8.5 shows that civic engagement in Los Angeles is lower than in the Bay Area in 1990, 1997, and 2005, and the gaps are statistically significant (i.e., greater than one standard deviation). Though the Bay Area does not have especially high levels of civic participation by the standards of other U.S. cities, Greater Los Angeles strikingly underperforms the national average. These results may in part reflect that the sample of metropolitan areas used in the construction of the mean include many smaller places, and many studies show that size of the region (population) and regional social capital tend to be inversely related (Putnam, 2007).

In order to verify this finding, we consulted the DDB *Lifestyle Survey* and constructed a broad measure of social capital, based on a composite average of responses to questions about generalized trust in the survey, most of which

TABLE 8.5 Social capital levels in Los Angeles and the Bay Area, 1990–2005

	Civic engagement		
	1990	*2000*	*2005*
Los Angeles	2.5	2.6	2.0
Bay Area	3.6	4.3	3.4
U.S. metro average	3.7 (SD = 1.04)	4.0 (SD = 0.92)	3.5 (SD = 0.90)

SOURCE: Civic engagement data calculated using Rupasingha and Goetz's (2008) county level social capital index for 326 metropolitan areas.

NOTE: Because of the switch from SIC to NAICS in 1998, the 2005 results are on a different scale from the 1990 and 1997 results. This means comparisons are best made within cross-sections, rather than across them. Generalized trust data from the *Social Capital Community Benchmark Survey* covers only Los Angeles and San Francisco counties, while U.S.-wide descriptive statistics come from a sample of 33 communities.

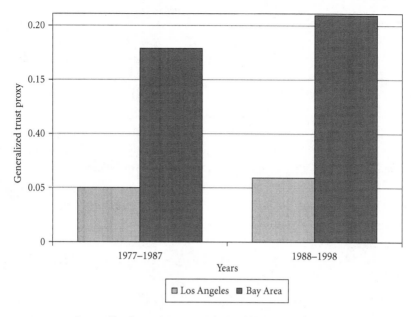

FIGURE 8.4 Generalized trust: Los Angeles and the Bay Area, 1977–1987 and 1988–1998

concern how people bridge to one another through trustful interactions with them. This survey was conducted for most years between 1977 and 1998. Figure 8.4 shows that the Bay Area's generalized trust proxy was fully 3.8 times that of Greater Los Angeles in the early 1980s and 3.5 times that of the early 1990s.

Conclusion: Surprisingly Different Relational Infrastructures

There are considerable differences in the relational infrastructures of the Bay Area and Greater Los Angeles. Business and civic networks are stronger and more centralized in the San Francisco Bay Area than in Los Angeles. University-industry ties are much stronger in Northern California, and there is more experience of managers and scientists having rotated through positions in the same firms in the Bay Area than in Los Angeles's more closed, corporate labor market. Indicators of civic involvement such as philanthropy are stronger in the Bay Area, and generalized social trust is stronger among Bay Area citizens than those of Greater Los Angeles. We could find no evidence of regionwide business leadership in Greater Los Angeles that is the equivalent of the Bay Area Council.

The evidence in this chapter suggests that there are stronger and more encompassing invisible colleges of actors in the Bay Area than in Greater Los Angeles. Instead of invisible colleges, Los Angeles has separate worlds. Some of the differences in relational infrastructure predate the economic divergence under examination, as in the inherited web of civic organizations and labor unions in the Bay Area that we documented in Chapter 7. But some of it emerged along with strong economic divergence. Initial modest differences around 1980 led to circular and cumulative causation processes in network structures, such that the initial differences have been magnified over time. Rather small differences, for example, in the ability to connect university-based researchers with entrepreneurs, venture capitalists, and other dealmakers, may have existed in the late 1970s and early 1980s. But as the Bay Area got ahead of Los Angeles, the people engaged in these practices got better and better at them in the Bay Area, and the most talented ones concentrated themselves increasingly there. As the buzz surrounding these practices and the learning spillovers increased in the Bay Area, they languished in Los Angeles. As the practices developed, so did the network connections among those engaged in them. Only many years later, when the Bay Area's success became highly apparent and commented upon, did Los Angeles–area universities and (to a limited extent) business and civic leaders realize that they needed to learn New Economy best practices. But as typically happens in economic development, by the time other nations or regions become aware of what they do not have, the advantages of the leaders are locked in.

9 Connecting the Dots

What Caused Divergence?

THE ROLE OF ACADEMIC RESEARCH IS SOMETIMES TO REVEAL what is not apparent to the naked eye, and sometimes to do the opposite by showing that what seems obvious is not what it appears to be. Both of these apply to the case of divergence between the Bay Area and Los Angeles.

A knowledgeable observer might say that the causes of divergence are obvious: the Bay Area won the information technology lottery, enjoyed the growth of IT-related corporate headquarters, and has recently become a significant hub of cutting-edge sectors such as biotechnology and mobile device applications. Los Angeles experienced dramatic downsizing of its mass manufacturing and aerospace/defense sectors and replaced them with lower-wage light manufacturing and international trade and logistics. Los Angeles's concentration of corporate headquarters declined and the region currently seems to be losing out in biotechnology.

But this intuitive and seemingly obvious story is deceptively simple. It says basically nothing about why, from their starting points, one economy has done so much better than the other. In previous chapters we have peeled away layers of the divergence that are not apparent to the naked eye. The two economies were also differently specialized in 1970, but the overall task content of work in the two economies was almost identical, and this was reflected in their similar levels of wages and incomes at that time. A large gap opened up in the quality of their tradable specialized sectors, and explaining this is not obvious.

The Usual Suspects: Causes or Effects?

Many different individual factors can be considered candidates for the divergent development of these two economies: immigration, housing costs, and cost-of-living differences in general; education and skills of the workforce; unique bad luck or good luck; business cost differences; and public policy. Let's recap why these commonly cited factors do not explain divergence.

We can begin with education and immigration. Chapter 4 shows in detail that during the study period Los Angeles migration was dominated by Latin Americans and especially Mexicans, while the Bay Area received a higher proportion of better-educated Asian immigrants. Differences in average levels of education and skills are sometimes offered as an explanation for the two regions' overall income divergence. In an accounting (but not explanatory) sense, only about half the average wage and income differences can be associated with differences in labor supply characteristics (education). Bay Area wage gaps for people with similar education, age, and national origin increased steadily over the period. By 2005–2010, Bay Area college degree holders earned about one third more than their Los Angeles counterparts. Wage differences were therefore not driven entirely by different types of in-migrants or educational levels. Even the 50 percent of wage differences that correspond statistically to different education levels of migrants raise the question of why the regions received such different migrants. They are only 360 miles apart, but Asian immigrants come from ten thousand miles away (including some low-skill ones, such as Pacific Islanders). For Latin American immigrants who make it from Mexico or Guatemala, the added distance is marginal (many of them do make it to Chicago, for example). The answer lies in the different structures of demand: on average, there are better jobs in the Bay Area but ultimately a limited absolute quantity of them. Jobs in Greater Los Angeles are lower in average quality, and Latin Americans on average are lower down the hiring queue than higher-skilled Asians for the Bay Area's higher-skill jobs. Latin Americans still do better in Los Angeles than they would be staying home.

Another line of reasoning holds that housing costs, or cost-of-living differences more generally, underlie divergent development by filtering for different populations and generating different population-to-job ratios. But evidence on housing costs and housing construction does not support this reasoning.

Still another claim about the Bay Area is that it is a unique case of success. Los Angeles's regional economy performed poorly compared to a wide variety of American metropolitan areas, including very big ones with a great deal of immigration such as New York and a set of other middle-size ones such as San Francisco, Washington, Boston, and Houston. The mirror image of the Bay Area luck argument is that somehow Los Angeles is a case of unusually bad luck due to the end of the Cold War and its effect on aerospace. But Boston had equally bad luck due to deindustrialization in the 1980s and bounced back (Glaeser, 2003); New York had worse luck in the 1970s and bounced back. Moreover, the Bay Area had a very big employment and investment shock at the end of the 1990s dot-com boom.

A common refrain in the local business press is that Los Angeles is "too expensive" and highly regulated to attract and retain firms. Chapters 1 and 6 showed that there is no reason to believe that there are systematic differences in factor costs, land prices, taxes, or regulation that could have driven these regions down such different pathways.

Finally, we can ask whether formal economic development policies and public spending differences drove the regions down different development pathways. Formal economic development strategies were not very different, though regionalism is more in evidence in the Bay Area, principally due to a combination of its natural and political geographies. The Bay Area has higher fiscal capacities than Los Angeles because of its higher tax receipts, but both regions' counties and cities spend a similar proportion of regional GDP (about 7 percent). Some differences in spending priorities are in evidence but are insufficient to explain such radical economic divergence.

There is no smoking gun in this list of standard arguments about the regions' differences. The causes of divergence are not obvious, and this list, taken together or separately, does little to lift the veil of causality. Unfortunately, the elements on this list command a great deal of attention on the part of politicians and the media, not only for this pair of cities, but more generally when the press and media speak of the different fates of regions. A deeper understanding of divergence is needed.

Economists' Stories: Shifting Regional Economic Equilibriums

Economists draw on some of the ingredients in the popular recipe for explanation, described earlier, but have a more sophisticated way of weaving them into a coherent overall story. To do so, economists employ what are known as simultaneous-causality models of regional factor markets and factor prices

(Richardson, 1979; Glaeser, 2008). Such stories go something like this. The change in Los Angeles's per capita income rank came about because of the declining share of high-wage employment there. This occurred because of the closing down of many capital-intensive manufacturing industries in the 1980s and then the weakening of the aerospace sector in the early 1990s. Concurrent to the weakening of relative demand for the highly skilled, the immigration wave of the 1980s augmented the supply of low-skilled workers. In the end, the region's rank in average wages and productivity shifted downward relative to the former position of the region and the U.S. mean.

In the Bay Area, the rise of the information technology sector and a smaller shock to capital-intensive manufacturing in the 1980s combined to maintain the region's high equilibrium wage. This in turn signaled to highly skilled immigrants that the region was a promising destination. The resulting increase in the supply of skilled workers was outweighed by increasing skill demand as the information technology sector undergoes strong agglomeration in the Bay Area. There were then strong wage spillovers to other tradable industries, as well as Balassa-Samuelson wage spillovers to the nontradable service sectors, except at the very bottom, where abundant supply from immigration to both regions maintained equally low wages.

The strength of this account is to link changes in factor supply and demand, showing how they shift together and respond to one another in each region. But notice that for all its sophistication, there is no causal explanation. The core events or factor demand changes that set off the movement to new equilibriums—such as changes in specialization—lie outside the model, as well as providing little insight into how the changes in specialization are sustained over time (Morck and Yeung, 2011; Leamer, 2012). Changes in specialization have to be tackled directly in order to explain divergence in incomes.

Specialization: A "Whodunit" Problem

There is no single elegant model that can account for the causes of specialization, if by causes we mean the sequence of events that leads to changes in what a region does in its tradable sectors. Many claims about the causes of specialized agglomerations exist. Considering them will clarify the meaning of the evidence presented thus far.

Was Silicon Valley's localization in Santa Clara County the result of a lucky break to the Bay Area? Were the aerospace and Hollywood agglomerations established because of historical accidents? Accidents can consist of one-off events in technology, personality, and organization that might cement the geography of major clusters in the economy. We can consider each in turn. First-mover agglomerations form where early breakthrough innovations in an industry occur, such as the superior semiconductors made by the first-mover firms Hewlett-Packard and Fairchild in the 1970s or the superior airplane, the DC-3, made by Douglas Aircraft in Santa Monica in the 1930s. To the extent that breakthrough innovations are accidental, then economic development is a lottery.

Other anecdotes emphasize accidents of personality as the key to specialization. In some accounts, Silicon Valley is where it is because of William Shockley's desire to live near his aging mother in Menlo Park, California, causing him to move from New Jersey. Another accident concerning Shockley is that after he attracted the best associates to his first-mover firm, his difficult management style and abrasive personality caused them all to quit, thus launching the Silicon Valley process of development through spin-off. These specific historical events are certainly not without consequence. In more flattering terms, we could call attention to Steve Jobs's marriage of functionality and aesthetics, Howard Hughes's zany technological imagination, Jack Warner's management skills, and so on. In the positive cases of breakthrough innovations associated with heroic individuals (Donald Douglas and Sergey Brin, for example), were these individuals not also encouraged by a welcoming regional environment, and hence were they not just responding to the demand for their industry-building entrepreneurship?

A third type of idiosyncratic influence on agglomeration is decisions by key firms at key moments. Motorola located the largest, earliest semiconductor facility in the world in Phoenix in the 1950s, for example, but this did not establish Phoenix as a subsequent center of the IT industry (Scott and Storper, 1987). Motorola was too early, and it made the further mistake of attempting to keep the production system for itself, vertically integrating in a technologically young industry, rather than participating in an open and flexible regional network. Amgen was an early mover in biotechnology but did not initiate a biotechnology cluster in Los Angeles for much the same reason.

Other explanations emphasize not so much the initial accidents, but what comes next. New Economic Geography models show how once a region has an early lead in an industry, there is a snowball process of drawing in supplier firms, human talent, and knowledge that drives a wedge between the leading region's productivity and innovation levels and the other regions that host the industry. Once this happens, the leading industry's position is said to be "locked in" (Thisse, 2010; Krugman, 1991b; Rosenthal and Strange, 2001).

Does this mixture of an initial accident (good luck in hosting the breakthrough innovation) and a big dose of lock-in explain the Bay Area's advance over Los Angeles? Once again, only partially. If it were a fully adequate explanation, Los Angeles should never have lost so much of its aerospace sector. Lock-in is not forever. Silicon Valley has been challenged since the beginning, because it has gone through unusually short product cycles. Mass semiconductor manufacturing moved out of Silicon Valley beginning in the late 1970s (Saxenian, 1994). What has kept Silicon Valley so viable as an agglomeration of IT activity is its capacity not just to generate the first breakthrough innovation in IT but to continue breaking through. As each previous innovation wave has matured, the Bay Area creates the next wave—from chips to personal computers, to servers and networkware, to the Internet, to mobile broadband hardware and applications.

A third type of accident argument about specialization is historicist: it makes it appear as a necessary and foreordained expression of the region's innate talents, the unique genius of the region (Storper, 2013). Such arguments confuse causes and effects. Consider the early days of industries, before lock-in occurs, such as IT in Silicon Valley in the 1960s and 1970s, aviation in Los Angeles in the 1920s and 1930s, the entertainment industry in Hollywood the 1910s, cars in Detroit in the 1890s, and mechanical engineering (e.g., agricultural equipment) in Illinois in the 1870s. All created complex business ecosystems in their principal regions (Klepper, 2009). These are the outcomes of their development, not the original causes of specialization. Along these lines, the dense concentration of venture capital firms, often cited as a reason for the Bay Area's leadership in IT, emerged through experimentation on the part of investors, and little by little became a recognized new branch of the investment industry. But it was not a pre-existing resource. Technological talent clearly existed in the Bay Area in the 1950s and 1960s, but it did not consist of what we now define as an organized field of "computer engineering."

Whodunit? Organizational Change Generates and Consolidates Specialization

The dynamic of economic transition, as we have seen, does not flow automatically from pre-existing factor endowments, accidents and shocks, lock-in dynamics, or deep genius. They are all part of the process (Feldman and Francis, 2003). They are tied together in particular ways: regions generate or attract the entrepreneurs who will build new industries or revolutionize existing ones; in order to do that, such entrepreneurs generate breakthrough innovations; those innovations are then transformed in new types of organizations (principally firms and networks of firms); the various actors in the emerging new ecosystem revise their views of their roles and develop conventions that allow them to coordinate the emerging ecosystem; and the conditions exist for some of the firms to grow into durable, bigger firms, but to remain open to innovations, in part by sustaining a robust and flexibly network of supplier and collaborator firms. This is a long list, but it captures the story of how dynamic, high-wage regional specializations emerge in the New Economy. What ties this complex process together is the region's capacity for organizational change.

Aerospace evolved over the twentieth century from the quintessential innovative frontier-pushing "tinkering" sector into one making large-scale highly planned systems for the Pentagon, as well as a mass manufacturing aircraft sector. It adopted the methods of large-scale and planned production; paradoxically, the much smaller Bay Area aerospace industry remained more on the tinkering edge of the sector, more experimental even if not nearly as significant in quantitative terms as its southern counterpart[1] (cf. Meisenzahl and Mokyr, 2012).

Nothing exemplifies the difference in how the two economies react to contemporary challenges and opportunities more than the radically different pathways they have traveled in the emerging biotechnology sector. Both the Bay Area and Los Angeles had firms that were among the first movers in biotechnology, especially Genentech up north and Amgen in the south. Both Genentech and Amgen were initially founded by venture capitalists, in concert with research scientists, at UCSF and UCLA, respectively. Amgen is the biggest and most successful biotechnology firm in California. From the beginning the firm adopted the scale-dominated managerial models that prevailed in Los Angeles. Powell and Sandholtz (2012: 411) call Amgen a "commerce dominated company" in contrast to the science-dominated major companies of the Bay Area. According to them,

> [the] commerce model builds on an alternate framework, with management in the lead role and science brought on board, though more as a passenger than driver ... important science was harnessed but an academic ethos was not

adopted. Publishing was not encouraged; the scientific advisory boards provided a seal of approval but did not dictate or set business strategy. (2012: 411)

Amgen's geography reflected this, as it was located near none of the major universities it drew upon, but equidistant to all three (USCB, UCLA, Caltech). Powell and Sandholtz (2012) continue:

> This geographical isolation is certainly one cause and consequence of Amgen's development as a sort of scientific island, manifest not only in its singular achievement of FIPCO (fully-integrated pharmaceutical company) status, but also in its aggressive (and on the whole, successful) legal battles to protect its core patents. (2012: 411)

The paradoxical outcome of this is that Los Angeles has a world-class biotechnology firm, and one that was a first-mover, but the company did not become the seed for a major biotech cluster. Initial favorable accidents, in this case, did not lead to cumulative causation and lock-in of a biotechnology agglomeration in Los Angeles.

The leading biotechnology firms in the Bay Area, such as Cetus, Genentech, Biogen, and Chiron, provide a striking contrast in their organizational practices. Founded in 1976, Genentech combined serious scientific guidance with venture capital funding. The firm's co-founders were UCSF biochemist Herb Boyer, who was among the inventors of recombinant DNA, and Robert Swanson, a young entrepreneur with whom Boyer agreed to work. An important element of this story is the kind of social networking that underlies it. The Genentech story revolves centrally around a young, relatively inexperienced entrepreneur and a world-class scientist, coming together to develop—in real time—new organizational practices, objectives, and procedures, more or less from scratch. This boundary-crossing networking occurred in the Bay Area starting in the late 1970s.

This same kind of mixing was attempted but did not take hold in Los Angeles. Boyer directed Swanson to contact researchers at the City of Hope Medical Center in Los Angeles, who were working at the cutting edge of synthetic genetics. Genentech financed work at City of Hope in Los Angeles. Genentech encouraged its scientists to publish their findings in academic journals and leveraged outside funding—including from the pharmaceuticals industry—for attaining scientific milestones. While Genentech's Boyer insisted on an open science model, Amgen's managers insisted on secrecy. Thus, Amgen's managers took a conception of how to succeed that borrowed from the standard playbook of the corporate world. The Genentech approach had much more favorable consequences for regional economic development in the Bay Area:

> Boyer's stature and Genentech's rapid ascendance as a premier scientific lab left a lasting legacy for subsequent biotech firms. . . . Both founders shared values around what motivates people (freedom, ownership) and how companies succeed (fiscal conservatism). Perhaps most crucially, they were unbiased by the conventions of commercial science. . . . They were able to create an entirely new hybrid: a world-class research lab funded by commercial means. (Powell and Sandholtz, 2012: 420)

Relational Networks Potentiate Entrepreneurship and New Organizational Practices

Chapter 8 argued that industry-building entrepreneurship is critical to the emergence of new industries or the adaptation of existing ones to economic change. New industries often draw from mature industries with big reservoirs of skills and knowledge, while in other cases of more radical technological change they draw directly from R&D. Conservatism and categorical thinking are natural features of corporate hierarchies and research labs, as well as of university-based R&D or practical innovation. This is why breakthrough entrepreneurship draws from networks that cross boundaries, mixing the old and the new, the seemingly far-fetched with the logical extension of today's reality.

In the early days of Bay Area IT, there was more than one community interested in new technologies, and there were people who spanned different networks, whose role as go-between enabled the mixing of sensibilities and knowledge (Turner, 2006). Padgett (2012) calls attention to the borrowing, importing, and transposing practices between organizations and systems as key to the evolution of such organizations:

> Organizational structure is the blending, transformation and reproduction, on-site, of networks and interaction rules transported by people into the site from numerous sources. People, conversely, are the hybridized residues of past networks and rules acquired through interaction at their previous organizational

sites. In other words, both organizations and people are shaped, through network co-evolution, by the history of each flowing through the other. (2012: 171)

Looking back, we know that the Bay Area would draw from widely different milieus to generate the lash-up that became the productive system of Silicon Valley. Let's revisit some of the elements of this process, drawing from Chapters 7 and 8.

In the Bay Area in the 1960s, there was already a widespread Bay Area fascination with new technologies, emanating not from the engineering communities but from these other milieus. Buckminster Fuller was the utopian alternative-technology guru who invented the geodesic dome and proposed alternative-technology futures for cities and modern life in general. He embodied the futuristic practicality that would later infuse the developers of personal computers (Foege, 2013b). Though he came from the East Coast, his principal breakthroughs occurred while in residence at San Jose State University. Shortly thereafter, Theodore Roszak documented the ways that Fuller and others were already creating a bridge between the Bay Area hippies and the techies in his 1969 book, *The Making of a Counter Culture* (Roszak, 1969). The key published forum for this meeting of counterculture and innovation culture was *The Whole Earth Catalog*, published in the late 1960s and early 1970s and cited by Steve Jobs in his 2005 commencement address at Stanford as one of the major sources of inspiration for the Apple PC and its operating system, and for the overall aesthetic of the company.

The catalog was published by Stewart Brand, a Stanford-educated biologist and Buckminster Fuller acolyte. As Foege (2013a) notes: "Besides its listings touting primitive tools and sustainable farming methods, the compendium included entries on stereo systems, welding equipment, cameras and computers." Brand was also a key figure in building the three-way relationship between tech, wealthy Bay Area elites, and the environmental movement. He was close to David Brower, who had been the executive director of the Sierra Club and founder of Friends of the Earth and Earth Island Institute. Important members of the San Francisco finance community were on their boards of directors. Their environmentalism not only consisted of a traditional focus on land conservation but was also fascinated with the utopian notion of using capitalism to make a better world through a rationalist and technological approach to better modern living.[2] The difference between alternative technologists and mainstream engineers was not about the virtues of technological solutions to social problems, but more that the former had an innate prefer-ence for decentralization and small scale, and the latter for centralization and scale (Turner, 2006).

This mixture of straight-laced elite and bohemian experimentalism co-existed, with certain boundary-spanners such as Brand moving between them. Brand and Ken Kesey (of *Magic Bus* fame) were the co-producers of the Trips Festival, a rock music gathering held in San Francisco with the world's first light show. By 1969, when Xerox founded the Palo Alto Research Center (PARC), the Bay Area had emerged as ground zero for the hippie countercul-ture but also for its associated techie culture, and PARC's first employees were academics with no experience of corporate culture and little interest in it. In 1972, *Rolling Stone* (then headquartered in San Francisco), published an article about PARC authored by Stewart Brand. In it, Brand described the employees of PARC as knowledge-fueled hippies, with computing as a utopian project to create more freedom and creativity. In 2013, in an article in *The New Yorker*, Nathan Heller described the current wave of applications developers locating in San Francisco in analogous terms, as technology-fueled youth seeking free-dom, creativity, and a nonconformist lifestyle, and cited other articles from the late 1960s that described San Francisco's cultural lash-up of that time in much the same terms (Heller, 2013a).

Steve Jobs and many other key figures in the ongoing evolution of both information technology and now life sciences and biotechnology are not—in the main—radical innovators. They are what Meisenzahl and Mokyr (2012: 45) call "tweakers," those who improve and debug major inventions, adapt them to new uses and combine them in new applications. As they put it,

> We should focus neither on the mean properties of the population at large nor on the experiences of the "superstars," but on the group in between, those who had the dexterity and competence to tweak, adapt, combine, improve and de-bug existing ideas, build them according to specifications, but with the knowl-edge to add in what the blueprints left out. (2012: 45)

A good amount of tweaking involves crossing boundaries, in the sense that it involves importing ideas or imagination or techniques from other fields. Jobs imported a sense of practical purpose and aesthetics from the al-ternative technology movement.

Greater Los Angeles's relational dynamics stand in sharp contrast to those of the Bay Area. In the middle of the twentieth century, Los Angeles County had a powerful urban elite network, the Committee of 20 (Jaher, 1982). Competing leadership groups emerged in the rest of the region, especially Orange County. When the New Economy began to emerge in the late 1960s, these different groups found themselves with few communication channels, and the leadership groups were unable to establish effective cross-regional "talking shops" where contact might be made and a broad regional vision secured. Even when New Economy opportunities like Amgen came their way, regional industrial leaders pulled them back to the existing practices they knew best: those inherited from a previous era of development.

Los Angeles was not fated to follow this pathway. One can imagine a counterfactual history of the Los Angeles economy, in which the equivalent of a Stewart Brand or a Steve Jobs had instead found himself in Hollywood, Orange County, or El Segundo (an epicenter of aerospace, near the Los Angeles International Airport). One can imagine, perhaps, a Herbert Boyer at UCLA or Caltech. One can imagine, in other words, some kind of major robust actor who would have changed the course of things for Los Angeles in the 1970s. Such robust actors existed at other points in Los Angeles's history: Jack Warner, Louis B. Mayer, and Donald Douglas come to mind.

But the environments of the two regions since the 1970s were not equally propitious to success by such out-of-the-box actors. By the time the New Economy was beginning to emerge, the maverick engineering talents of an earlier period were long gone from Los Angeles, absorbed by the massive operations funded by the Pentagon. In contrast, Hewlett and Packard, even though they had started in the 1930s, were continually brought into contact with experimental milieus, in a region where their social connections to downtown San Francisco elites and alternative-technology circles were likely to involve few degrees of separation and where the weight of the Pentagon was much smaller. In turn, the Bay Area and Los Angeles became magnets for different kinds of people.

The point of this example is not to claim that exactly this type of mixing of milieus and lashing up would have to have occurred in Los Angeles, or for any other region facing economic transition. When new high-wage activities emerge, they will be developed, captured, and locked in by agents or entrepreneurs in specific places. They are the economic development "accidents waiting to happen." The relational infrastructures of regions can exclude or, by contrast, potentiate the lash-up and organizational experimentation that steers these activities to some places and encourages their development, and away from others. Once that happens, cumulative lock-in processes reinforce divergence, at least until another major wave of technological and market change emerges and opens up a new game.

In this regard, Orange County's role in the nation's IT industry, as a second-rank high-tech agglomeration, seems to have similar causes to what Saxenian (1994) showed for Boston's early IT industry. Firms and managers there did not figure out how to organize themselves for an industry just beginning many waves of breakthrough innovations and organizational change. They stuck to classical managerial practices and attitudes and as a result tried to build organizations with economies of scale, just as did Amgen in Los Angeles's biotech industry. Seattle's recent success in the New Economy comes in a region that has similar antecedents to Los Angeles. Like Los Angeles, Seattle was host to big mature industries (natural resources and aviation) and faced a major challenge with the arrival of the New Economy. Unlike Boston and Los Angeles, it nonetheless attracted industry-building entrepreneurs such as Bill Gates and Jeff Bezos and allowed organizational ecologies to flourish around them. That Los Angeles did not enjoy the income success of Seattle is perplexing in light of the endowments of knowledge and talent the region possessed.

Contrasting Regional Zeitgeists: Conventions of Economic Actors

Paul Duguid, one of the participants in Xerox Corporation's PARC in the 1970s, uses the term *zeitgeist* to describe the Bay Area's "open source culture." He stresses that the zeitgeist is not "technology specific," by which he means that it is general to the region (Duguid, 2009). *Zeitgeist* is a German term that translates as the "spirit of the age," here meaning the spirit of the age in a certain region.

Zeitgeist comes from the shared ideas and practices and ways of organizing things that take hold in economic environments. These shared ideas, practices, and ways of doing are often not fully evident to the people who do them. They are conventions or rules of thumb. Most important about them is that for rules of thumb to work, those with whom we interact must use the same rules of thumb, so that we are coordinated or, as contemporary slang would have it, "on the same page." This is especially important in the environment of rapidly changing, highly innovative, knowledge-intensive economic activity, the kind that generates high incomes in cities. According to the analytical philosopher David Lewis, a convention consists of the following:

> A regularity, R, in the behavior of members of a population, P, when they act in a recurrent situation, S, is a convention . . . for the members of P, when:
>   Each conforms to R;
>   Each anticipates that others will conform to R;
>   Each prefers to conform to R on the condition that others do so. Since S is a problem of coordination, the general conformity to R results in coordination. (Lewis, 1969: 42).

Conventions belong to the wider family of attitudes and beliefs. Conventional attitudes and beliefs precede and enable economic change by helping large and decentralized communities of actors stay on the same page, underpinning the functioning of an organizational ecology.

Chapter 7 found that beliefs of leadership groups in Los Angeles and the Bay Area about the nature of economic possibilities and challenges have been strikingly different. Their conventional wisdoms were different from one another and diverged over time. We can give a broad brush picture of the different economic conventions of the two regions. Twentieth-century Los Angeles development was largely characterized by building up a set of super-efficient systems of large-scale production from IBE beginnings. Hollywood was started by visionary entrepreneurs and became a factory-like Hollywood studio system from the 1920s onward. Aviation started out through breakthrough innovation by the likes of Donald Douglas, continued to generate pioneering entrepreneurs for several decades, and then graduated to becoming a mass production chain for aviation in the 1940s. On top of these highly innovative activities, the Los Angeles region added a role as the West Coast center for branch plants of mass consumer durables production, as well as oil refining and a large port complex. With the rise of the Cold War, it created a hybrid world of production, involving large-scale, top-down industrial planning of large aerospace systems, sometimes produced in small numbers and sometimes in series. Los Angeles entrepreneurs also excelled in pioneering new areas of mass production: in housing and land development, mortgage financing, and fast food.

Bending the arc of this regional process of becoming a mass production economy, Hollywood dropped its mass production world starting in the 1950s. Responding to the twin challenges of television and U.S. Department of Justice antitrust action, it became a project-based industry with highly flexible firm networks. By the 1970s, it was already pioneering project-based, flexible combinations of firms and knowledge and inputs, and the roles of the giants firms (the studios) were changing into those of investors, product orchestrators, and marketers of films and their branded offshoots. With this shift in orientation came rapid and pronounced changes in forms of employment, organizational practices, and conventions.

Yet Hollywood's brilliant transformation into a new organizational ecology did not transform the wider Los Angeles economy. There are many reasons for this. Part of it is that the language of art, dominant in Hollywood, has few natural connections to the language of engineering, dominant in many of the other sectors in the Los Angeles region. This situation contrasts to Silicon Valley, which is based on engineering and thus has been able to draw from and contribute to engineering communities in that region. Indeed, according to economic historian Paul David, the aerospace community in the Bay Area was positively affected by the end of the Cold War. This is because it was involved much less in large-scale production than its counterpart in Los Angeles; it was considered a "boutique" and highly skilled part of aerospace, useful by the large defense contractors for making highly innovative new devices, often rather experimental. The successful ones would subsequently be transferred into large-scale systems (and moved down south).

William Hewlett and David Packard were tinkering in a garage in Palo Alto and founded Hewlett-Packard in 1938. Their first marketed product was a precision audio oscillator developed using an incandescent lightbulb as a pilot light. When the Cold War came to an end, many of those tinkerers had already smoothly moved into working in Silicon Valley, where engineering was the common language. Hollywood could not serve this function for Los Angeles when mass production manufacturing moved out and aerospace was downsized at the end of the Cold War, even though its organizational practices were very similar to those that came to dominate Silicon Valley. It is only now, as we write, that connections between Hollywood and the New Economy are deepening, but in areas that are linked to Hollywood's output specialization: visual and audio content.

In this sense, the conventional wisdoms of business leaders in the two regions (with the exception of Hollywood) were very different. It is easy to imagine why prospective entrepreneurs in the New Economy would have felt more at ease in the Bay Area than Los Angeles or Boston. And as leaders in

Los Angeles turned their attention to such industries as transport and logistics, the epistemic communities of the two regions increased their distance from one another. The zeitgeists, or overall spirits of the two regions, diverged as part of the process of diverging specialization. Since then, Los Angeles has had difficulty in creating a new zeitgeist that would enable it to perform as a high-income region.

10 Shaping Economic Development
Policies and Strategies

Imagining the Future

Imagine it is 1970: a time of unquestioned American global economic dominance. California is the star region of the day; people have flocked to California for decades, and residents have enjoyed persistently high incomes. California was also home to an education system from primary to university levels that was the envy of much of the world; in 1970 as today, California contained 6 of the top 20 world institutions of higher education. Fortunes were being made on land development, industrial agriculture, aerospace, petroleum, and entertainment. This feat of economic development, melded with folklore about Hollywood, Californian weather, landscapes, lifestyles, and quality of life, make the state an object of fascination, mixed with some condescension, from the Atlantic world of New York, London and Paris.

All was far from perfect, of course: there were widespread areas of poverty; Los Angeles was only five years out from a terrible race riot in Watts; and a good deal of inner-city San Francisco and Los Angeles had seriously deteriorated as suburbs drew middle classes away from cities. The people of California were also in the grips of a powerful wave of collective anguish about the environmental and social effects of the growth they had experienced, especially in the Bay Area. There were cultures of contestation—from the San Francisco Beats in the 1950s to the hippies, students, Black Panthers, and anti–Vietnam War protesters of the 1960s. They criticized the California growth machine, the society's "suburban assumptions," its dependence on military spending, and its crass materialism (Starr, 2011; Didion, 2004). The American economy, too, was starting to face challenges: manufacturing productivity growth declined and deindustrialization of the Northeast region began. California seemed immune to such distress. The contours of what would later be called the New Economy were starting to be glimpsed by prescient investors, who spoke to each other of Hewlett-Packard and Fairchild at poolside barbecues.

Roll this film forward about ten years, and much of the "coast of dreams" was embroiled in a wrenching deindustrialization (Starr, 2006). At the same time, by 1980, the cities in the suburban belt of San Mateo and Santa Clara County (Palo Alto, Cupertino, Menlo Park, San Jose) were consolidating themselves into Silicon Valley. Los Angeles had its own new industrial spaces in Orange County, by 1980 a prosperous domain of suburban industrial, postindustrial, and financial development (A. Scott, 1993; Sciesi, 1991). Los Angeles leaders were also beginning to implement a strategy that would place them closer to the heart of the global economy, by expanding their port infrastructure, seeking to become the West Coast gateway for Asian manufactures. If anything, Los Angeles's leaders were aggressively imagining their future.

Forward uncertainty is enormous when it comes to medium-term (30 to 50 years) processes of economic development, at any scale, from global to national to city-regional. Glaeser (2003: 119) remarks, along the lines that "an urban observer looking at Boston in 1980 would have every reason to believe that it would go the way of Detroit or Syracuse and continue along its sad path toward urban irrelevance." The U.S. national economy in the 1980s broadly moved toward new technology sectors, advanced services, and finance, but many analysts continued to believe that it should be reindustrialized (in the sense of manufacturing) (Bluestone and Harrison, 1984; Zysman and Cohen, 1988). The New Economy's highest-wage functions had a very selective geography, locating overwhelmingly in regions with structurally high land and labor costs, such as the Bay Area, New York, Boston, Chicago, and Washington, D.C. These members of the top development club of American metropolitan regions joined their counterparts abroad, such as London, Paris, Tokyo, Zurich, and Munich, to create a pattern of urban economic "resurgence" at the end of the twentieth century (Storper, 1995; Cheshire, 2006). They reversed a trend toward nonmetropolitan economic growth that had dominated the

United States from the 1950s to the early 1980s. This club of cities compensated their loss of Old Economy industries by raising their share of high-wage, high-skill, spatially concentrated, New Economy industries. Many other regions did not enjoy this type of transition, and it has therefore become a staple of economic development analysis to ask why certain regions have been more "resilient" than others (Christopherson and Clark, 2007; Christopherson et al., 2010; Storper, 2010; Feldman and Lowe, 2011). We have seen that the different fates of San Francisco and Los Angeles have many causes. But can anything be done to improve Los Angeles's performance and to avoid a future crash for the Bay Area?

The Great Divide in Policy Thinking: People or Places

The fields that think about economic development in general, and urban-regional economic development in particular—RSUE, NEG, and development studies—have fundamental divides when it comes to thinking about policy. The first such divide is about whether policy and strategy should target people and households, or places (Barca et al., 2012). RSUE models, in particular, believe that people and households choose to live according to their preferences and capabilities, and that jobs follow them. An extension of this basic way of thinking is that policy should concentrate on enhancing the capabilities of people to be productive, and places should then attract the right kind of people (Glaeser, 2000).

On the international scale, if people-only policies are implemented, such as training the workforce, but there is insufficient demand for their skills at home, there will be brain and body drain. This problem exists for metropolitan regions as well: if they have policies to improve the productivity and employability of their people, they will contribute to the economic welfare of the country as a whole and to other regions. This leakage of benefits is a reason that many people policies are funded at higher scales, such as by national or state governments. It is also the reason why no metropolitan area can afford to have only policies that shape the labor force; even in the counterfactual case where Los Angeles had poured resources into rapidly educating its immigrants from Mexico, many of them would have left in search of better jobs, and even higher proportions of the highly skilled would have left. To keep them or attract them, a region needs jobs that require their skills or develop their skills and experience.

NEG models and certain branches of development studies think about the place side of development in a different way. Their starting point is that the landscape of production—and thus labor demand—is inherently lumpy. High-skilled, high-wage activities have a high propensity to cluster because they need interaction, to be close to new sources of cutting-edge knowledge, and they draw from complex specialized local supply chains. The problem is that there is little consensus on what kinds of policies could help regions develop, capture, or keep these kinds of highly desired activities (Duranton, 2011).

Policies to shape specialization in the future, and hence the demand for labor, should not merely reflect the current state of regional factor endowments, especially labor supply. Los Angeles's big success in affecting its specialization has been in reinforcing its position as the West Coast international transport hub. Its port-logistics complex generates demand for labor with low to moderate skills. This strategy is said to respond to the abundant supply of low- to moderately educated people in the region. Meanwhile, a host of other metropolitan regions in the United States were increasing their proportions of college graduates, and thus widening their gap to Greater Los Angeles. Both the Bay Area and Los Angeles do have lower-cost border (interior) areas, such as the Inland Empire and the Central Valley counties, but these areas host employment that does not generate the high incomes required by the rest of their respective regions.

Should policies to shape specialization consist mostly of measures to reduce business taxes and regulations, and is there a case that these types of place policies are what have been lacking in Los Angeles? Within Los Angeles County, the localities with low employment creation and low income growth are not the most expensive or high-tax areas (Parent et al., 2013). There are four patterns of economic change in Los Angeles County. The first group consists of localities where there has been a steady *increase in both jobs and income* over the past 20 years. This group includes affluent communities like Calabasas and Beverly Hills, as well as Pasadena, Arcadia, and fast-growing industrial centers like Walnut and Diamond Bar. The second Los Angeles is comprised of areas where there has been *job gain, but income loss*, signaling a growth in service sector and administrative work. This includes a mix of cities including Burbank, Glendale, Torrance, and Carson. The third Los Angeles—which is the most expansive, including most of the Westside, the San Fernando Valley, and a swath of cities along the coast—is characterized by *job loss and income gain*, signaling an economy driven by real estate, services and private investment. Finally, the fourth Los Angeles, which is characterized by *job loss and income loss*, includes South Los Angeles, Compton, El Monte, Hawthorne, and Long Beach. Reinforcing the bleakness of this category, the data also revealed that after the City of Los Angeles itself, the cities that lost the most jobs over the past 20 years include El Segundo, San Fernando, El Monte, Compton, Hawthorne, Pomona, Thousand Oaks, and La Puente. (Parent et al., 2013)

The analysis performed by the UCLA Luskin report on Los Angeles County employment trends also found that many of the worst-performing areas had especially extensive policy offerings, such as enterprise zones, business improvement districts and generous tax and land-use policies. Many of the highest performers, places such as Santa Monica and the coastal cities, offered much more modest incentives, and in fact, have reputations for imposing more onerous regulations, taxes, fees, and permitting processes. In other words, across Los Angeles business is booming in many places noted for "poor business climates" (Parent et al., 2013)

Consistent with the preceding picture, policies designed merely to drive down business costs will be ineffective in Los Angeles. In other words, just as the United States and Turkey do not compete for the same sectors in the world economy, neither can Los Angeles, on balance, compete for cost-sensitive sectors with demand for low-skill employment in the United States. These activities sectors have better (interregional or international) choices of where to locate.

The other sorts of place policies recommended by RSUE theories concern the amenities that supposedly attract highly skilled workers (Glaeser and Maré, 2001). On the whole, as we showed in Chapter 4, the Bay Area does not rank higher in average amenity levels when compared to Los Angeles; nationally, both are high-amenity regions. Both regions are also internally diverse in terms of the amenities they offer, ranging from dense central city areas to sprawling suburbs. The amenity environments for the development of high-wage, high-skill employment are abundant in both metropolitan regions. This does not answer the question of why the Bay Area got so much more of it than did Los Angeles (Scott and Storper, 2009).

If quality of life and business cost/incentive policies are unlikely to solve the labor demand problem of Los Angeles and do not explain the success of the Bay Area, is there a case for more deliberate industrial policies at the regional scale (Barca et al., 2012; Chatterji et al., 2013)? This is an extremely complex topic, but two principal observations may be made at this point in the argument. First, many of the policy levers that lead to the development of high-wage, high-skill industries are principally—and rightly—organized and funded at national scale. They have to do with the R&D system, education, national scientific priorities, infrastructure, property rights, the judicial system, and the host of other institutional forces that make up a "national innovation system" (Lundvall, 2007). However, it is the most innovative, high-wage activities in the economy that have the strongest natural agglomeration economies, so the national policies that stimulate them are always going to have spatially selective and uneven effects. The question, then, is whether additional regional policies toward economic development should attempt to direct the "where" of these developments toward themselves.

In the latter vein of place-oriented, activity-specific policies—those that attempt to attract desired industries to places—are what are known today as cluster policies, which we also discussed in Chapter 6. Theory tells us that cluster policies can only be justified when they would enhance clustering above and beyond the natural level that market forces would generate, and where by so doing, the industry in question becomes more efficient at the policy-induced level of clustering than the market-generated one (in technical terms, clustering has a nonlinear economic benefit and is subject to a market failure). Unless this specific condition is met, clustering policies undertaken by one region merely "beg thy neighbor" by siphoning off some of the cluster to itself, but reducing the optimal level of clustering of the industry for the economy as a whole (Nathan and Overman, 2013). The available statistical evidence shows that most deliberate cluster policies fail to meet these two criteria (Duranton, 2010, 2011).

In any case, in neither the Bay Area nor Los Angeles in the period under study did we detect the existence of comprehensive regional cluster strategies to create the IT and biotech clusters, just as the Los Angeles aerospace and Hollywood clusters emerged were not induced, planned, or implemented by regional authorities. Aerospace was supported by federal military procurement and Hollywood has subsequently been the object of local support policies, but they cannot be said to have been principally the result of deliberate cluster strategies. Paradoxically, Orange County industrialization was the object of much more deliberate planning than Silicon Valley. The Irvine Company did this through top-down urban land use planning, rather than a cluster policy per se. The Los Angeles–Long Beach port industry was developed through active, strategic regional industry policy, but it has the limited economic benefits shown in previous chapters.

The preceding discussion does not mean that deliberate regional economic development strategy is necessarily pointless, but rather that cluster policies as undertaken to date have largely missed their target and need to be reformulated (Farole et al., 2011; McCann, 2015, Duranton, 2011).

The Elements of a High-Wage Specialization Strategy

The first step in such a reformulation is clarity about what it takes to build high-wage regional economic specialization today. The comparative case studies of this book show that there are eight principal components.

First, all cases of high-wage specialization start out with a wave of entrepreneurship, either via individuals leaving existing firms to explore new technologies and markets in related areas, or via the formation of a critical mass of regional industry-building entrepreneurs in an innovation-prone field. Often, these entrepreneurs draw on boundary-spanning economic and social networks, enabling them to draw knowledge from different fields and recombine them.

Second, though the first process may occur in more than one region, the regions that ultimately get ahead have what Padgett and Powell (2012) call "robust actors" who draw the entrepreneurs together at an early stage, giving them a focus and some institutional support in the stage before breakthrough market-shaping innovations have occurred. This is what Fred Terman did in the Bay Area.

Third, the regions that become leading clusters are host to applications of breakthrough innovations. This was the case for aerospace in Los Angeles in the 1930s, with Donald Douglas's invention of the DC-3, or of Silicon Valley in the case of Fairchild's breakthrough chip in the early 1970s. It important to clarify what is meant by breakthrough innovation. Some breakthrough innovations are radical new technologies, as in Karl Benz's motorcar in Germany in the 1880s. But Fairchild's chip was not radical in the way that Shockley's 1954 invention of the chip was radical; both Douglas in Los Angeles's aircraft industry and Fairchild in Silicon Valley's chip industry transformed radical breakthroughs into commercially viable breakthroughs. This is an opportunity open in principle to all regions.

Fourth, the breakthrough is accompanied by the development of organizational practices that externalize parts of the supply system, so that the demand for industry-building entrepreneurship increases. This stimulates relational networks among people through shared experience in different firms and organizations, many of which fail. What should not happen too early is dominance of the regional organizational ecology by a single firm that internalizes a lot of its activity, as happened with high-tech in Phoenix in the 1950s (Motorola) or with biotech in Los Angeles with Amgen in the 1970s.

Fifth, the emerging system can draw from a supportive overall relational infrastructure, where it draws in entrepreneurship, labor, and knowledge from other domains of the regional economy, transforming them in the process. The regional leadership class comes to be deeply involved in the emerging industry. The milieu of entrepreneurs and highly skilled labor is formed through the mobility of people between firms and new ventures, so that they build extensive interpersonal networks.

Sixth, following upon the early boost given by robust actors, new types of dealmakers and brokers emerge and take their place in the emerging system. In Hollywood, they were agents and other organizers of relationships such as attorneys and talent scouts; in Silicon Valley, they were venture capitalists and hippie engineers, and in biotechnology, they are science-based capitalists.

Seventh, the industry invents conventions—for entrepreneurship, interfirm relations, relations, R&D, and labor market mobility—that coordinate the emerging organizational ecology and set examples for new norms that are subsequently formalized in some cases and diffused beyond the region. These epistemic communities transform their host regions, melding together to shape its zeitgeist. In later phases of the maturation of these industries, elements of the region's zeitgeist are borrowed by people in other regions (many regions now have San Francisco–like "geek" milieus today) (Heller, 2013a).

Finally, major firms emerge in the industry from its industry-building entrepreneurship, but they do not initially substitute for spin-off and start-up. Instead, they draw on, and often acquire, start-ups that allow them to prolong the industry's innovative period even as it develops mass scale and market power (Klepper, 2010).

Barriers to Strategy

The barriers to intentionally shaping the eight features mentioned previously are considerable. For one thing, the outcomes of efforts will emerge over long time periods and hence will be uncertain, and the benefits are likely to be unknown and their distribution different from the costs incurred and effort dispensed. Some of the principal hurdles are as follows:

- Organizational practices have considerable inertia, even in the presence of market sanctions for getting it wrong. The aerospace industry in Los Angeles did transform itself in the face of the end of the Cold War, but it did so in part by shrinking and changing locations, rather than transposing skills from the New Economy to existing firms and the regional engineering community.
- The relational networks of a region are dispersed, with a variable geometry and nobody in control. Seeing them clearly (even with advanced network tools) is difficult and there are few robust actors with the potential to reshape them.
- If public policy is brought into the effort to change visions and beliefs, organizational practices, and networks, struggles over resource allocation and dominant ideas are likely to reflect existing interests. Sometimes today's economic winners have interests that are different from the long-term interests of a regional economy, involving future workers or firms rather than existing wealth holders or workers. Even when they become political losers, they can sometimes have enough power to block reorientation of priorities (Acemoglu and Robinson, 2000).
- But neither do winner firms, those favored by the direction of change, always do what is required to create a general direction of change. The Amgen case in Los Angeles exemplifies this; all the while pursuing an effective business strategy for itself, Amgen's leaders did not institutionalize new organizational practices or create the relational infrastructure that would have led to a biotech cluster in Los Angeles, much like the successful but cloistered success of Hollywood in prior decades. Firm-based policies are generally not successful for this reason.

Reshaping Organizational Practices and Relational Infrastructure

The history of economic development also contains examples of successful changes in organizational practices and key relational networks. Boston was not among the top ten metropolitan areas in per capita income in 1970, whereas Detroit was a member of this privileged club. Boston was a declining mill and manufacturing region, whereas today it is the third wealthiest metro area in the United States. Some of this was good luck, with Boston holding resources in R&D that would become more valuable with the advent of the New Economy, and Detroit having the opposite, an economy overly concentrated on a de-agglomerating old manufacturing sector, where technological change was eliminating employment and global competition threatened market share.

But in both cases, more than these accidents of specialization were responsible. In Detroit, the regional economy generated considerable growth in New Economy sectors, but this occurred in its suburbs of Oakland County. Automobile industry leaders foundered in their responses to foreign imports, and in this atmosphere of permanent crisis, they had little interest in regional and central city economic regeneration. As in Detroit, in Boston many of the working-class groups present in the central city (Irish and Italian "white ethnics" rather than inner-city African Americans, as in Detroit) were unlikely to directly benefit from the New Economy. Early successes of the Boston area IT economy succumbed to traditional corporate practices (Saxenian, 1994). Unlike in Michigan, however, in the Boston case the Commonwealth of Massachusetts, under the leadership of Governor Michael Dukakis, set up a "growth cabinet," the first of its kind in the United States (Peirce, 1983). Dukakis convened the groups that were until then unable to talk to one another. The cabinet also harnessed other forces in the region's hospitals and biomedical research establishments. An extended conversation among different groups was thus opened up. Governor Dukakis, of course, did not create this from whole cloth; he astutely built on the leadership of the region's existing universities and hospitals. But he helped boost them into a new entrepreneurial mode, with attention to social inclusion of the core working-class constituencies of the metropolitan region of Boston. In so doing, he also helped the foundering high-tech industry, until then based on suburban Route 128, to get a new lease on life, as young technologists were drawn into the Cambridge–Kendall Square area.

Economic sociology has now accumulated some understanding of these processes of blockage and change (North, 1990; Acemoglu and Robinson, 2012). Puga and Trefler (2012) show how merchant groups in medieval Venice (eleventh century), favored by the expansion of world trade, did more than profit from that trade; they pushed for new rules and institutions that enabled trade to expand and displace the hereditary ruling group. Yet later on (late thirteenth century), the rich merchants who emerged reinstated hereditary participation in the most lucrative parts of long-distance trade, ushering in a new oligarchic period, derailing institutional dynamism, and leading to Venice's ultimate stagnation. In another regional example, Padgett and Ansell (1993) take up the case of Cosimo de Medici in medieval Florence, showing how Cosimo took advantage of the ways that economic change strengthened and weakened certain pre-existing actors. For his own personal ends, he knit together a coalition containing many of the economy's "new men." A by-product of this new relational network was, in essence, a newly functioning type of state. The winners created both hard institutions and changed the regional zeitgeist.

San Diego built a coalition to help the nascent biotechnology industry, which never occurred in Greater Los Angeles in spite of the latter's early advantages (Casper, 2009; Kenney, 1986). There have been no Cosimos in Los Angeles's economic development since 1970. The Bay Area has had many of them.

Changing Beliefs and Worldviews

Putative Cosimos can be found in many places; they succeed from a mixture of luck and determination but also when they are in the right time at the right place. Part of conditions being right for them is when the beliefs and worldviews of leaders are aligned with what they want to do (North, 2005). By the early 1980s, the Bay Area Council did just that: it began to educate Bay Area leadership on the way the New Economy functions. It focused attention on the structural position of the Bay Area in this new world, as a high-cost region that could succeed only by enhancing the capabilities of its economy to generate high-wage jobs and accommodate high-wage workers. The council regularly called attention to the need to moderate housing costs and other business costs and regulations, but it did not place all of its eggs in this basket. Its members explicitly acknowledged that the Bay Area would be the brains, while the hands of the economy—the manual work—would be elsewhere. Apple's mantra captures this zeitgeist perfectly: "designed in California, manufactured in China."

Though an element of luck is involved in where the great entrepreneurs go at the critical moment where activities are establishing their regional clusters, it is striking that people such as Bill Gates or Jeff Bezos went to Seattle and not to Los Angeles. Seattle was another regional economy in trouble in the 1980s, with a declining natural resources industry and an industrial behemoth—Boeing—going through difficulties and restructuring itself to locate more of its activities in other regions. Seattle had a reputation as a high-cost, highly unionized town. Its universities were, and are, much less prestigious than those of Los Angeles. A realistic counterfactual is that a coherent leadership class with beliefs adapted to the zeitgeist of a New Economy age could have helped more visionary entrepreneurs flourish in Los Angeles.

Changing the perceptions and analyses of regional leadership groups would not be a magic wand. But in light of the analysis of this book, a conversation about a new vision is a necessary step to make the region more hospitable to game-changing innovation, industry-building entrepreneurship, and twenty-first-century organizational ecologies. Without such a conversation, this new zeitgeist will be stifled by existing structures.

Who Is in the Conversation?

If changing the zeitgeist of an economy were merely a question of reading a few well-done academic reports, all regions would do it. But it is a contested terrain of perceptions and interests. Who occupied this turf in 1970? In Los Angeles, the kaleidoscopic range of actors might have included the downtown elites organized around the Chandler family; the remains of the Group of 20 and the downtown clubs; the aerospace engineers and companies and their lobby; the leaders of Hollywood; the Irvine Company, the new city government of Irvine, and the social and economic leaders in Irvine and Newport Beach; the leaders of UCLA, UC Irvine, USC, and Caltech, especially Franklin Murphy and Charles Young; the garment industry in downtown Los Angeles; the big manufacturing firms from downtown Los Angeles to Long Beach; the regional banks and their owner-managers; SCAG; the major industrial unions in the Los Angeles County Federation of Labor; and the oil and agribusiness companies headquartered in Los Angeles. There were also some suburban community groups, the beginnings of an environmentalist movement, and the community groups in the African American neighborhoods. In the 1970s, the community groups were at the margins, but by the 1980s, things were changing, with the advent of the coalition that elected Tom Bradley mayor of Los Angeles. Dramatic events, such as the riots of 1992, the real estate collapse in the early 1990s, and the bleeding of jobs from aerospace led to the creation of showcase "grand coalitions" to turn the economy around in Los Angeles. They all failed. Rebuild LA was a victim of lackadaisical business leadership, weak coalitional forces in Los Angeles, and the absence of a broad conversation about the New Economy in Los Angeles County.

Orange County had its own conversation. The strategically planned development of the new core of Orange County, centered on Irvine, is one of the greatest success stories of metropolitan development in recent history. Land development was the motor of this expansion, supercharged by the power of a single large landowner (the Irvine Company) to rapidly plan and implement development of this new metropolitan core. Major companies established themselves in the belt from Costa Mesa southward, creating one of the great "new industrial spaces" of the time (A. Scott, 1993).

And so a sort of New Economy was in fact built in Greater Los Angeles. But it is not a New Economy in the same sense as Silicon Valley or the other great IT centers of the world. As a second-mover, it was in many ways, a 1970s version of what had already worked in Los Angeles County way back in the 1950s: large-scale land development coupled to the location of large firms, carrying out scale-oriented production in relatively new industrial branches of the economy. In the end, for all its spanking-new appearance (and physical resemblance to Silicon Valley), Orange County's strategy was classical midcentury Southern California.

The Bay Area had a different mix of groups in the conversation. Its downtown elite was more powerful than that of Los Angeles and more broadly based. Politically it consisted of moderate Republicans (in tense relationship to ethnic white groups) strongly based in natural resources industries, and it brought a New England style sense of civic responsibility to the Bay Area that Los Angeles downtown elites had not been able to sustain in midcentury (Walker, 2008). As we pointed out in Chapter 7, by 1970 the Bay Area had many layers of social involvement. The conservationist movement had spun off major environmentalist organizations, which were powerful civic actors from different parts of the Bay Area society. The port unions were in retreat but still had significant influence. The environmentalists were talking to the alternative-technology movement, centered on San Francisco, Marin County, and UC Berkeley, and even to some of the more iconoclastic scientists working at Lawrence Berkeley National Laboratory. Some of them were talking to people in the South Bay, at Stanford and Xerox PARC (Duguid, 2009). San Francisco itself became transformed from a Republican city to America's first true postmodern urban political coalition, an odd mix of well-educated elites, social progressives, technologists, environmentalists, and bohemians. The Dianne Feinstein mayoral coalition, tame as it seems in retrospect, was the leading edge of America's new urban politics, very different from the more traditional bigcity black-Jewish-liberal Bradley coalition in Los Angeles. Both were radically different from the top-down landowner dominance of Orange County politics. A different set of participants in the conversation would have been required to maintain Los Angeles's position in the high-income development club.

Alternative Conversations: What Should We Have Talked About?

Regional leaders need to have a basic understanding of economic geography and the map of development clubs. With each major phase of economic development, a geographical pattern of comparative advantages is defined: development clubs. The conversation in Los Angeles did not revolve around the development clubs of the New Economy but around an older, less relevant set of concerns about business taxes, housing costs, and regulatory burdens. These were the equivalent of Los Angeles attempting—in a futile way—to become Phoenix.

A second theme of the conversation must concern the organizational practices and skills that the region needs in order to be in a certain club. As an example, Casper (2007, 2009) identifies the requirements of building a successful biotechnology agglomeration in Los Angeles, along the lines of what happened in San Diego. The key is to build an appropriate relational infrastructure. In order to do this, there must be repair work to the weak connections between researchers and firms, weak connections from end-use firms (such as medical device firms) and biotech producers, and weak interconnections between researchers as they move through different roles in the private sector (weak "invisible colleges") or "career affiliation" networks. Casper summarizes this problem with the pithy phrase that there is a weak "marketplace for ideas" in the region.

There are many practical barriers to alternative conversations. Indeed, even in the Bay Area, there was no spontaneous and easily achieved consensus about the new economy in the 1970s. In vast parts of the Bay Area, and notably the central city and the old industrial belt of the East Bay, powerful interests had little perception of a New Economy or its potential benefits. The downtown corporate elites were comfortably related to their traditional positions in natural resource industries and banking headquarters built up when San Francisco was California's leading city. The robust actors who emerged could have been stopped at certain early points in the process. Imagine a Fred Terman having been frustrated in his efforts to build links to business, or Steve Jobs being considered too weird to attract engineers or financers, or for that matter, Xerox PARC never having entered the Bay Area because of a hostile or unresponsive local culture. Imagine even further, as the Bay Area high-tech industry hit its first of many crises (with the first wave of commodification of chips in the late 1970s, whence its own firms moved production out of the Valley and even out of the Bay area [Saxenian, 1983]), that there had been no culture of further experimentation, or that the Bay Area Council had settled on analyses similar to those of SCAG in Los Angeles. The Bay Area development pathway was the result of much more than talk, conversation, and emerging understandings; it involved fortunate breakthroughs and powerful circular and cumulative agglomeration processes. As the experiment unfolded, so did its cross-domain communities of practice, well-organized firms, labor market networks, professional associations, legions of new kinds of dealmakers, and vast quantities of capital, all of which complemented the zeitgeist with broad conversations. The emerging zeitgeist could have been derailed or shaped differently had the conversations not taken place.

What Should We Talk About Now?

There are many possible conversations Greater Los Angeles could have in the future: expanding the Hollywood-based content industries into the digital economy; breaking down Amgen's isolation and building a robust biotechnology agglomeration; attracting or developing a bigger investment finance industry; building on Hollywood to become a bigger media center; somehow turning around the region's weak role as a corporate headquarters city (possibly by becoming a key location for developing world multinationals' foreign subsidiaries, as these expand in the developed countries); transforming the region's great importance in producing art into a business-arts complex, where art is sold as well as produced; and upgrading its craft and fashion industries to specialize in higher-quality (and higher-priced) clothing, furniture, and other products.

It may seem odd even to suggest changes to the Bay Area's conversations, given the region's economic success. And yet, all economies ultimately face external shocks and internal challenges. The Bay Area has become dependent on a specific kind of entrepreneurial process, based on rapid commercialization of new ideas, using an amalgam of talents and dealmakers, with short creation cycles. Economic history once again suggests that entrepreneurship of this type comes and goes in waves (Klepper and Sleeper, 2005; Klepper, 2010). The Bay Area IT industry has now matured, consisting of a set of world-spanning corporate juggernauts, surrounded by this start-up penumbra. In 2009, the Bay Area Council argued that there are "one million jobs at risk" in the Bay Area as the physical production parts of IT become more oriented toward timely delivery and customization, and involving high capital intensity and high customer service requirements (Bay Area Economic Forum, 2005). The Bay Area will face the inevitable maturation of the IT sector, where radical entrepreneurialism alone is not going to maintain incomes forever.

This notion may seem odd, given the latest wave of Bay Area technology development, consisting of the vigorous start-up of firms creating mobile applications and largely located in San Francisco proper, rather than Silicon Valley. But these firms, high as their market capitalization might ultimately be, do not generate major new waves of employment and are being taken over by the Silicon Valley giants. Moreover, the current managers of the Silicon Valley giants are a different generation from the scientists and entrepreneurs who built the IT industry and Silicon Valley. The giant firms of the Valley now have increasingly traditional forms of corporate management, in spite of the hip images they project to the public and to young college graduates. As one recent commentator has it:

> New corporations usually insist on what they're not; behind them looms the heavy shadow of the sprawling, narrow-minded greedy companies of yore. "Think different" Apple's famous ad campaign implored. . . . [N]ew corporate guys vaunt their ingenuity and their exceptionalism, even as their business goals are standard issue. . . . [L]ife in a new-corporate company differs little from life elsewhere. (Heller, 2013b: 69)

Returning to the theories reviewed in Chapter 2, the Bay Area might be at the beginning of a "Chinitz" problem, where it is becoming a one-horse town. Its factor markets, political attention, managerial talent, and worldviews are dominated by one type of activity. Moreover, the traditional managers and engineers of the corporate Valley are increasingly disconnected from the "geek" milieus of San Francisco. They do not devote themselves to large-scale radical problem solving that will be needed to ensure the industry's growth (Lu, 2014). Thus, the boundary-spanning lash-ups that created this economy are weaker than they used to be. This is what started to happen in Detroit in the 1950s, when Detroit's wealth was at its peak.

Oddly enough, the Bay Area might face a double paradox of its success. On the one hand, it is a one-horse town with a zeitgeist of disruption in a sector that is consolidating and coming to be dominated by corporate giants. Company towns are rarely disruptively innovative over the long-run (Agarwal et al., 2010). On the other, the giants are becoming successful at normal corporate management, and when that happens, we can be sure that weakening of clustering is not far behind.

Not Allowing Certain Conversations to Crowd Out the Essential Ones

The conversation in Los Angeles has changed. Two big new conversations revolve around Los Angeles's rising status as a creative arts capital and around the need to integrate equity concerns into its development strategies. We confirmed that Los Angeles hosts one of the United States' two biggest creative arts concentrations, along with New York. The creative arts and entertainment industries are iconic parts of the region's identity and lifestyle, founts of talent for associated activities and underpinnings to Los Angeles's cultural vibrancy. But Chapter 5 demonstrates that even an extremely high concentration of creative arts does not solve Los Angeles's income problem. Under the best of circumstances, the sector will be neither big enough nor high-wage enough to lift Los Angeles back up to its previous rank in its development club. Los Angeles's location quotients in arts and entertainment are so high that they are at their natural ceilings. Supporting and even strengthening the creative arts industries is desirable for the intrinsic value that the arts and entertainment have, as long as it does not crowd out other fundamental tasks in developing specializations that can raise the region's per capita income.

Los Angeles's social mobilization sector is growing, and a key concern of this sector is to address the region's high level of income and quality-of-life inequalities. Much of this necessarily takes the form of job development in disadvantaged communities and among disadvantaged groups. Inequality is growing in the United States as a whole, and there is a lively debate over its causes and effects. We produced evidence in Chapter 1 that San Francisco has generated much higher per capita income than Los Angeles, but both regions have similar levels of income inequality (and both have high levels of inequality relative to the United States and developed-world averages). It has become increasingly common to argue that more equitable regions develop more successfully than more unequal ones (Benner and Pastor, 2014). It may be desirable to have lower levels of inequality in both regions. But this does not obviate the fact that at every level in the income distribution, people are better off in real terms on average in the Bay Area than they are in Los Angeles.

Our evidence suggests that equity conversations without conversations about per capita income have two weaknesses. On one hand, they could unleash the famous "dividing a shrinking pie" problem; this is what has happened in Los Angeles, with tragic effect. On the other, they could crowd out conversations about high-wage growth strategies; this is what occurred with Los Angeles's focus on the port-logistics industry. The contrast to San Diego's focus on gaining biotechnology to replace its shrinking military economy is very sharp. This is a cautionary tale about well-meaning conversations that are not sufficiently anchored in the realities of economic geography and the structural nature of development clubs.

Institutional Arrangements and Institutional Strategies

Rodríguez-Pose (2013) makes a useful distinction between economic development strategies and institutional arrangements for promoting regional economic development. Chapter 6 reviewed the institutional arrangements in the United States, noting that a complex layer cake of agencies and governments is involved in shaping regional economic development. At the same time, metropolitan regions rarely have agencies whose role is to promote regional economic development but instead rely on a patchwork of cities and counties and their many departments and agencies. Moreover, we have no accurate comprehensive data on what they actually do or what it costs. All of this is a problem because economies operate at regional scales, with causes and effects that do not respect the borders of cities and counties or the different powers of their dizzying array of agencies and policies.

In light of these arrangements, it is not realistic to propose that regions devise formal strategies for regional economic development in the United States. There would be no agency to implement them even if they were well designed. Should we create such agencies and authorities? There is an opportunity to eliminate waste by defining more clearly what economic development policies should be, putting them in the light of day by labeling them clearly, and eliminating competition and overlap between cities, counties, and their departments, and special authorities. But economic development is too complex a problem to be assigned to any single agency or level of government. In addition, existing interests in fragmentation and overlap are entrenched and supported by a widely shared ideology of community economic development and local control.

A more modest proposal is to develop informational tools to label what all these governments and agencies do, to reveal their costs, and to bring this information together to be able to evaluate the effects of the measures on regional economic development. Merely having an up-to-date database on economic development policies would be a major advance (Storper, 2014). Once we know reliably what cities and counties and special agencies do and how much it costs, then we could initiate conversations about reform of the institutional arrangements that are used to promote economic development.

11 Improving Analysis of Urban Regions
Methods and Models

ECONOMIC DEVELOPMENT IS FORTUNATELY THE OBJECT OF attention by many academic disciplines and draws on a rich variety of theories and methods. Four principal theories—development, urban and regional economics, New Economic Geography, and institutions—have been mobilized to frame this deep empirical dive into just two regions, the San Francisco Bay Area and Greater Los Angeles. The purpose of this dive was not only to shed light on the specific case of these two great California urban regions, but to use the comparison as a device for understanding divergent economic development more widely. In light of this, what has been learned about theories of urban and regional economic development and the methods and data used to make claims about urban economies?

What Is Development? Development Clubs

Economic development is the ultimate noisy social science problem, which means that there are many variables that change in concert as part of the development process; land prices, traffic congestion, specialization, population, output, output per capita, income, income per capita, foreign trade, education levels, ethnic diversity, segregation, office space, manufacturing space, tax receipts, and many more variables are related to development. But not all of these variables are equally good synthetic indicators of the overall nature of the development process.

Growth variables (such as population or output change) do not, in and of themselves, proxy for development. Growth can occur without development if there is a decline in per capita income or if the distribution of income worsens such that a significant part of the population becomes worse off. Regions can also de-develop if their level of output population declines, and even more so if shrinking population is combined with decreasing per capita income. In the language of modeling, growth processes are independent or intermediate variables (contributing forces) in development, but development itself is not synonymous with growth.

The club metaphor that is used widely in international development theory is appropriate for the comparative study of metropolitan economic development. It provides a structural picture of similar groups of metropolitan economies. Between clubs, there is significant covariation of the quality of specialization, income levels, labor skills, and organizational forms and conventions. The movement of regions between clubs is not continuous or smooth. Using the concept of club membership and possible changes in position within and between clubs is a useful guide to summarizing the effects of changes in the quality of specialization and level and rank of real per capita income, which are the most reliable proxies of development.

Going forward, the field of comparative regional development should use consistent dependent variables, combining real per capita income and the income distribution, and should tease out changes in development by being attentive to noncontinuous initial takeoff processes and middle-income traps. For high-income metropolitan regions, we need to develop analytical tools for systematically detecting differences between renewal of membership in the high-income club versus shocks and adjustment processes that kick metropolitan areas out of that club. We should not, therefore, extrapolate from per capita income levels as if they change in a smooth, continuous way, whether upward or downward.

What Is a City-Region? Getting the Unit of Analysis Right

Research on urban economies has long been afflicted by a problem of definition. Cities and regions vary greatly in physical, economic, and population size. This is also a problem in comparative research on national economic development, since nation-states vary enormously in size. How meaningful is it to compare Denmark or Switzerland to the United States, or El Salvador to Brazil?

In comparative research on large samples of regions even within the same country, there is no single standard for the definition of region. In the United States, one can find some research using MSAs (e.g., San Francisco–Oakland), some others using just CSAs (the entire Bay Area), and still others that use and mix both. A typical example of the latter can be found in *Forbes* magazine on November 18, 2011, which lists the American metro areas with the highest rates of employment growth in high technology (Forbes, 2011). But it switches between MSAs and CSAs, thus leading it to claim, for example, that one of the subregions of Southern California (Riverside–San Bernardino) has a higher rate of high-tech job growth than the entire San Francisco Bay Area CSA, a meaningless observation if there ever was one.

The appropriate scale at which to investigate and compare regional economic performance is the extended metropolitan region; in the United States this is the CSA, and in the European Union, it is the Functional Urban Region or the Larger Urban Zone. This scale captures extended regional economies, such as the Île-de-France with Paris at its center and eleven million residents, the San Francisco Bay Area, or Greater São Paulo. The theoretical basis for this choice is clear. A functional economic region is a scale at which principal economic interactions occur, which determine the prices of labor and land in the region. The key price systems of a regional economy, notably wages and land and housing, are strongly (albeit imperfectly) integrated at the scale of the metropolitan region. This integration is reflected in the fact that, once factors are adjusted for quality (of workers, and type and location for housing and land), the Samuelson "law of one price" operates at the extended regional scale. There is a steep slope of such prices, which defines the border between the region and the nonmetropolitan space beyond it.

These market borders of functional or extended metropolitan regions obviously do not uniquely determine per capita income. The "national effect" is powerful, reflecting the strong role of national borders in trade intensity, monetary and fiscal policy, and institutions, even in this era of strong globalization; thus, most of the top 50 metropolitan regions in the world in per capita income are in the United States. But regional effects can be powerful as well; for example, London, Paris, Vancouver, and Sydney appear at the top of their respective national rankings and also enter into the top class of internationally ranked metro regions, because their regional specialization and productivity levels are much greater than those of their respective national averages.

Subregional scales are relevant as well. All regions are complex systems that sort factors of production and activities into a geographical mosaic of people, land, housing, transport, production, and leisure. These smaller scales of selected and intensive interactions are commonly called communities or neighborhoods. For the purposes of understanding economic performance, neighborhood-scale effects are relatively unimportant. The very high incomes we observe in certain neighborhoods of metropolitan regions have little to do with local productivity and interaction effects; they are the result instead of the self-sorting of a region's high-income people, who group themselves together through their residential choices. The extremely low incomes found in poor neighborhoods are also mostly the result of the forced sorting—segregation—of low-income people to those places; this is why even very wealthy metro areas have poor neighborhoods. Some of this is clearly a regional effect; in a poor metropolitan area, there are probably more poor neighborhoods, though ultimately that depends on the level of segregation in relationship to the region's income level. Some additional neighborhood effects may then come about. In poor neighborhoods, for example, the concentration of poor people may intensify local interactions that perpetuate isolation, deprivation, and low productivity of those populations even in the midst of regional prosperity (Sampson, 2012). But to state the case as bluntly as possible, incomes for African Americans are determined more by national and regional effects than they are by neighborhood effects: national effects are both positive (a wealthy and productive economy) and negative (racial discrimination in labor markets and education); regional effects are both positive (regional price system and labor market) and potentially negative (racial discrimination and geographical sorting). The strictly local or neighborhood effect is very small. So it is safe to say that our use of the functional urban region as the principal scale in regional economic development analysis, at least within a country, is the right one.

In this book, we operationalize this scale as the five counties of metropolitan Los Angeles, and ten counties of the San Francisco Bay Area. We analyzed some border issues in our research. For example, part of the Bay Area workforce commutes in from counties just outside the ten that were included, in the nearby San Joaquin Valley. These border areas have steadily become part of the Bay Area economy, in a natural process of expansion during the study period. This was recognized in the redefinition of the Bay Area Core Based Statistical Area (CBSA) by the Office of Management and Budget, to enlarge that region from ten to twelve counties following the 2010 census. Comparative research over a long time period has to decide whether to use the original ten-county definition of the Bay Area in 1970 or the most recent twelve-county definition; this is a general issue for the field.

We dealt with this problem by calculating the influence of incomes of Bay Area workers who live outside the ten counties on Bay Area per capita income and workforce characteristics. Since these interior areas concentrate lower-income workers, they may lead us to exaggerate Bay Area income levels. But inclusion of those workers did not change the Bay Area ranking nor its income gap to Greater Los Angeles, because the commuting workforce is a small minority of the regional workforce. In parallel fashion, we considered whether the inclusion of large low-income inland counties—Riverside and San Bernardino, part of whose workforce is in territories that clearly lie partly outside the reach of metropolitan Los Angeles—would lead to underestimating Los Angeles per capita income. We verified this by isolating the wages, incomes, and attributes of those counties' working populations that clearly work in metropolitan Los Angeles. Both of these exercises confirm the divergence of the two regions' per capita income and in this case introduced negligible changes in the numbers.

The lesson is that the field of development analysis needs consistent definitions of the regional scale of economic performance and income determination and procedures for dealing with cross-border commuting and regional expansion. It also needs to accumulate a larger body of work based on this scale.

An additional challenge for research on urban regions is that these regions are not the same size. Any urban system has a size distribution of regions within it, which is the subject itself of a specialized area of theory and data. But when we try to detect development patterns in a system consisting of units that are not equally sized, results are extremely sensitive to whether they are adjusted for size. For example, if we say that per capita incomes converged between cities in a system, but it turns out that the higher-income cities are systematically bigger than the lower-income ones, then we might instead conclude that per capita incomes are diverging if we weight cities by their population (or some other relevant denominator). This is even more problematic for simple ranking exercises (e.g., "most high-tech city").

What Is Regional Economic Specialization?

A key task of comparative economic research is to identify patterns of specialization and their role in regional economic performance. In order to do this, we must define the components of specialization, which are industries or economic activities. Research that compares large numbers of metropolitan regions generally uses broad categories for describing their economies; in technical parlance, these are two- and three-digit industrial economic census categories. They are too aggregated to shed light on specialization in the contemporary economy, where increasingly narrow slices of activity are allocated to different regions. We showed this by decomposing IT at the *six*-digit level and by comparing wages of the two regions' electronics-related occupations, and cross-checking this by showing the different proportions of nonroutine work within the same detailed occupational and industrial categories.

We were able to examine in detail the heterogeneous nature of activities in our two economies, because we examined only two regions. Doing this for large samples of city-regions could easily lead to overwhelming quantities of data and limited degrees of freedom in the statistical analysis. However, over-aggregation that wipes clean the heterogeneity of economic reality cannot be defended on the grounds of convenience. So the field needs new measures that can cope with this heterogeneity. We used two of them actively in this book. We detected heterogeneity through wages within industries. And we used recent indexes of routineness or nonroutineness in tasks to establish how homogeneous sectors really are across regions. These are promising approaches for wide application in better measuring regional economic specialization. However, they open up the "Humpty Dumpty" problem: once we have disaggregated, how do we put it back together into a comprehensive comparative vision?

There may also be undetected forms of similarity in specialization that are not apparent. For example, there are many activities that have strong interrelations (whether as suppliers to one another, or sharing one another's labor pool, or exchanging technological knowledge with one another) (Kemeny and Storper, 2014). Such relatedness is not captured by census categories. So in order to make progress in comparing regional economies, we need both to disaggregate the overly heterogeneous categories into finer ones, and sometimes to recombine them into larger related groups. The current state of analysis of specialization is far from this ideal and thus prone to many inaccuracies.

What Are the Workforce and Population Characteristics?

The best news for comparative analysis comes with respect to data on the composition of the workforce. Labor economics has long used sophisticated controls when analyzing wages: for age, education, ethnicity, gender, and immigration status. In this book, we analyzed detailed micro-data on individuals (IPUMS—Integrated Public Use Micro Series). There are some limits to those data too; for example, education is not a perfect proxy for skill, and there may be unobserved heterogeneity among people in a skill-occupation category. Experience is also hard to detect, and different experience of people with the same observable characteristics could, in principle, lead to some of the wage and income differentials detected in this research. Indeed, we believe (as stated in Chapter 4) that different regional economies lead to progressively different experience patterns, and are likely to be one of the reasons for regional economic divergence (De la Roca and Puga, 2012; Davis and Dingel, 2013). If this regional experience effect is confirmed, it creates a wedge between wage/income differences that can be attributed to workforce composition (age, ethnicity, education, immigration, etc.), economic specialization (the mix of industries in a region), and resulting regional wages and incomes. Wages and incomes should ideally be decomposed into the effect of what activities people are in, their initial skill endowments, and then how they acquire experience in a particular regional context. Carrying this out for large samples of regions would require considerable methodological innovation, effectively modifying the unit of analysis of both individual and occupation.

Thus, our basic categories of analysis—region, industry, individual, and occupation—are in need of overhaul in order to be able to accurately describe regional economies and determine the causes of their development.

Regional Science/Urban Economics (RSUE)

What has the comparison of the Bay Area and Greater Los Angeles taught us about the substantive theories of regional economic development that were identified in Chapter 2? In the standard RSUE theory, there are two regions with high levels of openness. They trade products and services with one another and their capital, labor, and knowledge can freely migrate from one region to another. They also have similar formal institutions and rules, so there is a high degree of comfort in their economic exchanges. Under these conditions, RSUE predicts that real incomes of regions will tend to converge. The migration of factors between them will be strong (equalizing their prices), and firms will arbitrage locations, leading to similar productivity levels between the two regions.

Firms, individuals, and households choose locations by arbitraging between money wages, land and housing prices, and nonpriced amenities. Individual and household location decisions, when taken together, drive regional population dynamics. The productive sector is backgrounded in almost all of its models, resting on the assumption that jobs follow people and that housing-driven cost-of-living differences are reflected in nominal wage differences between regions, so that firms and households arbitrage in the same direction. This leads to the key unifying notion of RSUE that the space-economy tends to an interregional real income or utility equalization, a form of convergent development of regions. RSUE thus holds that population change is the only valid indicator of regional development, since income and utility are effectively assumed to be equalized or on the way to being so.

Several of the findings reported in Chapters 1, 2, and 3 go against the grain of this theory:

- In a detailed analysis of wages, incomes, and housing costs, we did not find real wage or income equalization between the two regions, whether on a per capita basis or for particular subgroups in the population, and over time we found sharp divergence.

- Differences in housing costs do not appear to be less driven by differences in regulation or supply, as held by RSUE models, than by differences in demand. Therefore, they seem to be generated by a regional spillover from nominal wage levels into the regional housing market. This implies that the direction of causality can under some circumstances be the opposite from that built into most RSUE models, at least in the case of the two regions at hand.

- Unpriced amenities (quality of life) are not sufficiently different between the two regions to drive any additional wedge between nominal and real wages and incomes. This may not be true in different samples of regions. However, in other research (Kemeny and Storper, 2014), we found that metro areas in the Sun Belt with high population growth have *lower* levels of unpriced and priced amenities than many older regions with lower levels of population growth.

- Some international migration (immigration) patterns do not seem well accommodated by RSUE models. It makes sense that more highly skilled immigrants migrated to the Bay Area, since its real wages and incomes are higher than in Los Angeles for them. But this is true as well for low-skilled immigrants, yet more of them went to Los Angeles. Population change, then, must be driven not only by real wage arbitraging but by some other factor that does not figure prominently in RSUE models.

RSUE tries to explain these anomalies through add-ons to its basic models. They assume that entrepreneurs and the highly skilled agglomerate together in order to interact with one another (Chatterji et al., 2013). It is descriptively plausible that technology workers are attracted to the Bay Area for the rich, large, and diverse milieu of skills and information with which it might be advantageous for any such individual to co-locate; the same would be true of, say, people in the entertainment industry for the case of Hollywood. But what is the chicken and what is the egg of this process? As firms of a certain type of activity agglomerate, they generate a bigger labor and entrepreneur pool and a local knowledge pool as well. This concentration in turn makes interaction more valuable to individuals, already in the region and far away from it. The desire for interaction is not an independent cause that arises on its own and then subsequently generates specialization; it is more the other way around.

We believe that the research reported in this book backs up a case for the reformulation of RSUE models, which focus excessively on convergence forces to the detriment of explaining divergence and the economy's developmental dynamic, and which have no consistent view of specialization, clustering, and labor demand.

New Economic Geography

The weak point of RSUE is the strong point of the New Economic Geography: the geographical dynamics of production, clustering, and specialization. The NEG has developed a strong body of theory and evidence on the three principal underpinnings of agglomeration—sharing of input structures, matching in labor markets, and learning through knowledge exchange. Though this book does not test NEG theories in any formal way, we interpret our results as being broadly consistent with the NEG's emphasis on agglomeration as a source of regional specialization, and in this case as a source of regional divergence in wages and incomes.[1]

The NEG also has gaps in its theory of specialization. The NEG does not have a good theory of the origins of specialization in particular regions (Storper, 2013). It holds, with some plausibility, that once an agglomeration reaches a certain size threshold, it grows through cumulative causation, in a snowball process. But this says little about the origins of that process in the Bay Area, and nothing about Greater Los Angeles. Chapters 5 through 9 attempt to plug this gap.

Institutions: Politics, Policies, Economic Sociology

Chapters 5 through 9 emphasize the role of a variety of institutional factors in driving the divergence of Los Angeles and the Bay Area economies. Rodríguez-Pose (2013) argues that there is a widespread consensus that "institutions are important to development," but there is less consensus about what we mean by institutions or how they shape development. Granovetter (2005) argues that norms and network density are critical to the deployment and redeployment of factor endowments in an economy. Owen-Smith and Powell (2012) hold that there is also a high degree of recursiveness between networks, organizational forms, and institutions, as well as feedbacks between beliefs and practices and networks. Going after the role of institutions in shaping the geographical pattern of development thus offers promise but also poses great challenges.

Let us examine some of these, with a view toward what the field needs to achieve to improve them.

Formal local economic development policies. Chapter 6 argues, by process of elimination, that formal local and regional economic development policies were not very important in driving divergence. The problem, as we noted there in considerable detail, is that there are no reliable data on the policies implemented by local and regional bodies. The field urgently needs to find ways to construct these data.

Moreover, in all countries, a fair amount of explicit policy that shapes metropolitan economic development is national in nature, or comes about through the delegation of nationally determined policies and programs to regions. Once again, there are crippling gaps in the information we have on the geographical effects of those programs.

Beyond these data and measurement deficiencies, there is little theoretical sophistication on how innumerable local and regional policies might interact and add up to steer the regional economy in the medium run. Do thousands of land use decisions add up in a way that systematically shapes regional productivity, specialization, and incomes? Does the local construction of mega-facilities shape regional specialization and incomes? RSUE claims that the housing/land use nexus shapes spatial arbitraging of people and firms, so that it concentrates on the effects of land use regulation on housing supply and prices as the key vector of that effect. We argued that the causality likely runs largely in the other direction. Additional formal models of all these effects and involve testable causal sequences, are thus needed.

Economic sociology: Organizational practices, relational infrastructure, transposition, robust action. Our integrative argument about divergence in Chapter 9 draws heavily on concepts from economic sociology. Ultimately, wider use of these concepts would require the following:

- More standardized ways of detecting transposition of practices and their recombination in growing sectors, and the role of networks in transposition
- Better data on regional elite and non-elite networks, and not only on their architecture, but on what people actually do inside networks, and hence on economic outcomes
- Better data on the structure of communities or groups in regions, and how they do or do not build bridges to become part of broader networks (Rodríguez-Pose and Storper, 2005)

Events and Structures: From Models to Causal Stories

In the economic development field, data represent large-scale regularities or repeating processes, such as urban growth and income change. But NEG models, and some historical knowledge, both suggest that there may be decisive events that generate turning points in the geography of the economy. This seems to be the case in the comparison of Los Angeles and the Bay Area. We know major turning points have occurred in world economic development, such as the industrial revolution in Europe and the subsequent Great

Divergence in world incomes from 1750 to 1980, or perhaps in the twenty-first century with the reappearance of East Asia as a center of the world economy. Agglomeration processes are circular and reinforcing, and we therefore model these regularities of cluster growth. But this tells us nothing about how clusters are set off, or precisely where they are set off. Their growth is also nonlinear in their early phases, which complicates the way data are analyzed. Moreover, they are only self-reinforcing until some dramatic new force such as technical change in products (especially breakthrough innovations) or transport shocks undermines them. Our data sets do not have the categories of "events" and "shocks" in them. An ideal data set would combine information on the establishment and lock-in of agglomerations, along with other shocks, breakthrough innovations, or sharp switches in consumer preferences.

In this inquiry into two regions, we consider the contributions of both regular processes and key events or turning points in the unfolding process of divergence, as well as circular and cumulative reinforcement after turning points. This has required a lot of information—a deep dive into two regions—and it runs up against the constraint of larger-scale generalization. Our integration of them in Chapter 9 also tries to maintain a link to theory, by creating a narrative that is attentive to sequence, and deductive with respect to alternative hypotheses for how to explain the sequence. And so this represents still another challenge for the field: how to perfect the field's norms for the elements of such comparative case studies, their evidentiary basis, and the method for integrating them into more convincing causal stories.

Parallel challenges apply to formal approaches. Most research makes a choice between cross-sectional approaches and fixed effects and panel data (for detecting linear changes), and there is relatively little attention to discontinuities and selection forces. With better and bigger data now emerging from such diverse theoretical fields as urban and regional economics, economic geography, economic sociology, and so on, it is time to reconsider the field's use of econometrics. Leamer (2010, 2012) has long eloquently pleaded for realism in the use of econometrics, and especially the use of techniques for winnowing out econometrically solid but implausible conclusions. He argues that a succession of ever more powerful techniques—instrumental variables, nonparametric methods, consistent standard errors, and randomized experiments—have in some ways just contributed to a deeper problem. They are often mobilized in an attempt to draw conclusions that conform to the researcher's underlying belief that the world is asymptotic, behaving in a regular way according to secure and knowable laws (cf. Morck and Yeung, 2011). Leamer calls for building realistic frameworks for use of econometric techniques by triangulating with external validation, using broad and deep substantive knowledge of the processes that are being explained, and using realistic assumptions about agent behavior. To this we have added the need to consider both structural determinants and one-off events and shocks that switch the system from one pathway to another and reinforce themselves through their collateral effects in the regional economy. These key events could then be combined with large-number, large-scale regularities, adjustments, and the search for convergence processes (mean reversions) to generate models that integrate processes of divergence (from innovation and clustering) and convergence (from labor migration and maturing technologies) and how they relate to one another over time and place (Storper, 2013).

The research reported in this book, then, opens up some new frontiers in regional economic analysis. Addressing the sources of divergent regional economic development is a critical issue for humanity in the twenty-first century, as our planet becomes more and more urbanized. This comparison of the different ways two great California cities have entered the New Economy should be useful to those studying economic development in established and emerging cities around the world, and to those who work on the ground to improve economic development for the well-being of humanity.

Notes

Chapter 1

1. And specifically, in the United States, this corresponds roughly to the Combined Statistical Area (CSA), which is larger than the Metropolitan Statistical Area (MSA).

2. Urban gross domestic product (GDP) data in this paragraph are taken from the Regional Economic Accounts of the Bureau of Economic Affairs. International data are taken from the World Bank's *World Development Indicators* database.

3. In this book, we use the Combined Statistical Area (CSA) boundaries as defined in June 2003 by the U.S. Office of Management and Budget (OMB) with reference to the 2000 decennial census. The 2010 census produced new area definitions for San Francisco to include two additional counties. CSAs combine government-defined Metropolitan Statistical Areas (MSAs), each measuring a central core that contains a concentrated population as well as adjacent communities having a high degree of economic and social integration.

4. There are areas adjacent to the ten-county Bay Area in the Central Valley that are commuter zones to the Bay Area. Two of the Inland Empire counties, San Bernardino and Riverside, have areas that are part of the functional urban region of Southern California and parts that are not because they are large counties and much of them is too remote for its residents to be employed in coastal Southern California. We tested the effects of these areas on our levels and rankings of per capita income for the two regions by adding in the commuting workers from Central Valley counties to the Bay Area and by subtracting the residents of San Bernardino and Riverside from metropolitan Southern California. These methods generated statistically insignificant changes in our results. We therefore concluded that using a ten-county Bay Area

definition and a five-county Southern California definition leaves our calculations of the economic performance of the two regions robust and unbiased.

5. Per capita personal income includes income from wages as well as from other sources, such as rental property and investments. It is used here largely because it is one of only a few choices for detailed, long-running annual measures of economic well-being at the metropolitan scale. The Bureau of Economic Affairs (BEA) also estimates average wage per job as well as gross domestic product per capita. The latter ties most closely to equivalent metrics at the national scale; however, the BEA has tracked this figure only since 2000. Measures of the average wage per job do not account for workers who hold multiple jobs. Nonetheless, results using average wages per job do not markedly differ from those estimated using per capita personal income (PCPI) (although the gap between the group of metros and Los Angeles is smaller). Later in the chapter we use wage data from the decennial census and the *American Community Survey*. These paint a highly consistent picture of the evolution of PCPI; however, the census wage data are not available as an annual series from 1970.

6. This threshold is arbitrary and is chosen chiefly for clarity of presentation. However, the story does not materially change with a more inclusive cutoff.

7. Estimates were produced using a 2 percent extract of the *American Community Survey*.

8. Households are the smallest possible unit of observation for this exercise, because multiple residents of the same housing unit often contribute to its maintenance.

9. The fact that the real income premium in San Francisco is larger than the difference between nominal wages suggests that the median worker spends a larger percentage of his or her income on housing in the Southland than in the Bay Area. This curious finding reveals serious problems with using median housing costs to characterize the broad set of costs facing households in entire regional economies. However, the gaps between real and nominal income premiums are fairly modest. In 1980, they amounted to only 2 percent, while in 2010 they appeared larger but much of the gap simply reflects the shift from one unit of measurement (per capita personal income) to another (household wage and salary income). The difference between the nominal household wage and salary income gap and the real household wage and salary income gap is only 3 percent. The bottom line is that when we compare housing-cost-adjusted incomes in our two case study regions, the Bay Area's advantage is in no way diminished.

10. In 1980, the mean Gini coefficient among 288 metropolitan areas was 0.477, with a standard deviation of 0.02. In 1990, Los Angeles was almost one standard deviation above San Francisco, and the gap may have been larger in 1990.

Chapter 2

1. Each of these is internally heterogeneous; we will simplify here.

2. "Economic geography" as used here covers a wide variety of perspectives from

the disciplines of geography and spatial economics. In the latter, there is a specific body of theory known as New Economic Geography, based on a specific set of models that explain spatial concentration of firms. We will distinguish among different specific models within economic geography as necessary in later chapters; for present purposes, they are considered together.

3. Though the Greater Los Angeles area's abundant sunshine and varied scenery reportedly had considerable appeal in the early days of filmmaking, the shift from the East Coast of the United States to Hollywood was premised on filmmakers' desire to avoid paying patent dues to Edison, the inventor of the first motion picture device, the Kinetoscope. Moreover, sunshine quite evidently has little to do with the resilience of the filmed entertainment sector, which has preferred indoor film shoots, offering a controlled environment.

Chapter 3

1. Specifically, they calculate a Theil index for contributions to income inequality between 1994 and 2000. Interestingly, the largest negative change in the Theil index was found in Los Angeles County.

2. This section has focused on specialization as described by the top handful of sectors. But, using measures such as the Herfindahl index or locational Gini coefficients, researchers also try to gauge specialization by considering the relative sizes of all the sectors found in a region or country (at the national scale; see Sapir, 1996; Amiti, 1999). Such measures capture the extent to which the distribution of employment across these sectors indicates concentration in just a few activities, or a more "even" pattern. Calculating the Herfindahl index using four-and-six-digit industry data from the Census Bureau's *County Business Patterns* dataset, we found that San Francisco appears more specialized than Los Angeles in both 1970 and 2010. In both years, however, the difference is very small relative to the distribution across all U.S. cities. The same kinds of results are found using the locational Gini index. This approach again has the problem of assuming that detailed sectors are meaningfully independent of one another.

3. We use the Census Bureau's *County Business Patterns* series to examine specializations at the highest available level of detail.

4. Indeed, distinguishing between tradable and nontradable sectors is a challenging task. Not only may similar-seeming functions be tradable or nontradable according to context, but what was once nontradable may become tradable over time. Radiology services, for instance, are now being offshored from some hospitals in the United States to board-certified specialists located in India, Israel, and a few other countries, as a result of technologies that facilitate the delivery of this kind of work across great distances (Levy and Goelman, 2005). Radiology was nontradable before the advent of these technologies, except when people traveled long distances to consult a highly specialized radiologist—a tiny minority of all radiology visits.

In order to differentiate tradable from nontradable industries, we adopt a method developed by Bradford Jensen and Lori Kletzer (2006) that classifies sectors that are geographically concentrated within the United States as tradable and those that are spatially ubiquitous as nontradable. Jensen and Kletzer's method has a number of advantages, including that it distinguishes proportions of industries that are tradable—so, in theory at least, it might distinguish between retail shops on Rodeo Drive that draw tourists from around the world (hence they are part of the tradable economy of Los Angeles) from a neighborhood nail salon (most likely a purely locally serving establishment). However, their method also produces some anomalies that prove problematic in the context of our two regions; in particular it classifies the entertainment industry as nontradable, which might be true for many cities where such activity consists of movie and stage theaters and amusement parks but does not work for Hollywood. Hence we used our judgment to selectively adjust the results of Jensen and Kletzer's approach applied to the California context.

5. In practice, this means four-digit SIC codes up to 1997, and six-digit NAICS codes thereafter. Unfortunately, no sufficiently detailed data exists that uses a consistent system of industrial classification system over time. In the United States, the NAICS system replaced SIC in 1997. Only imperfect crosswalks exist between the two systems, making examinations across time challenging. As a result, the employment shares in Table 3.1 are best understood cross-sectionally, rather than being effectively comparable over time.

6. "Communication transmitting equipment" (SIC 3662), also known as "Radio and TV communication equipment," also contains certain subcomponents that form part of Los Angeles's specialization in guidance and control systems for aircraft and aerospace. However, these subcomponents cannot be properly extracted from published four-digit data, and as a result the estimates presented here undercount the true size of each region's aerospace agglomeration. See Stekler (1965: 30–31) for further discussion.

7. "Software publishers," "Custom computer programming services," "Electronic parts and equipment wholesalers," "Computer systems design services," "Computer and peripheral wholesalers," "Data processing," and "Semiconductor and related device manufacturing."

8. If port size is a function of the number of containers, Los Angeles–Long Beach ranked first in the United States in 2009; when measured by volume, it ranked behind South Louisiana, Houston, and New York–New Jersey (American Association of Port Authorities, 2010).

9. Authors' calculations based on California Economic Development Department data from 2010, combining both manufacturing and services involving computers, electronics, and professional and technical consulting.

10. But the wages in the tradable and nontradable parts of the regional economy are interrelated, through what economists call "human capital externalities." A yoga teacher in a rich metropolitan area such as San Francisco will generally earn more, even after adjusting for the cost of living, than a yoga teacher in a city with lower

wages in its core tradable industries (Moretti, 2012). We will explore this point in more detail in our analysis of the labor market in Chapter 4.

11. Moreover, some ideas cannot be patented: utility patents, which account for 90 percent of patents in the United States, cover new machines, processes, or otherwise material inventions; they do not cover the production of new plant species, nor design and immaterial knowledge production like software.

12. On the other hand, a reasonable number of software patents are subsequently overturned on the basis that they are overly broad.

13. Using inventors' locations listed on utility patent applications, as well as data on the broad industrial class to which an invention belongs, we allocate patented inventions to sectors in particular places. There are some challenges in using patents in this manner. Chiefly, patent classes do not neatly concord with standard industrial classifications. We use a bridge created by Jaffe (1989), while acknowledging its imperfections (Thompson and Fox-Kean, 2005).

14. For a detailed description of the DOT, see Cain and Treiman (1981) and Peterson et al. (2001). DOT has been replaced by O*Net, maintained by the Bureau of Labor Statistics; however, this only covers occupations from 2001 forward, making it hard to examine the earlier part of the study period. We decided to opt for the older system, acknowledging its imperfection in the postmillennium context.

15. While the distinction between routineness and nonroutineness chiefly comes from national-level studies of international and labor economics, other scholars have exploited occupational variation to capture industrial structure at the metropolitan scale. Relevant studies include Feser (2003), Barbour and Markusen (2007), and Bacolod et al. (2009). Although these papers model specialization in different ways, they share with the present study the notion that occupations are a complementary lens into understanding the industrial makeup of regional economies.

16. In many ways, the same can be said for nonroutine manual tasks—the kinds of activities undertaken by a craftsperson in, say, furniture making or weaving. In some cases, these activities are also well paid, and there is a growing niche interest in craft work ("makers," etc.).

17. The Census data are public-use extracts from the Decennial Census and the American Community survey, available from IPUMS. Individual workers are weighted by the involvement in the labor market, as measured by usual hours worked.

18. These data are more aggregated than much of the data used in the rest of this chapter, but they are the most detailed for which detailed occupational data are available.

19. This pattern also holds for "Electrical machinery." The pattern of employment in "Legal services" in San Francisco appears more sophisticated, but for both it and "Insurance," t-tests indicate that the differences between nonroutineness levels in each region are not statistically significant.

20. With t-tests indicating statistically indistinguishable differences.

21. The idea that economies are composed of tightly integrated subspaces of linked activities is generally attributed to Perroux (1950), and then technically

developed in input-output economics, stemming from Leontief (1954), and has been used in empirical regional economics for many decades. The notion of "relatedness" is more expansive, including not only trade between sectors, but also technologically cognate activities and similar types of skills as possibly linking the development of some sectors to that of others.

22. "Milken Institute has this measure of diversity of high-tech economies and Orange County's always first or second. I think the last recording time we were second. Boston is usually neck and neck with us. . . . [We] have a higher per capita probably patent rate than other counties, but we don't have the management talent as much for those high-tech operations that the Bay Area has" (Walrod, 2009).

23. "[Orange County] seemed to be down there that was kind of compartmentalized, different kinds of technologies, industries, companies that were doing well. It was not like here [Silicon Valley]. . . . not as synergistic" (Scalice, 2009). "Companies in Southern California want to do everything themselves . . . so they don't leverage the relationships that, maybe because they don't exist" (Bergeron, 2009).

Chapter 4

1. In Chapter 1, we reported per capita personal income (PCPI) data from the Bureau of Economic Analysis. We chose this data because it reported annual measures of per capita personal income. In this chapter, however, we use somewhat different data from another source—wage and salary income from U.S. decennial Census public-use microdata. We opt for the decennial data chiefly because it permits us to decompose the city-level picture into results that can help us isolate the deeper forces at work that shape that overall picture. Per capita personal income and wage and salary income are not identical: the former are mostly a function of the latter, but PCPI also includes income from investments, dividends, and rental property, as well as net government transfers. Nonetheless, while not identical, these two methods should not produce materially different results, in terms of how each describes the relative situation of our two case study regions.

2. Student t-statistic tests at each cross-section in Table 3.2 confirm the existence of statistically significant differences between mean education levels in the two regions (with a p-value of 1 percent).

3. For instance, according to the authors' calculations based on IPUMS census data, average educational attainment for Hispanic workers active in the labor market in 2005–2010 was approximately 11.4 years, as compared with 13 years for American workers on the whole.

4. For syntactic convenience, we assume that workers with at least four years of college have earned a bachelor's degree.

5. This is also true inside particular occupations. To take a few of many examples from 2005–2010: financial managers in San Francisco are paid 38 percent more than

workers in this same occupation in Los Angeles; software engineers earn a 32 percent premium in the Bay Area.

6. Note that Los Angeles represents about a quarter of the population of its metropolitan region, and the three largest cities of the Bay Area (San Francisco, Oakland, San Jose) together account for about the same proportion of theirs. They therefore make a sensible comparison group.

7. We assume that regulation levels are relatively stable over time. We do not have much specific information for or against this hypothesis, though we will explore some other measures of restrictiveness that suggest that the broad findings from the price-cost ratio are durable over time.

8. Since this index depends on survey results in which individuals report perceived restrictiveness, rather than objectively measuring actual restrictiveness, we cannot know precisely how reliable it is. However, these findings converge with those produced using other measures.

9. For cities in our two regions, the correlation between per capita income and Wharton restrictiveness is statistically insignificant, with a coefficient of 0.04.

10. Chetty and colleagues (2014) show also that there is no difference in intergenerational income mobility in the two regions, even controlling for ethnicity, as we reported in Chapter 1.

Chapter 5

1. Aviation and aerospace were located across the Greater Los Angeles region. The heart of the complex was located in coastal Los Angeles County from Santa Monica to Palos Verdes, including Torrance, Hawthorne, Inglewood, Culver City, El Segundo, Manhattan Beach, Hermosa Beach, Redondo Beach, and Long Beach. But it also included major outposts elsewhere in the region, such as in the San Fernando Valley (Lockheed in Van Nuys and Burbank, Woodland Hills and Canoga Park); the San Gabriel and Pomona Valleys (Aerojet in Azusa; North American in Pomona); the Antelope Valley (abutting Edwards Air Force Base); the aerospace-dominated parts of Los Angeles's traditional manufacturing belt (North American Aviation in Downey); and Orange County, with Hughes and other companies establishing branch plants in Fullerton and Anaheim. Top management resided in Palos Verdes and, to a lesser extent, upper Santa Monica and, later, the upper-class neighborhoods of Long Beach.

2. Fairchild Semiconductors received its initial capital from Fairchild Camera, a New York–based corporation. The money was provided by Sherman Fairchild, who provided the money on the condition that he would be able to purchase the equity of the eight founding members for $300,000 per member, should the firm prove successful. Within three years, the founding members were bought out. This led to a number of engineers leaving the firm to start their own enterprises (Kenney and Florida, 2000b; Klepper and Sleeper, 2005).

3. http://www.nytimes.com/interactive/2013/09/08/technology/myspace-off shoots.html?ref=technology

4. http://www.laobserved.com/biz/2013/07/report_amazon_near_d.php

5. http://venice.patch.com/groups/business-news/p/silicon-beach-google-ven ice-los-angeles-opening-reception

6. For the purpose of tracking changes in the local industry over time, we adopt a commonly accepted definition of Hollywood, encompassing a number of SIC codes covering classes of activity up to 1997, as well as NAICS codes that capture changes since 1998. The switch between these two primary systems of industrial classification in 1998 makes it difficult to tell a perfectly coherent story about filmed entertainment over time; as a result of the switch, one important subsector, "Services allied to motion picture production" (SIC 7819) cannot be traced after 1997.

Subsectors in the filmed entertainment industry

NAICS	Subsector	Years
512110	Motion picture and video production	1998–2006
512191	Teleproduction and other postproduction services	1998–2006
512199	Other motion picture and video industries	1998–2006

SIC	Subsector	Years
7812	Motion picture and video tape production	1988–1996
7813	Motion picture and video tape production	1968–1987
7814	Motion picture and video tape production	1968–1987
7819	Services allied to motion picture production (teleproduction and postproduction services)	1974–1996

7. The industry also has classical multiplier effects in the regional home market in terms of spending of high wages; in addition to higher-than-average wages it has a highly skewed income structure, analogous to the finance industry in New York, with a small class of industry elites enjoying extravagant income from profit participation. Together these wealthy consumers have fueled the growth of large luxury sectors such as high-end interior decorators, retail shopping districts, and restaurants, much in the way that financiers do this for New York or technologists for the Bay Area.

8. **Definition of the port-logistics sector in NAICS and SIC codes**

NAICS	Subsector
481112	Scheduled freight air transportation
481212	Nonscheduled chartered freight air transportation
482111	Line-haul railroads
482112	Short line railroads
483111	Deep sea freight transportation
483113	Coastal and Great Lakes freight transportation

483211	Inland water freight transportation
484110	General freight trucking, local
484121	General freight trucking, long-distance, truckload
484122	General freight trucking, long-distance, less than truckload
484220	Specialized freight (except used goods) trucking, local
484230	Specialized freight (except used goods) trucking, long-distance
488310	Port and harbor operations
488320	Marine cargo handling
488330	Navigational services to shipping
488510	Freight transportation arrangement
488991	Packing and crating
493110	General warehousing and storage
493120	Refrigerated warehousing and storage
493130	Farm product warehousing and storage
493190	Other warehousing and storage
541614	Process, physical distribution, and logistics consulting services

SIC	Sector
4512	Air transportation, scheduled (freight)
4522	Air transportation, nonscheduled (freight)
4011	Railroads, line-haul operating
4013	Railroad switching and terminal establishments (short line railroads)
4412	Deep sea foreign transportation of freight
4424	Deep sea domestic transportation of freight
4499	Water transportation services, NEC (lighterage)
4212	Local trucking without storage (general freight)
4213	Trucking, except local (general freight, truckload)
4213	Trucking, except local (general freight, less than truckload)
4212	Local trucking without storage (specialized freight)
4213	Trucking, except local (specialized freight)
4491	Marine cargo handling (dock and pier operations)
4491	Marine cargo handling (all but dock and pier operations)
4492	Towing and tugboat services
4731	Arrangement of transportation of freight and cargo (except freight rate auditors, private mail centers, and tariff consultants)

SIC	Sector
4783	Packing and crating
4225	General warehousing and storage (except self-storage and mini-warehouses)
4222	Refrigerated warehousing and storage
4221	Farm product warehousing and storage
4226	Special warehousing and storage, NEC (except fur storage and warehousing in foreign trade zones)
8742	Management consulting services (manufacturing management, physical distribution, and site location consulting)
4741	Rental of railroad cars
4785	Fixed facilities and inspection and weighing services for motor vehicle transportation (marine cargo checkers)
4789	Transportation services, NEC (pipeline terminals and stockyards for transportation)
4231	Terminal and joint terminal maintenance facilities for motor freight transportation
4499	Water transportation services, NEC (lighterage)

Chapter 6

1. This used to be the case in California, which for many decades had higher-than-average unemployment rates than the United States as a whole, because even though it created many jobs, it was a magnet for in-migrants.

2. For the most part, these local agencies are funded from programs that are funded by the State of California, through its Economic Development Department, which administers the Workforce Investment Act, or from the federal government's Employment Training Administration.

3. A large international literature on taxation and development has not uncovered a clear inverse relationship between the level of taxation and the rate of growth of output or incomes; it has instead found that it is the type of taxation used to generate a given level of revenue that determines whether taxation produces "dead weight losses" to the economy in the medium and long run (Lindert, 2004). This is why, for example, Sweden was able to have very high economic growth in the twentieth century along with a very high level of taxation, and why some countries with lower tax levels performed comparatively poorly.

4. The California State Controller requires all cities and counties to submit a budget each year, detailing how revenues were deployed; here, we analyze city and county budgets from 1991 to 2007. While this does not cover the entire period of our study, it does enable us to look at differences in government actions over part of the period during which divergence occurred between our two regions. City and county budgets

are not comparable, because the two levels of government have different responsibilities. It is, therefore, necessary to analyze them separately and see how each may signal differences in policy priorities. We face the additional challenge that San Francisco is both a city and a county. For the purpose of reporting to the state controller, the expenditures of San Francisco are classified as municipal expenditures. This means that when we compare city budgets between the two regions, there is a bias in terms of total expenditures in favor of the Bay Area, since San Francisco's figures include expenditures for county responsibilities. The opposite is true for counties. Bay Area aggregate county expenditures will be lower than they should be since there will be no expenditures for San Francisco. To put these irregularities into perspective, note that San Francisco City and County contain about 10 percent of the Bay Area's population; we find ways to work around this constraint in the analysis that follows.

Chapter 7

1. The ABAG and SCAG reports analyzed in research for this chapter are as follows:

ABAG Reports

1984   ABAG, MTC, and California State Department of Transportation, 1984, "1984–1989 Overall Work Program: For Planning Activities in the San Francisco Bay Area," April 1984 (Major Report).

1985   ABAG, 1985, "Projections—1985: Forecasts for the San Francisco Bay Area to the Year 2005," July 1985 (Major Report).

1987   MTC, Caltrans, and ABAG, 1987, "Overall Work Program: For Planning Activities in the San Francisco Bay Area, 1987–1992," Draft January 1987 (Major Report).

1989   ABAG, 1989, Center for Analysis and Information Services, "Special Report: San Francisco Bay Area Economy: 1989 and 1990," January 25, 1989 (Major Report).

1990   ABAG and the Bay Area Council's LHEAP, 1990, "Blueprint for Bay Area Housing" (Major Report).

1998   ABAG, 1998, "Trends and Challenges Facing the Future of the San Francisco Bay Area" (Major Report).

2001   ABAG-sponsored report, 2001, "Blueprint 2001, Housing Element Ideas and Solutions for a Sustainable and Affordable Future" (Major Report).

2009   ABAG, 2009, "Projections and Priorities 2009: Building Momentum" (Major Report).

2009   ABAG, 2009, "Projections 2009: What If?" (Major Report), http://www.abag.ca.gov/rss/pdfs/whatif.pdf.

SCAG Reports

1984   SCAG, 1984, "Profile of an Economic Transition: A Status Report on the Southern California Economy" (Major Report).

1986   SCAG, 1986, "Draft Appendix III-D Baseline Projection," August 1986 (Pamphlet).

1988	South Coast Air Management District and SCAG, 1988, "Solutions for Southern California's Air Pollution, Growth and Mobility: Choices for Action" (Pamphlet).
1990	SCAG, 1990, "Economic Profile of the SCAG Region," SCAG regional economic profile, December 1990 (Major Report).
1991	SCAG, 1991, "Facts About Growth" (Pamphlet).
1992	SCAG, 1992, "Regional Comprehensive Plan," Volume 1, No. 1 (Pamphlet).
1992	SCAG, 1992, "Regional Comprehensive Plan," Volume 1, No. 2 (Pamphlet).
1993	SCAG, 1993, "Regional Comprehensive Plan," Volume 1, No. 4 (Pamphlet).
1993	SCAG, 1993, "Regional Comprehensive Plan," Volume 1, No. 5 (Pamphlet).
1993	SCAG, 1993, "DRAFT: Regional Comprehensive Plan," December 1993 (Major Report).
1993	SCAG, 1993, "State of the Region Report," December 23, 1993 (Major Report).
2001	SCAG, 2001, "State of the Region Report" (Major Report), http://www.scag.ca.gov/publications/sotr01/sortofc.html.
2002	SCAG, 2002, "State of the Region Report" (Major Report), http://www.scag.ca.gov/publications/sotrpast.htm#sotr02.
2004	SCAG 2004, "2004–2005 Overall Work Program" (Major Report), http://www.scag.ca.gov/owp/pdf/104.pdf.
2004	SCAG, 2004, "Southern California Compass: Charting the Course for a Sustainable Southland" (Major Report), http://www.compassblueprint.org/files/scag-growthvision2004.pdf.
2005	SCAG, 2005, "Regional Airport Management Study," (Major Report).

2. Henceforth in this chapter, the references to reports are contained in endnotes, rather than in the list of works cited at the end of the book.

3. Bay Area Forum/Bay Area Council Economic Institute reports analyzed for this chapter:

2012	The Bay Area Innovation System
2012	The Economic Impact of Caltrain Modernization
2012	The Economic Impact of the Affordable Care Act on California
2012	The Culture of Innovation: What Makes San Francisco Bay Area Companies Different?
2012	Innovation and Investment: Building Tomorrow's Economy in the Bay Area
2012	Accelerating Job Creation in California Through Infrastructure Investment: Opportunities for Infrastructure Asset Formation and Job Creation Using Public-Private Partnership Procurement Methods
2012	Innovation and Investment: Building Tomorrow's Economy in the Bay Area
2011	Benchmarking the Bay Area's Environment for Entrepreneur-Led Start-Ups
2011	Roadmap to a High-Value Health System: Addressing California's Healthcare Affordability Crisis

2011   Options for Financing the Restoration of San Francisco Bay Wetlands

2011   Employment in the Bay Area's Emerging Clean Economy

2011   World Expo 2020, Silicon Valley—USA: Economic Impacts

2010   International Trade and the Bay Area Economy: Regional Interests and Global Outlook 2010–2011

2010   Global Competitiveness, China and California's Emerging Clean Energy Economy

2010   Framework Conditions for Foreign and Domestic Private Investment in California's Infrastructure: Seizing the P3 Opportunity

2010   The America's Cup: Economic Impacts of a Match on San Francisco Bay

2010   Public-Private Partnerships: Alternative Procurement Methods for Campus Development in the University of California System

2010   Recession and Recovery: An Economic Reset

2009   Global Reach: Emerging Ties Between the San Francisco Bay Area and India

2009   Managing Recession: Strategic Responses to the Economic Downturn

2008   California High-Speed Rail: Economic Benefits and Impacts in the San Francisco Bay Area

2008   The Innovation-Driven Economic Development Model: A Practical Guide for the Regional Innovation Broker

2008   Human Capital in the Bay Area: Why an Educated, Flexible Workforce Is Vital to Our Economic Future

2008   Sustaining the Bay Area's Competitiveness in a Globalizing World

2007   Toward a California Trade and Investment Strategy: Potential Roles for the State in Global Market Development

2007   Innovative Energy Solutions from the San Francisco Bay Area: Fueling a Clean Energy Future

2007   BASIC Innovators Series, Number 2

2007   Measures to Reduce the Economic Impacts of a Drought-Induced Water Shortage in the San Francisco Bay Area

2007   Bay Area Innovation Network Roundtable: Identifying Emerging Patterns of the Next Wave of Innovation

2007   Shared Values, Shared Vision: California's Economic Ties with Canada

2006   Ties That Bind: The San Francisco Bay Area's Economic Links to Greater China

2006   BASIC Innovators Series, Number 1

2006   The Innovation Edge: Meeting the Global Competitive Challenge

2006   Investing in California's Infrastructure: How to Ensure Value for Money and Protect California's Competitive Position in the National and Global Economy

2006   Employer Mandates and the Health Care Crisis: Economic Impacts in California and the Bay Area

2006   The Innovation Economy: Protecting the Talent Edge

2005   International Trade and the Bay Area Economy: Regional Interests and Global Outlook 2005–2006

2005   Visas for Higher Education and Scientific Exchanges: Balancing Security and Economic Competitiveness

2005   One Million Jobs at Risk

2004   Economic Impacts of Competitive Air Service at San Francisco International Airport

2004   The Future of Bay Area Jobs: The Impact of Offshoring and Other Key Trends

2004   Supercenters and the Transformation of the Bay Area Grocery Industry: Issues, Trends, and Impacts

2004   Nanotechnology in the San Francisco Bay Area: Dawn of a New Age

2004   Downturn and Recovery: Restoring Prosperity

2003   Meeting the Challenge of Homeland Security, 2nd Edition

2002   Hetch Hetchy Water and the Bay Area Economy

2002   Air Transport and the Bay Area Economy—Crisis in Air Travel: Weathering the Downturn

2002   After the Bubble: Sustaining Economic Prosperity

2001   International Trade and the Bay Area: Air Cargo, Technology and the Economy of Silicon Valley

2000   Air Transport and the Bay Area Economy—Phase Two

2000   Air Transport and the Bay Area Economy—Phase One

1999   The Bay Area: Winning in the New Global Economy

4. Joint Venture Silicon Valley reports analyzed:

1992   An Economy at Risk

1995   The Joint Venture Way: Lessons for Regional Rejuvenation, Vol. 1

1998   Silicon Valley 2010: A Regional Framework for Growing Together

1998   The Joint Venture Way: Lessons for Regional Rejuvenation, Vol. 2

1999   Workforce Study

2000   Index of Silicon Valley

2000   Internet Cluster Analysis

2001   Index of Silicon Valley

2001   Next Silicon Valley: Riding the Waves of Innovation

2002   Index of Silicon Valley

2002   Next Silicon Valley: Opportunities and Choices

2002   Workforce Study: Connecting Today's Youth with Tomorrow's Technology

2003   Index of Silicon Valley

2003   Building the Next Silicon Valley: Strategy and Actions

2003   Preparing Tomorrow's Innovators

2003   Tax Principles Workbook: A Tool for Critiquing Tax and Fiscal Proposals

2004   Statement of Principles: California Budget and Tax Reform Initiative

2004   Index of Silicon Valley

2004   Main Street Silicon Valley: Shared Issues, Snapshots of Success and Models for Moving Forward

2004   The Future of Bay Area Jobs

2005   A Vision of a Wireless Silicon Valley

2005   Index of Silicon Valley

2006   Index of Silicon Valley

2007   Index of Silicon Valley

2008   Index of Silicon Valley

2008   Smart Valley and Smart Health: A Final Report to the Community

2008   Cell Phone Coverage Primer

2009   Index of Silicon Valley

2009   Special Analysis: Economic Restructuring and Workforce Transitions

2009   Climate Prosperity: A Greenprint for Silicon Valley

2010   Silicon Valley Index

2010   Workforce Study

2011   2011 Silicon Valley Index

2011   Cross-Jurisdiction Collaboration: New Models for State, Regional, and Local Governments

2011   Purchasing Power: Best Practices Guide for Collaborative Solar Procurement

2012   2012 Silicon Valley Index

5. Los Angeles Economic Roundtable reports analyzed:

2012   Getting to Work: Unemployment and Economic Recovery in Los Angeles

2012   Equity Below the Wing

2012   Rental Housing 2011: The State of Rental Housing in the City of Los Angeles

2009   Ebbing Tides in the Golden State

2009   Economic Study of the RSO and the Los Angeles Housing Market

2009   Ebbing Tides in the Golden State

2009   Benchmark for a Family-Sustaining Wage in Los Angeles

2008   Op-Ed: Organized Labor Lifts LA Economy

2008	Concentrated Poverty in Los Angeles
2007	Planning Economic Growth
2007	Economic Footprint of Unions in Los Angeles
2006	Public Outlays, Local Jobs
2006	Jobs in LA's Green Technology Sector
2006	From the Pockets of Strangers: Economic Impacts of Tourism in LA
2006	Poverty, Inequality and Justice
2006	LA Workforce Investment
2005	Hopeful Workers, Marginal Jobs
2004	Benefits of CRA/LA Social Equity Policies
2003	Prisoners of Hope: Welfare to Work in Los Angeles
2002	Running Out of Time: Voices of Parents Struggling to Move from Welfare to Work
2002	Workers Without Rights
2001	When The Big Wheel Turns
1998	Survival Skills: Welfare to Work in Los Angeles
1998	Ventura Capital Market Connection Survey
1996	Post Cold War Frontiers: Defense Downsizing and Conversion in Los Angeles
1994	Technology and Jobs: Defense Conversion in the Los Angeles Region
1994	Fuel Cells for Transportation: Technical Feasibility and Economic Impacts
1993	Creating Transportation Jobs: Aerospace Industrial and Workforce Capabilities for Surface Transportation Manufacturing
1993	Air Quality Rules in the South Coast Basin: Industrial and Geographic Impacts
1992	Los Angeles County Economic Adjustment Strategy for Defense Reductions

6 See note 5.

7. We first built a timeline of regional projects and initiatives, from interviews and archival research. In the second stage we carried out in-depth research on each regional initiative. We corroborated our findings with interviews.

8. In order to make a comparison of the 501(c)(3) public charities sector in a way that takes into account the difference in our two regions' population sizes, we calculated total revenues per capita. Our analysis runs from 1989 to 2004, the years for which data was available from the National Center for Charitable Statistics (NCCS). Furthermore, we removed one outlier from our analysis, Kaiser Foundation Healthcare, which alone contributed $20 billion in total Bay Area revenues in 2003, accounting for 30 percent of total Bay Area revenues that year. As it is a California-wide health care system that happens to be headquartered in the Bay Area, removing it from our analysis introduces no bias into the analysis.

9. Ballot measures analyzed:

Year	Proposition	Ballot title	Bay Area	Los Angeles
1990	116	Authorized a bond of $1.99 billion for passenger and commuter rail administered through the Public Transportation Account (PTA)	9–1	2–3
1990	118	Would have made changes in the legislative reapportionment process, in the timing of election of state senators, and in laws regarding ethical standards for members of the California State Legislature	0–10	0–5
1990	136	Would have imposed a variety of limits on state and local taxes in California	1–9	4–1
1992	165	Would have changed California's budget process in several ways and increased the governor's control over state spending	0–10	2–3
1992	167	Would have increased the tax burden on California taxpayers by an estimated $340 million, through a variety of changes to income taxes, sales tax, renters' tax credits, taxes on corporations, and taxes on oil and gas	2–8	0–5
1994	180	Would have authorized an approximately $2 billion bond issue for the acquisition and development of parks, historic sites, and recreational facilities	5–5	1–4
1994	185	Would have imposed an additional 4 percent tax on retail sales of gasoline	0–10	0–5
1994	186	Would have established a single-payer health care system	1–9	0–5
1996	208	Campaign Contributions and Spending Limits Initiative	10–0	5–0
1996	212	Campaign Contributions and Spending Limits Initiative	8–2	2–3
1996	217	Annual increase in state personal income tax revenues of about $700 million, with about half the revenues allocated to schools and half to other local governments	9–1	0–5
1996	218	Requires the local government to have a vote of the affected property owners for any proposed new or increased assessment before it could be levied	7–3	5–0
1998	7	Proposition 7 would have provided tax credits to individuals and corporations for certain expenditures they made that would have reduced emissions of pollutants into the air	2–8	0–5

Year	Proposition	Ballot title	Bay Area	Los Angeles
1998	10	Proposition 10 imposed additional tax on cigarettes of 50 cents/pack, as well as additional taxes on other tobacco products, with which the state government created state and county commissions to establish early childhood development and smoking prevention programs	8–2	2–3
1998	11	Authorized the creation of the California Citizens Redistricting Commission, to set legislative boundaries in the state instead of the state legislature	8–2	4–1
1998	226	Would have established new requirements with regard to payroll deductions for political activities and established a provision prohibiting campaign contributions from a foreign national for a candidate for public office	0–10	2–3
2000	12	Proposition 12 authorized a $2.1 billion bond for various land and water quality programs	10–0	5–0
2000	14	Proposition 14 authorized a $350 million bond for public libraries and literacy programs	10–0	5–0
2000	25	Proposition 25 would have revised state laws on political campaigns for candidates and ballot measures beginning in 2001, expanded campaign contribution disclosure, and required ballot pamphlets to list top contributors on ballot measures	10–0	0–5
2000	34	Proposition 34 limited the amount of money an individual could contribute to candidates for the California State Legislature and for statewide elective offices	10–0	5–0
2000	35	Amends the constitution to provide that in the design, development, and construction of public works projects, state government may choose to contract with private entities for engineering and architectural services without regard to certain existing legal restrictions that apply to the procurement of other services	0–10	4–1
2000	39	The primary impact of the measure was to reduce the threshold required to pass local California school district bond issues from a two thirds vote to a 55 percent vote	9–1	3–2
2002	40	Should the state borrow $2,600,000,000 through the sale of general obligation bonds for development, restoration, and acquisition of state and local parks,	10–0	5–0

Year	Proposition	Ballot title	Bay Area	Los Angeles
		recreation areas, and historical resources, and for land, air, and water conservation programs?		
2003	53	Should the state dedicate up to 3 percent of General Fund revenues annually to fund state and local (excluding school and community college) infrastructure projects?	0–10	0–5
2006	89	Proposition 89 was a failed 2006 California ballot initiative that would have offered clean elections centered on campaign finance reform	1–9	0–5
2006	82	Would have made a free, voluntary, half-day public preschool program available to all four-year-olds in California	2–8	0–5
2008	1A	The Safe, Reliable High-Speed Passenger Train Bond Act for the 21st Century	10–0	1–4

Chapter 8

1. These three time periods coincide well with economic cycles, with major recessions in 1979 and the early 1990s and the recent global recession of 2008, and capture the network structures ahead of important economic restructuring due to globalization and technological change in the 1980s.

2. Form 10-K data for 1982, the first available year, come from *Dun's Business Rankings*. Data for the 1995 snapshot come from both the Wharton Research Data Service (WRDS) and *Dun's Business Rankings*. Data for 2010 were sourced from Dun and Bradstreet's *Million Dollar Directory* (MDD) and the *10-K Wizard* database from Morningstar Inc.

3. The largest component in an industry network is the one with the greatest number of industrial sectors that are linked through board cross-memberships. It follows that the maximum possible number of nodes in a component is equal to the number of nodes in the overall network (for example, if all the corporations in a network are directly or indirectly connected to one another, then network analysis describes this as all the nodes belonging to one single component; if the network is one of industries, then all the industries would be in one component).

4. Before interpreting the data, it should be noted that research of this type is sensitive to the industry categories that are used and is not perfect. This is due to the issue we discussed in Chapter 3, of industry relatedness. It is possible that a certain related set of activities could be classified as being in two separate industries (for example, software reproduction is in industry 33 but software publishing is in industry 51, and this might make them appear as interindustry pairs when they are closely related). In spite of this possibility, the differences reported here are of such a magnitude that

we can be sure that we are finding significant real differences between the degree of interindustry connection in our two regions.

Chapter 9

1. Paul David, Stanford University, personal communication to Michael Storper, February 2013.

2. One of the authors of this book, Michael Storper, was employed by Friends of the Earth in the late 1970s and early 1980s and was acquainted with some of the people discussed in this paragraph.

Chapter 11

1. It would have been preferable to measure sharing, matching, and learning more directly. The reason we did not do so is that we chose to examine specialization, labor dynamics, and technological profiles of our three regions at the regional scale, but using industrial, labor, and technology categories that were as specific as possible (e.g., six-digit industry and occupation codes and extremely detailed breakdown of labor force and tasks). This had the advantage of allowing us to profile specialization, the labor force, and innovation in much more detail than usual. But doing so made it impossible to use published data to look at input-output relations within the region. Even with broadly defined industries, this would have been challenging, but with the finely disaggregated industries used to detect specialization in Chapter 3, it is impossible. Likewise, data on regional labor matching of industries to disaggregated, tightly defined sectors is not available in published form. And though we have some evidence of different patent profiles and how this is consistent with regional specialization, it was impossible to trace learning directly from patent statistics, except through the Net Local Citation Percentage index presented in Chapter 8. Thus, if future research is to peer into the actual processes of how clusters work, it will have to find or create data sources that are not currently publicly available.

Works Cited

Acemoglu, D., Johnson, S., Robinson, J., 2004. *Institutions as the fundamental cause of long-run growth*. National Bureau of Economic Research, working paper 10481. http://www.nber.org/papers/w10481.pdf.

Acemoglu, D., Robinson, J. A., 2000. Political losers as a barrier to economic development. *American Economic Review* 90,2: 126–130.

———, 2012. *Why nations fail: The origins of power, prosperity, and poverty*. Profile Books, London.

Acs, Z. J., Audretsch, D. B., Carlsson, B., 2010. The missing link: Knowledge diffusion and entrepreneurship in endogenous growth. *Small Business Economics* 34,2: 105–125.

Acs, Z. J., Storey, D., 2004. Introduction: Entrepreneurship and economic development. *Regional Studies* 38,8: 871–877.

Adler, S., 1987. Why BART but no LART? The political economy of rail rapid transit planning in the Los Angeles and San Francisco metropolitan areas, 1945–57. *Planning Perspectives* 2: 149–174.

———, 1991. The transformation of the Pacific Electric Railway: Bradford Snell, Roger Rabbit, and the politics of transportation in Los Angeles. *Urban Affairs Review* 27,1: 51–86.

Agarwal, A., Cockburn, I., Rosell, C., 2010. Not invented here? Innovation in company towns. *Journal of Urban Economics* 67,1: 78–89.

Agarwal, A., Giuliano, G., Redfearn, C., 2004. *The Alameda Corridor: A white paper*. Los Angeles: University of Southern California, Price School of Public Policy. http://www.metrans.org/pdfs/AlamedaCorridorWhitePaper.pdf.

Air Quality Management District (Southern California), 1997. *The Southland's war on smog: Fifty years of progress toward clean air*. http://www.aqmd.gov/home/library/public-information/publication/50-years-of-progress.

Albouy, D., 2008. Are big cities bad places to live? Estimating quality of life across metropolitan areas. National Bureau of Economic Research, working paper 14472. http://www.nber.org/papers/w14472.pdf.

Alchian, A. A., 1950. Uncertainty, evolution, and economic theory. *Journal of Political Economy* 58,3: 211–221.

Alesina, A., Spolaore, E., 2003. *The size of nations.* Cambridge, MA: MIT Press.

Almeida, P., Kogut, B., 1999. Localization of knowledge and the mobility of engineers in regional networks. *Management Science* 45,7: 905–917.

American Association of Port Authorities, 2010. *World port rankings.* http://www .aapa-ports.org/Industry/content.cfm?ItemNumber=900&navItem Number=551.

Amiti, M., 1999. Specialization patterns in Europe. *Weltwirtschaftliches Archiv* 135,4: 573–593.

AMPTP (Alliance of Motion Picture and Television Producers), 2011. Ratification of WGA agreement [press release]. April 27, 2001. http://www.amptp.org/state ments/2011_0427.html.

Amsden, A. H., 1992. *Asia's next giant: South Korea and late industrialization.* Oxford: Oxford University Press.

———, 2001. *The rise of "the rest": Challenges to the west from late-industrializing economies.* Oxford: Oxford University Press.

Area Development Online, 2009. Taxation: A decisive factor in location selection. http://www.areadevelopment.com/taxesIncentives/sept2010/taxation-decision -location-selection3991.shtml.

Armington, C., Acs, Z., 2002. The determinants of regional variation in new firm formation. *Regional Studies* 36,1: 33–45.

ABAG (Association of Bay Area Governments), 1985. *Projections 85: Forecasts for the San Francisco Bay Area to the year 2005: Population, households, income, employment.* Oakland, CA: Association of Bay Area Governments.

Audretsch, D. B., Falck, O. M., Feldman, M. P., Heblich. S., 2012. Local entrepreneurship in context. *Regional Studies* 46,3: 379–389.

Audretsch, D. B., Feldman, M. P., 1996. R&D spillovers and the geography of innovation. *American Economic Review* 86,3: 630–640.

Audretsch, D. B., Keilbach, M., 2004. Entrepreneurship, capital and economic performance. *Regional Studies* 38,8: 949–959.

Autor, D. H., Dorn, D., 2013. The growth of low-skill service jobs and the polarization of the US labor market. *American Economic Review* 103,5: 1553–1597.

Autor, D. H., Levy, F., Murnane, R. J., 2003. The skill content of recent technological change: An empirical exploration. *Quarterly Journal of Economics* 118,4: 1279–1334.

Baade, R., Sanderson, A., 1997. The employment effect of teams and sports facilities. In R. Noll and A. Zimbalist, eds., *Sports, jobs and taxes*, 92–118. Washington, DC: Brookings Institution Press.

Bacolod, M., Blum, B. S., Strange, W. C., 2009. Skills in the city. *Journal of Urban Economics* 65,2: 136–153.

Balassa, B., 1964. The purchasing power parity doctrine: A reappraisal. *Journal of Political Economy* 72,6: 584–596.

Barbour, E., 2007. *State-local fiscal conflicts in California: From Proposition 13 to Proposition 1A*. Occasional paper. San Francisco: Public Policy Institute of California.

Barbour, E., Markusen, A., 2007. Regional occupational and industrial structure: Does one imply the other? *International Regional Science Review* 30,1: 72–90.

Barca, F., McCann, P., Rodríguez-Pose, A., 2012. The case for regional development intervention: Place-based versus place-neutral approaches. *Journal of Regional Science* 52,1: 134–152.

Barnes, R. C., Ritter, E. R., 2001. Networks of corporate interlocking: 1962–1995. *Critical Sociology* 27,2: 192–220.

Barro, R., 1997. *Determinants of economic growth: A cross-country empirical study*. Cambridge, MA: MIT Press.

Bartik, T. J., 1991. *Who benefits from state and local economic development policies?* Kalamazoo, MI: Upjohn Institute for Employment Research.

———, 2003. *Local economic development policies*. Kalamazoo, MI: Upjohn Institute for Employment Research, working paper 03-91.

———, 2005. Solving the Problems of Economic Development Incentives. *Growth and Change* 36,2: 139–166.

———, 2012. The future of state and local economic development policy: What research is needed. *Growth and Change* 43,4: 545–562.

Bartik, T. J., Erickcek, G., 2010. *Simulating the effects of Michigan's MEGA tax credit program on job creation and fiscal benefits*. Kalamazoo, MI: Upjohn Institute for Employment Research, working paper 12-185.

Bay Area Air Quality Management District, 2011. History of Air Districts 1955–1960. http://www.baaqmd.gov/Divisions/Communications-and-Outreach/News-Media-and-Features/History-of-Air-District-2005/1955-1960.aspx.

Bay Area Economic Forum, 2005. *One million jobs at risk: The future of manufacturing in California*. http://www.bayareaeconomy.org/media/files/pdf/CAManufacturing Report.pdf.

Bay Area Council Economic Institute, 2012a. *The Bay Area innovation economy*. San Francisco: Bay Area Science and Innovation Consortium.

———, 2012b. *The Bay Area: A regional economic assessment*. http://www.bayareaeconomy.org/media/files/pdf/BAEconAssessment.pdf.

Beaudry, C., Schiffauerova, A., 2009. Who's right, Marshall or Jacobs? The localization versus urbanization debate. *Research Policy* 38: 318–337.

Benhabib, J., Spiegel, M. M., 1994. The role of human capital in economic development: Evidence from aggregate cross-country data. *Journal of Monetary Economics* 34,2: 143–173.

Benner, C., 2003. Learning communities in learning regions: The soft infrastructure of cross-firm learning networks in Silicon Valley. *Environment and Planning A* 35,10: 1809–1830.

Benner, C., Pastor, M., 2014. Whither resilient regions? Equity, growth and community. *Journal of Urban Affairs* (forthcoming).

Bergeron, D., 2009. Personal interview, March 6. San Jose, CA: Silicon Valley Technology Center.

Berke, P., 1983. San Francisco Bay: A successful case of coastal zone planning legislation and implementation. *Urban Law* 15: 487–501.

Beugelsdijk, S., Van Schaik, T., 2004. Differences in social capital between 54 Western European regions. *Regional Studies* 39,8: 1053–1064.

Bhide, A., 2000. *The origin and evolution of new businesses.* New York: Oxford University Press.

Blackwood, A. S., Roeger, K. L., Pettijohn, S. L., 2012. *The non-profit sector in brief: Public charities, giving, and volunteering.* Washington, DC: Urban Institute. http://www.urban.org/UploadedPDF/412674-The-Nonprofit-Sector-in-Brief.pdf.

Blakely, E. J., Bradshaw, T. K., 2002. *Planning local economic development: Theory and practice.* Thousand Oaks, CA: Sage.

Blau, F. D., Kahn, L. M., 2000. Gender differences in pay. *Journal of Economic Perspectives* 14: 75–100.

Blinder, A., 2009. How many US jobs might be offshorable? *World Economics* 10: 41–78.

Blinder, A. S., Krueger, A. B., 2013. Alternative measures of offshorability: A survey approach. *Journal of Labor Economics* 31: S97–S128.

Bloch, R., 1983. *The rise of the US aerospace industry, 1945–1960,* PhD major field paper. Los Angeles: UCLA Department of Urban Planning.

Bluestone, B., Harrison, B., 1984. *The deindustrialization of America.* New York: Basic Books.

Boarnet, M. G., Bogart, W. T., 1996. Enterprise zones and employment: Evidence from New Jersey. *Journal of Urban Economics* 40,2: 198–216.

Bonacich, E., Wilson, J. B., 2008. *Getting the goods: Ports, labor, and the logistics revolution.* Ithaca, NY: Cornell University Press.

Borgatti, S. P., Foster, P. C., 2003. The network paradigm in organizational research: A review and typology. *Journal of Management* 29,6: 991–1013.

Bourdieu, P., 1986. The forms of capital. In J. Richardson, ed., *Handbook of theory and research for the sociology of education,* 241–258. New York: Greenwood Press.

Brechin, G. A., 2006. *Imperial San Francisco urban power, earthly ruin.* Berkeley: University of California Press.

Breschi, S., Malerba, F., 2005. *Clusters, networks and innovation.* Oxford: Oxford University Press.

Bresnahan, T., Gambardella, A., eds., 2004. *Building high-tech clusters.* Cambridge: Cambridge University Press.

Brodkin, K., 2007. *Making democracy matter: Identity and activism in Los Angeles.* New Brunswick, NJ: Rutgers University Press.

———, 2009. *Power politics: Environmental activism in south Los Angeles.* New Brunswick, NJ: Rutgers University Press.

Burdett, K., Coles, M., 2010. *Tenure and experience effects on wages*. Northwestern University, working paper. http://www.econ.northwestern.edu/seminars/Mortensen/Burdett.pdf.

Bureau of Labor Statistics, 2014. *Occupational employment and wages in Los Angeles-Long-Beach-Glendale, May 2013*. http://www.bls.gov/r09/oeslosa.html.

Bureau of Transportation Statistics, 2012. *Border crossing/entry data: Quick search by rankings*. http://www.bts.gov/programs/international/transborder/TBDR_BC/TBDR_BC_QuickSearch.html.

Busso, M., Gregory, J., Kline, P. M., 2010. Assessing the incidence and efficiency of a prominent place-bound policy. National Bureau of Economic Research, working paper 16096. http://www.nber.org/papers/w16096.pdf.

Button, K., Lall, S., Stough, R., Trice, M., 1999. High-technology employment and hub airports. *Journal of Air Transport Management* 5,1: 53–59.

Cain, P., Treiman, D. J., 1981. *The Dictionary of Occupational Titles* as a source of occupational data. *American Sociological Review* 46,3: 253–278.

Cambridge Systematics, 2009. *Institutional arrangements for freight transportation systems*. National Cooperative Freight Research Program, Report 2. http://online pubs.trb.org/onlinepubs/ncfrp/ncfrp_rpt_002.pdf.

Carruthers, J., Mulligan, G. F., 2012. The plane of living and the precrisis evolution of housing values in the USA. *Journal of Economic Geography* 12,4: 739–773.

Casper, S., 2007. How do technology clusters emerge and become sustainable? Social network formation and inter-firm mobility within the San Diego biotechnology cluster. *Research Policy* 364: 438–455.

———, 2009. *The marketplace for ideas: Can Los Angeles build a successful biotechnology cluster?* Los Angeles, CA: John Randolph Haynes and Dora Haynes Foundation.

———, 2012. The spill-over theory revisited: The impact of regional economies on the commercialization of university science. *Research Policy* 42,8: 1313–1324.

Castilla, E. J., 2003. Networks of venture capital firms in Silicon Valley. *International Journal of Technology Management* 25,1/2: 113–135.

Chapman, J. I., 1998. *Proposition 13: Some unintended consequences*. San Francisco: Public Policy Institute of California.

Chatterji, A., Glaeser, E. L., Kerr, W., 2013. *Clusters of entrepreneurship and innovation*. Paper prepared for the Innovation Policy and the Economy forum. Cambridge, MA: Harvard University.

Cheshire, P., 2006. Resurgent cities, urban myths and policy hubris: What we need to know. *Urban Studies* 43,8: 1231–1246.

———, 2013. Land market regulation: Market versus policy failures. *Journal of Property Research*, 30,3: 170–188.

Cheshire, P., Nathan, M., Overman, H. O., 2013. *Urban economics and urban policy*. Cheltenham, UK: Elgar.

Chetty, R., Hendren, N., Kline, P., Saez, E., 2014. Where is the land of opportunity? The geography of intergenerational mobility in the United States. National Bureau

of Economic Research, working paper 19843. http://www.nber.org/papers/w19843
.pdf.

Chinitz, B., 1961. Contrasts in agglomeration: New York and Pittsburgh. *American Economic Review* 51,2: 279–289.

———, 2003. The limits to "New Regionalism." *Geoforum* 34,4: 413–415.

———, 2006. Behind the scenes: How transnational firms are constructing a new international division of labor in media work. *Geoforum* 37,5: 739–751.

Christopherson, S., Clark, J., 2007. *Remaking regional economies: Power, labor and firm strategies in a knowledge economy.* London: Routledge.

Christopherson, S., Michie, J., Tyler, P., 2010. Regional resilience: Theoretical and empirical perspectives. *Cambridge Journal of Regions, Economy and Society* 3,1: 3–10.

Christopherson, S., Storper, M., 1988. Effects of flexible specialization on industrial politics and the labor market: The motion picture industry. *Industrial and Labor Relations Review* 42,3: 331–347.

Clagett, M. G., 2006. *Workforce development in the United States: An overview.* Paper prepared for the New Commission on the Skills of the American Workforce. Washington, DC: National Center on Education and the Economy. http://www.skillscommission.org/wp-content/uploads/2010/05/ACII_WIA_Summary.pdf.

Coleman, J. S., 1988. Social capital in the creation of human capital. *American Journal of Sociology* 94 (supplement): S95–S120.

Combes, P.-P., Duranton, G., Gobillon, L., 2008. Spatial wage disparities: Sorting matters! *Journal of Urban Economics* 63: 723–742.

Cooke, P., 1995. Keeping to the high road: Learning, reflexivity and associative governance in regional economic development. In P. Cooke, ed., *The rise of the rustbelt*, 231–245. London: UCL Press.

Cooke, P., Morgan, K., 1998. *The associational economy: Firms, regions and innovation.* Oxford: Oxford University Press.

Cosio, T., Fertig, M., Lopez, S., Shinde, D., 2005. *Economic development activities in Los Angeles: An inventory and analysis.* Los Angeles: Office of the Los Angeles City Controller.

Crescenzi, R., Gagliardi, L., Percoco, M., 2013. Social capital and the innovative performance of Italian provinces. *Environment and Planning A* 45,4: 908–929.

Crescenzi, R., Rodríguez-Pose, A., 2012. Infrastructure and regional growth in the European Union. *Papers in Regional Science* 91,3: 487–513.

Cunningham, W. G., 1951. *The aircraft industry: A study in industrial location.* Los Angeles: Morrison.

Currid, E., 2006. New York as a creative hub: A competitive analysis of four theories on world cities. *Economic Development Quarterly* 20,4: 330–350.

Currid-Halkett, E., 2007. *The Warhol economy: How fashion, art, and music drive New York City.* Princeton, NJ: Princeton University Press.

Dardia, M., McCarthy, K. F., Schoeni, R. F., Vernez, G., 1996. *Defense cutbacks: Effects on California's communities, firms, and workers.* Santa Monica, CA: Rand National Defense Research Institute.

Davis, D. R., Dingel, J. I., 2013. *A spatial knowledge economy.* National Bureau of Economic Research, working paper 18188. http://www.nber.org/papers/w18188.pdf.

Davis, G. F., 1996. The significance of board interlocks for corporate governance. *Corporate Governance: An International Review* 4,3: 154–159.

Davis, G. F., Yoo, M., Baker, W. E., 2003. The small world of the American corporate elite, 1982–2001. *Strategic Organization* 1,3: 301–326.

De la Roca, J., Puga, D., 2012. Learning by working in big cities. London: Centre for Economic Policy Research, discussion paper DP 9243. http://papers.ssrn.com/sol3/papers.cfm?abstract_id=2210212.

Dibner, M., 1999. *Biotechnology guide USA,* 5th ed. Basingstoke, UK: Macmillan.

Dickens, W. T., Sawhill, I., Tebbs, J., 2006. *The effects of investing in early childhood education on economic development.* Washington, DC: Brookings Institution. http://www.brookings.edu/~/media/Research/Files/Papers/2006/4/education%20dickens/200604dickenssawhill.PDF.

Didion, J., 2004. *Where I was from.* New York: Vintage Books.

Dolfman, M. L., Holden, R. J., Fortier Wasser, S., 2007. The economic impact of the creative arts industries: New York and Los Angeles. *Monthly Labor Review,* October: 21–34.

Dollar, D., Kraay, A., 2004. Trade, growth, and poverty. *Economic Journal* 114, F22–F49.

Donahue, J. D., 1997. *Disunited states: What's at stake as Washington fades and the states take the lead.* New York: Basic Books.

Dosi, G., 1982. Technological paradigms and technological trajectories: A suggested interpretation of the determinants and directions of technical change. *Research Policy* 11,3: 147–162.

Dosi, G., Freeman, C., Nelson, R., Soete, L., eds., 1988. *Technical change and economic theory.* London: Pinter.

Drabenstott, M. R., 2005. *A review of the federal role in regional economic development.* Kansas City, MO: Federal Reserve Bank of Kansas City, Center for the Study of Rural America.

Dreier, P., Mollenkopf, J. H., Swanstrom, T., 2001. *Place matters: Metropolitics for the twenty-first century.* Lawrence: University Press of Kansas.

Drennan, M. P., Lobo, J., 1999. A simple test for convergence of metropolitan income in the United States. *Journal of Urban Economics* 46: 350–359.

Duguid, P., 2009. Personal interview, January 23. University of California at Berkeley, School of Information.

Duranton, G., 2010. *The economics of clusters: Lessons from the French experience.* Oxford: Oxford University Press.

———, 2011. California dreamin': The feeble case for cluster policies. *Review of Economic Analysis* 3,1: 3–45.

Duranton, G., Puga, D., 2004. Micro-foundations of urban agglomeration economies. In J. V. Henderson and J.-F. Thisse, eds., *Handbook of regional and urban economics,* vol. 4, 2063–2117. Amsterdam: Elsevier.

Earle, C., 1992. *Geographical inquiry and American historical problems.* Stanford, CA: Stanford University Press.

Easterly, W., 2006. *The white man's burden.* New York: Penguin.

Ebenstein, A., Harrison, A., McMillan, M., Phillips, S., 2009. *Why are American workers getting poorer? Estimating the impact of trade and offshoring using the CPS.* National Bureau of Economic Research, working paper 15107. http://www.nber.org/papers/w15107.pdf.

Eichengreen, B., Park, D., Shin, K., 2013. *Growth slowdowns redux: New evidence on the middle-income trap.* National Bureau of Economic Research, working paper 18673. http://www.nber.org/papers/w18673.pdf.

Eisinger, P., 2000. The politics of bread and circuses: Building the city for the visitor class. *Urban Affairs Review* 35,3: 316–333.

Eisinger, P. K., 1988. *The rise of the entrepreneurial state: State and local economic development policy in the United States.* Madison, WI: University of Wisconsin Press.

Elmer, G., Gasher, M., 2005. *Contracting out Hollywood: Runaway productions and foreign location shooting.* Lanham, MD: Rowman and Littlefield.

Elvery, J. A., 2009. The impact of enterprise zones on resident employment: An evaluation of the enterprise zone programs of California and Florida. *Economic Development Quarterly* 23,1: 44–59.

Erie, S. P., 1992. How the west was won: The local state and economic growth in Los Angeles, 1880–1932. *Urban Affairs Review* 27,4: 519–554.

———, 2004. *Globalizing L.A.: Trade, infrastructure, and regional development.* Stanford, CA: Stanford University Press.

Euchner, C. C., McGovern, S. J., 2003. *Urban policy reconsidered: Dialogues on the problems and prospects of American cities.* New York: Routledge.

Fairlie, R., 2013. *Kauffman Index of Entrepreneurial Activity, 1996–2012.* Kansas City, MO: Kauffman Foundation.

Falck, O., Heblich, S., Kipar, S., 2010. Industrial innovation: Direct evidence from a cluster-oriented policy. *Regional Science and Urban Economics* 40,6: 574–582.

Fallick, B., Fleischman, C., Rebitzer, J., 2006. Job hopping in Silicon Valley: Some evidence concerning the microfoundations of a high technology cluster. *Review of Economics and Statistics* 88,3: 472–481.

Farole, T. C., Rodríguez-Pose, A., Storper, M., 2010. Human geography and the institutions that underlie economic growth: A multidisciplinary literature review. *Progress in Human Geography* 35,1: 58–80.

———, 2011. Cohesion policy in the European Union: Growth, geography, institutions. *Journal of Common Market Studies* 49,5: 1089–1111.

Federal Bureau of Investigation, 2012. *Crime statistics.* Washington, DC: U.S. Department of Justice. http://www.fbi.gov/news/pressrel/press-releases/fbi-releases-preliminary-annual-crime-statistics-for-2010.

Feldman, M., Audretsch, D. B., 1999. Innovation in cities: Science-based diversity, specialization, and localized competition. *European Economic Review* 43,2: 409–429.

Feldman, M., Zoller, T. D., 2012. Dealmakers in place: Social capital connections in regional entrepreneurial economies. *Regional Studies* 46,1: 23–37.

Feldman, M. P., 2014. The character of innovative places: Entrepreneurial strategy, economic development and prosperity. *Small Business Economics* 43,1: 9–20.

Feldman, M. P., Francis, J., 2003. Fortune favours the prepared region: The case of entrepreneurship and the Capitol region biotechnology cluster. *European Planning Studies* 11,7: 765–788.

Feldman, M. P., Francis, J., Bercovitz, J., 2005. Creating a cluster while building a firm: Entrepreneurs and the formation of industrial clusters. *Regional Studies* 39,1: 129–141.

Feldman, M. P., Lowe, N., 2011. Restructuring for resilience. *Innovations: Technology, Governance, Globalization* 6,1: 129–146.

Ferrary, M., Granovetter, M., 2009. The role of venture capital firms in Silicon Valley's complex innovation network. *Economy and Society* 38,2: 326–359.

Feser, E. J., 2003. What regions do rather than make: A proposed set of knowledge-based occupation clusters. *Urban Studies* 40,10: 1937–1958.

Fisher, P. S., Peters, A. H., 1998. *Industrial incentives: Competition among American states and cities.* Kalamazoo, MI: Upjohn Institute for Employment Research.

Flanigan, J., 2009. *Smile Southern California, you're the center of the universe: The economy and people of a global region.* Stanford, CA: Stanford General Books.

Florida, R., 2002. *The rise of the creative class.* New York: Basic Books.

Flyvbjerg, B., 1998. *Rationality and power: Democracy in practice.* Chicago: University of Chicago Press.

———, 2005. Design by deception: The politics of megaproject approval. *Harvard Design Magazine* 22, June: 50–59.

Flyvbjerg, B., Bruzelius, N., Rothengatter, W., 2003. *Megaprojects and risk: An anatomy of ambition.* Cambridge: Cambridge University Press.

Foege, A., 2013a. *California's successful dilettantes.* Zocalo Public Square, February 27. http://www.zocalopublicsquare.org/2013/02/27.californias-successful-dilettantes.

———, 2013b. *The tinkerers: The amateurs, DIYers, and inventors who make America great.* New York: Basic Books.

Fogelson, R. M., 1993. *The fragmented metropolis: Los Angeles 1850–1930.* Berkeley: University of California Press.

Forbes, 2011. November 18. http://www.forbes.com/the-best-cities-for-technology -jobs.html.

Frank, L., Wong, K., 2004. Dynamic political mobilization: The Los Angeles County Federation of Labor. *Working USA* 8: 155–181.

Freedman, M., 2012. *Place-based programs and the geographic dispersion of unemployment.* Ithaca, NY: Cornell University, Department of Economics, working paper.

Frenken, K., Van Oort, F., Verburg, T., 2007. Related variety, unrelated variety and regional economic growth. *Regional Studies* 41,5: 685–697.

Fritsch, M., Mueller, G., 2004. Effects of new business formation on regional development over time. *Regional Studies* 38,8: 961–975.

Fujita, M., Krugman, P. R., Venables, A. J., 1999. *The spatial economy: Cities, regions and international trade*. Cambridge, MA: MIT Press.

Fujita, M., Thisse, J.-F., 2002. *Economics of agglomeration: Cities, industrial location, and regional growth*. Cambridge: Cambridge University Press.

Fukuyama, F., 1995. *Trust: The social virtues and the creation of prosperity*. New York: Free Press.

Fulton, W., Pendall, R., Nguyen, M., Harrison, A., 2001. *Who sprawls most? how growth patterns differ across the U.S.* Washington, DC: Brookings Institution.

Funderburg, R., Bartik, T., Peters, A. H., Fisher, P. S., 2013. The impact of marginal business taxes on state manufacturing. *Journal of Regional Science* 53,4: 557–582.

Gabe, T., Abel, J., Ross, A., Stolarick, K., 2009. Knowledge in cities. *Urban Studies* 49: 1179–1200.

Gabriel, S. A., Rosenthal, S., 2004. Quality of the business environment vs. quality of life: Do firms and households like the same cities? *Review of Economics and Statistics* 86: 438–444.

Galbraith, J. K., Hale, T., 2008. *American inequality: From IT bust to big government boom*. Austin: University of Texas Inequality Project, working paper 40. http://utip.gov.utexas.edu/papers/utip_40.pdf.

Ganong, P., Shoag, D., 2012. Why has regional income convergence in the US stopped? Cambridge, MA: Harvard University Kennedy School, working paper RWP12-028. http://papers.ssrn.com/sol3/papers.cfm?abstract_id=2081216.

Glaeser, E. L., 2000. Places, people, policies. *Harvard Magazine*, November–December. http://harvardmagazine.com/2000/11/places-people-policies.html.

———, 2003. Reinventing Boston: 1640–2003. *Journal of Economic Geography* 5,2: 119–153.

———, 2008. *Cities, agglomeration, and spatial equilibrium*. Oxford: Oxford University Press.

Glaeser, E. L., Gyourko, J., Saks, R., 2005. Why is Manhattan so expensive? regulation and the rise in housing prices. *Journal of Law and Economics* 48,2: 331–369.

Glaeser, E. L., Gyourko, J., Saks, R. E., 2006. Urban growth and housing supply. *Journal of Economic Geography* 6,1: 71–89.

Glaeser, E. L., Maré, D. C., 2001. Cities and skills. *Journal of Labor Economics* 19: 316–342.

Glaeser, E. L., Tobio, K., 2008. The rise of the sunbelt. *Southern Economic Journal* 74,3: 610–643.

Goos, M., Manning, A., 2007. Lousy and lovely jobs: The rising polarization of work in Britain. *Review of Economics and Statistics* 89,1: 118–133.

Granovetter, M., 1985. Economic action and social structure: The problem of embeddedness. *American Journal of Sociology* 91,3: 481–510.

———, 2001. A theoretical agenda for economic sociology. In M. Guillen, R. Collins, P. England, and M. Meyer, eds., *The new economic sociology: Developments in an emerging field*, 35–59. New York: Russell Sage Foundation.

———, 2005. The impact of social structure on economic outcomes. *Journal of Economic Perspectives* 19,1: 33–50.

Graves, P. E., 1980. Migration and climate. *Journal of Regional Science* 20: 227–237.

Grossman, G. M., Rossi-Hansberg, E., 2008. Trading tasks: A simple theory of offshoring. *American Economic Review* 98,5: 1978–1997.

Guiso, L., Sapienza, P., Zingales, L., 2010. *Civic capital as the missing link.* National Bureau of Economic Research, working paper 15845. http://www.nber.org/papers/w15845.pdf.

Gyourko, S., Saiz, A., Summers, A., 2008. A new measure of the local regulatory environment for housing markets: The Wharton Residential Land Use Regulatory Index. *Urban Studies* 45,3: 693–729.

Haas, G., 2009. Personal interview, May 23.

Haezendonck, E., 2001. *Essays on strategy analysis for seaports.* Leuven, Belgium: Garant. Publisher, Leuven, Belgium.

Hall, P. A., Soskice, D. W., 2001. *Varieties of capitalism: The institutional foundations of comparative advantage.* New York: Oxford University Press.

Hanson, A., Rohlin, S., 2013. Do spatially targeted redevelopment programs spillover? *Regional Science and Urban Economics* 43,1: 86–100.

Harlan, N. E., 1956. *Management control in airframe subcontracting.* Boston: Division of Research, Graduate School of Business Administration, Harvard University.

Heller, N., 2013a. Bay watched: How San Francisco's new entrepreneurial culture is changing the country. *New Yorker,* October 14: 67–79.

———, 2013b. Naked launch: What's really new about the big new tech companies? *New Yorker,* November 25: 68–76.

Helpman, E., 2011. *Understanding global trade.* Cambridge, MA: Harvard University Press.

Henken, A., 2014. *More accountability needed in workforce training programs.* Washington, DC: Council of State Governments. http://knowledgecenter.csg.org/kc/content/more-accountability-needed-workforce-training-programs.

Hidalgo, C. A., Klinger, B., Barabási, A.-L., Hausmann, R., 2007. The product space conditions the development of nations. *Science* 317,5837: 482–487.

Hill, L., 2004. Can media artists survive media consolidation? *Journal of the Caucus of Television Producers, Writers and Directors* 22: 17–21.

Hirschman, A. O., 1967. *Development projects observed.* Washington, DC: Brookings Institution Press.

Hollenbeck, K., Huang, W.-J., 2006. Net impacts and cost-benefit estimates of the workforce development system in Washington state. Kalamazoo, MI: Upjohn Institute for Employment Research, technical report 06-020. http://research.upjohn.org/up_technicalreports/20.

Holzer, H. J., Block, R. N., Cheatham, M., Knott, J. H., 1992. Are training subsidies for firms effective—the Michigan experience. *Industrial and Labor Relations Review* 46: 625–636.

Hurd, R. W., Milkman, R., Turner, L., 2003. Reviving the American labor movement: Institutions and mobilization. *European Journal of Industrial Relations* 9,1: 99–117.

Ikhrata, H., 2011. Personal interview, February 24. Los Angeles: Southern California Association of Government headquarters.

Jacobs, W., 2007. *Political economy of port competition: Institutional analyses of Rotterdam, Southern California and Dubai*. Nijmegen, Netherlands: Academic Press Europe.

Jacobs, W., Ducruet, C., De Langen, P., 2010. Integrating world cities into production networks: The case of port cities. *Global Networks* 10,1: 92–113.

Jacobs, W., Koster, H., Hall, P., 2011. The location and global network structure of maritime advanced producer services. *Urban Studies* 48,13: 2749–2769.

Jaffe, A., 1989. Real effects of academic research. *American Economic Review* 79,5: 957–970.

Jaher, F. C., 1982. *The urban establishment: Upper strata in Boston, New York, Charleston, Chicago, and Los Angeles*. Urbana: University of Illinois Press.

Jensen, J. B., Kletzer, L., 2006. Tradable services: Understanding the scope and impact of services offshoring. In L. Brainard and S. M. Collins, eds., *Offshoring white-collar work—issues and implications*. Washington, DC: Brookings Trade Forum.

Jobs, S., 2005. Commencement speech, Stanford University. http://www.network world.com/community/blog/apples-steve-jobs-stanford-commencement-speech -transcript.

Jones, B. D., Baumgartner, F. R., 2005. *The politics of attention: How government prioritizes problems*. Chicago: University of Chicago Press.

Kaldor, M., 1982. *The baroque arsenal*. New York: Hill and Wang.

Kasindorf, M., 2003. Ueberroth called "sleeper" in race. *USA Today*, August 19: 3A.

Kemeny, T., 2010. Does foreign direct investment drive technological upgrading? *World Development* 38,11: 1543–1554.

Kemeny, T., Rigby, D., 2012. Trading away what kind of jobs? Globalization, trade and tasks in the US economy. *Review of World Economics* 148,1: 1–16.

Kemeny, T., Storper, M., 2012. The sources of urban development: Wages, housing, and amenity gaps across American cities. *Journal of Regional Science* 52,1: 85–108.

Kemeny, T., Storper, M., 2014. Is specialization good for regional economic development? *Regional Studies*, May 8.

Kenney, M., 1986. *Biotechnology: The university-industrial complex*. New Haven, CT: Yale University Press.

Kenney, M., Florida, R., eds., 2000a. *Understanding Silicon Valley: The anatomy of an entrepreneurial region*. Stanford, CA: Stanford University Press.

———, 2000b. Venture capital in Silicon Valley: Fueling new firm formation. In M. Kenney and R. Florida, eds., *Understanding Silicon Valley: The anatomy of an entrepreneurial region*, 99–122. Stanford, CA: Stanford University Press.

Kenney, M., Mowery, D., eds., 2014. *Public universities and regional growth: Insights from the University of California*. Stanford, CA: Stanford University Press.

Kenney, M., Patton, D., 2005. Entrepreneurial geographies: Support networks in three high-technology industries. *Economic Geography* 81,2: 201–228.

Kerr, W., 2010. Breakthrough innovations and migrating clusters of innovation. *Journal of Urban Economics* 67,1: 46–60.

Khanna, D. M., 1997. *The rise, decline, and renewal of Silicon Valley's high technology industry.* New York: Garland.

Kirzner, I. M., 1979. *Perception, opportunity, and profit: Studies in the theory of entrepreneurship.* Chicago: University of Chicago Press.

Kleinhenz, R. A., Ritter-Martinez, K., De Andra, R., 2012. *The aerospace industry in Southern California.* Los Angeles: Kyser Center for Economic Research. http://laedc.org/reports/AerospaceinSoCal_0812.pdf.

Klepper, S., 2009. "Silicon Valley, a chip off the old Detroit bloc." In Z. Acs, D. B. Audretsch, and R. Strom, eds., *Entrepreneurship, growth and public policy,* 79–117. Cambridge: Cambridge University Press.

———, 2010. The origin and growth of industry clusters: The making of Silicon Valley and Detroit. *Journal of Urban Economics* 67,1: 15–32.

Klepper, S., Sleeper, S., 2005. Entry by spinoffs. *Management Science* 51,8: 1291–1306.

Knack, S., Keefer, P., 1995. Institutions and economic performance: Cross-country tests using alternative measures. *Economics and Politics* 7,3: 207–227.

Kolko, J., 2002. Silicon mountains, silicon molehills: Geographic concentration and convergence of internet industries in the US. *Information Economics and Policy* 14: 211–232.

Kolko, J., Neumark, D., Mejia, M. C., 2013. What do business climate indexes teach us about state policy and economic growth? *Journal of Regional Science* 53,2: 220–255.

Kotz, D. M., 1978. *Bank control of large corporations in the United States.* Berkeley: University of California Press.

Krugman, P. R., 1991a. *Geography and trade.* Cambridge, MA: MIT Press.

———, 1991b. Increasing returns and economic geography. *Journal of Political Economy* 99: 483–499.

Kucera, R. P., 1974. *The aerospace industry and the military: Structural and political relationships.* Beverly Hills, CA: Sage.

LAEDC (Los Angeles Economic Development Corporation), 2012. *The aerospace industry in Southern California.* http://www.laedc.org/reports/Aerospacein SoCal_0812.pdf.

LAEDC (Los Angeles Economic Development Corporation) and Kyser Center for Economic Research, 2011. *Manufacturing: Still a force in Southern California.* http://www.laedc.org/reports/Manufacturing_2011.pdf.

Lanier, J., 2013. *Who owns the future?* London: Penguin.

Laslett, J. H. M., 2008. Playing catch-up: The labor movement in Los Angeles and San Francisco, 1985–2005. *California Policy Options.* Los Angeles: UCLA Luskin School of Public Affairs. https://escholarship.org/uc/item/6rc8z30g.

Laursen, K., Masciarelli, F., Prencipe, A., 2011. Regions matter: How localized social capital affects innovation and external knowledge acquisition. *Organization Science* 23,1: 177–193.

Lazarus, J., 2009. Personal interview, March 6. San Francisco, CA.

Lazega, E., 2001. *The collegial phenomenon.* Oxford: Oxford University Press.

———, 2014. *Réseaux sociaux et structures relationnelles (Social networks and relational structures).* Paris: Presses Universitaires de France.

Leamer, E. E., 2010. Tantalus on the road to asymptopia. *Journal of Economic Perspectives* 24,3: 31–46.

———, 2012. *The craft of economics: Lessons from the Heckscher-Ohlin framework.* Cambridge, MA: MIT Press.

Lécuyer, C., 2006. *Making Silicon Valley: Innovation and the growth of high tech, 1930–1970.* Cambridge, MA: MIT Press.

Leontief, W., 1954. Domestic production and foreign trade: The American capital position re-examined. *Economia Internazionale* 7: 9–45.

Leslie, S. W., 1993. *The Cold War and American science: The military-industrial -academic complex at MIT and Stanford.* New York: Columbia University Press.

Levy, F., Goelman, A., 2005. Offshoring and radiology. *Brookings Trade Forum*, 411–423.

Lewis, D. K., 1969. *Convention: A philosophical study.* Cambridge, MA: Harvard University Press.

Lindert, P. H., 2004. *Growing public: Social spending and economic growth since the eighteenth century.* Cambridge: Cambridge University Press.

Littleton, C., 2007. Showrunners swaying strike script. *Daily Variety*, November 26: 2.

Los Angeles Economic Roundtable, 1992. *Public policy analysis: Los Angeles County economic adjustment strategy for defense reductions.* http://www.economicrt.org/download/form.html.

Los Angeles Times, 2012. L.A. city council backs proposed $1.2-billion downtown NFL stadium. http://latimesblogs.latimes.com/lanow/2012/09/nfl-stadium-los -angeles-city-council.html.

Lotchin, R. W., 1992. *Fortress California, 1910–1961: From warfare to welfare.* New York: Oxford University Press.

Lu, Y., 2014. Silicon Valley's youth problem. *New York Times Magazine*, March 12: 28–33. http://www.nytimes.com/2014/03/16/magazine/silicon-valleys-youth -problem.html.

Lundvall, B.-A., 2007. National innovation systems—analytical concept and development tool. *Industry and Innovation* 14,1: 95–119.

Malecki, E. J., 2012. Regional social capital: Why it matters. *Regional Studies* 46,8: 1023–1039.

Markusen, A., Glasmeier, A., 2008. Overhauling and revitalizing federal economic development programs. *Economic Development Quarterly* 22,2: 83–91.

Markusen, A., Schrock, G., 2006. The artistic dividend: Urban artistic specialization and economic development. *Urban Studies* 43,10: 1661–1669.

Markusen, A. R., Hall, P., Campbell, S., Deitrick, S., 1991. *The rise of the gunbelt: The military remapping of industrial America.* New York: Oxford University Press.

Martin, P., Mayer, T., Mayneris, F., 2011. Public support to clusters: A firm level study of French "local productive systems." *Regional Science and Urban Economics* 41,2: 108–123.

McCann, P., 2015. *The regional and urban policy of the European Union: Cohesion, results-orientation, and smart specialisation.* Cheltenham, UK: Edward Elgar.

McKinsey Corporation, 2011. *Urban world.* San Francisco: McKinsey Global Institute. http://www.mckinsey.com/insight/urbanization/urban_world.

Meisenzahl, R. R., Mokyr, J., 2012. The rate and direction of invention in the British industrial revolution: Incentives and institutions. In S. Stern and J. Lerner, eds., *The rate and direction of inventive activity revisited*, 443–479. Chicago: University of Chicago Press.

Mercury Corporation, 2014. Air cargo salaries, Los Angeles. http://www.salarylist .com/company/Mercury-Air-Cargo-Salary.html.

Merk, O., ed., 2013. *The competitiveness of global port-cities: Synthesis report.* Paris: Organisation for Economic Co-operation and Development.

Milkman, R., 2006. *L.A. story: Immigrant workers and the future of the U.S. labor movement.* New York: Russell Sage.

Mintz, B. A., Schwartz, M., 1985. *The power structure of American business.* Chicago: University of Chicago Press.

Mokyr, J., 1991. *The lever of riches: Technological creativity and economic progress.* New York: Oxford University Press.

Molotch, H., 2002. Place in product. *International Journal of Urban and Regional Research* 26,4: 665–688.

Montgomery, M. S., 2011. *Organizing for regime change: An analysis of community unionism in Los Angeles, 2000–2010.* PhD dissertation. New Brunswick, NJ: Rutgers University.

Morck, R., Yeung, B., 2011. *Economics, history, and causation.* National Bureau of Economic Research, working paper 16678. http://www.nber.org/papers/w16678.pdf.

Moretti, E., 2004. Human capital externalities in cities. In J. V. Henderson and J.-F. Thisse, eds., *Handbook of regional and urban economics*, vol. 4, 2243–2291. Amsterdam: Elsevier.

———, 2010. Local multipliers. *American Economic Review, Papers and Proceedings* 100, May: 1–7.

———, 2012. *The new geography of jobs.* Boston: Houghton Mifflin Harcourt.

———, 2013. Real wage inequalities. *American Economic Journal: Applied Economics* 5,1: 65–103.

Mowery, D. C., Simcoe, T., 2002. Is the Internet a US invention?—an economic and technological history of computer networking. *Research Policy* 31: 1369–1387.

Muth, R. F., 1971. Migration: Chicken or egg? *Southern Economic Journal* 37,3: 295–306.

Myers, D., Goldberg, S., Mawhorter, S., Min, S., 2010. Immigrants and the new maturity of Los Angeles. Los Angeles: University of Southern California School of Policy, Planning and Development.

Nathan, M., Overman, H., 2013. Agglomeration, clusters and industrial policy. *Oxford Review of Economic Policy* 29,2: 383–404.

NCCS (National Center for Charitable Statistics), 2012. *Business master files.* Washington, DC: Urban Institute. http://nccs.urban.org/database/overview.cfm.

Neiman, M., 2009. Personal interview, February 6. San Francisco: Public Policy Institute of California.

Neiman, M., Andranovich, G., Fernandez, K. L., 2000. *Local economic development in Southern California's suburbs: 1990–1997.* San Francisco: Public Policy Institute of California.

Neiman, M., Krimm, D., 2009. *Economic development: The local perspective.* San Francisco: Public Policy Institute of California. http://www.ppic.org/content/pubs/report/R_509MNR.pdf.

Nelson, R. R., Winter, S. G., 1973. Toward an evolutionary theory of economic capabilities. *American Economic Review* 63: 440–449.

———, 1982. *An evolutionary theory of economic change.* Cambridge, MA: Harvard University Press.

Neumark, D., Kolko, J., 2010. Do enterprise zones create jobs? Evidence from California's enterprise zone program. *Journal of Urban Economics* 68,1: 1–19.

Noll, R., Zimbalist, A., eds., 1997. *Sports, jobs, and taxes.* Washington, DC: Brookings Institution Press.

North, D. C., 1990. *Institutions, institutional change, and economic performance.* Cambridge: Cambridge University Press.

———, 1993. *Economic performance through time.* Nobel Prize lecture, December 9. http://www.nobelprize.org/nobel_prizes/economic-sciences/laureates/1993/north-lecture.html.

———, 2005. *Understanding the process of economic change.* Princeton, NJ: Princeton University Press.

Norton, R. D., Rees, J., 1979. The product cycle and the spatial decentralization of American manufacturing. *Regional Studies* 13,2: 141–151.

Oden, M., Markusen, A., Flaming, D., Feldman, J., Raffel, J., Hill, C., 1996. *From managing growth to reversing decline: Aerospace and the Southern California economy in the post Cold War era.* Project on Regional and Industrial Economics. New Brunswick, NJ: Rutgers University Press.

Ó hUallacháin, B., 2012. Inventive Mega-regions of the United States: Technological Composition and Location. *Economic Geography* 88,2: 165–195.

O'Mara, M. P., 2005. *Cities of knowledge: Cold War science and the search for the next Silicon Valley.* Princeton, NJ: Princeton University Press.

O'Rourke, K. H., Williamson, J. G., 1999. *Globalization and history: The evolution of a nineteenth-century Atlantic economy.* Cambridge, MA: MIT Press.

Otis College of Art and Design, 2013. Otis creative economy report. http://www.otis .edu/creative-economy-report.

Owen-Smith, S. J., Powell, W. W., 2012. Networks and institutions. In R. Greenwood, C. Oliver, R. Suddaby, and K. Sahlin-Andersson, eds., *The Sage handbook of organisational institutionalisms*, 594–621. Los Angeles: Sage.

Padgett, J., 2012. Transposition and functionality: The birth of partnership systems in Renaissance Florence. In J. F. Padgett and W. W. Powell, eds., *The emergence of organizations and markets*, 168–207. Princeton, NJ: Princeton University Press.

Padgett, J. F., Ansell, C. K., 1993. Robust action and the rise of the Medici, 1400–1434. *American Journal of Sociology* 98,6: 1259–1319.

Padgett, J. F., Powell, W. W., eds., 2012. *The emergence of organizations and markets*. Princeton, NJ: Princeton University Press.

Painter, G. D., Yu, Z., 2009. *Leaving gateway metropolitan areas in the United States: Immigrants and the housing market*. Los Angeles: University of Southern California. http://lusk.usc.edu/research/research-briefs/leaving-gateway-metropolitan -areas-united-states-immigrants-and-housing.

Papke, L. E., 1994. Tax policy and urban development: Evidence from the Indiana enterprise zone program. *Journal of Public Economics* 54,1: 37–49.

Parent, W., Drennan, M., Osman, T., 2013. *A view of the region*. Los Angeles: UCLA Luskin School of Public Affairs, working paper. http://luskin.ucla.edu/sites/ default/files/laulcommonground.pdf.

Parkes, C., 2004. California's decade of flux. *Financial Times*, October 14: 13.

Partridge, M. D., 2010. The duelling models: NEG vs amenity migration in explaining US engines of growth. *Papers in Regional Science* 89,3: 513–536.

Partridge, M. D., Rickman, D. S., 2006. *The geography of American poverty: Is there a role for place-based policies?* Kalamazoo, MI: Upjohn Institute for Employment Research.

Pastor, M., 2010. Contemporary voices: Contradictions, coalitions, and common ground. In W. Deverell and G. Hise, eds., *A companion to Los Angeles*, 250–266. Chichester, UK: Wiley-Blackwell.

Pastor, M., Benner, C., Matsuoka, M., 2009. *This could be the start of something big: How social movements for regional equity are reshaping metropolitan America*. Ithaca, NY: Cornell University Press.

Peck, M. J., Scherer, F. M., 1962. *The weapons acquisition process: An economic analysis*. Boston: Division of Research, Graduate School of Business Administration, Harvard University.

Peirce, N., 1983. Dukakis winning "industrial policy." *Eugene Register Guard*, September 6: 6. http://news.google.com/newspapers?nid=1310&dat=19830906&id=Sm8 RAAAAIBAJ&sjid=PeIDAAAAIBAJ&pg=3702,1383446.

Peri, G., Shih, K., Sparber, C., 2014. *Foreign STEM workers and native wages and employment in US cities*. National Bureau of Economic Research, working paper 20093. http://www.nber.org/papers/w20093.pdf.

Perroux, F., 1950. Economic space: Theory and applications. *Quarterly Journal of Economics* 64,1: 89–104.

Peters, A. H., Fisher, P. S., 2002. *State enterprise zone programs: Have they worked?* Kalamazoo, MI: Upjohn Institute for Employment Research.

Peterson, N., Mumford, M., Borman, W., Jeanneret, P., Fleishman, E., Levin, K., Campion, M., et al., 2001. Understanding work using the occupational information network (O*NET): Implications for practice and research. *Personnel Psychology*, 54,2: 451–492.

Pfeffer, J., Salancik, G. R., 1978. *The external control of organizations: A resource dependence perspective.* New York: Harper and Row.

Pisano, M., 2009. Personal interview, January 30. Los Angeles: University of Southern California.

Pomeranz, K., 2000. *The great divergence: China, Europe, and the making of the modern world economy.* Princeton, NJ: Princeton University Press.

Porter, M. E., Rivkin, J. W., Kanter, R. M., 2013. *Competitiveness at a crossroads.* Boston: Harvard Business School. http://www.hbs.edu/competitiveness/pdf/competitiveness-at-a-crossroads.pdf.

Powell, W. W., Packalen, K., Whittington, K. B., 2012. Organizational and institutional genesis: The emergence of high-tech clusters in the life sciences. In J. F. Padgett and W. W. Powell, eds., *The emergence of organizations and markets*, 434–465. Princeton, NJ: Princeton University Press.

Powell, W. W., Sandholtz, W., 2012. Chance, nécessité, et naïveté: Ingredients to create a new organizational form. In J. F. Padgett and W. W. Powell, eds., *The emergence of organizations and markets*, 379–433. Princeton, NJ: Princeton University Press.

Puga, D., 2010. The magnitude and causes of agglomeration economies. *Journal of Regional Science* 50,1: 203–219.

Puga, D., Trefler, D., 2012. *International trade and institutional change: Medieval Venice's response to globalization.* National Bureau of Economic Research, working paper 18288. http://www.nber.org/papers/w18288.html.

Purcell, M., 2000. The decline of the political consensus for urban growth: Evidence from Los Angeles. *Journal of Urban Affairs* 22,1: 85–100.

———, 2002. Politics in global cities: Los Angeles charter reform and the new social movements. *Environment and Planning A* 34,1: 23–42.

Putnam, R. D., 2001. *Bowling alone: The collapse and revival of American community.* New York: Touchstone.

———, 2007. E pluribus unum: Diversity and community in the twenty-first century. 2006 Johan Skytte Prize Lecture. *Scandinavian Political Studies* 30: 137–174.

Rae, J. B., 1968. *Climb to greatness: The American aircraft industry, 1920–1960.* Cambridge, MA: MIT Press.

Rand, C., 1967. *Los Angeles: The ultimate city.* New York: Oxford University Press.

Randolph, S., 2009. Personal interview, February 6. San Francisco: Bay Area Council Economic Institute.

Rao, A., Scaruffi, P., 2011. *A history of Silicon Valley: The largest creation of wealth in the history of the planet: A moral tale.* Palo Alto, CA: Omniware Group.

Rappaport, J., 2007. Moving to nice weather. *Regional Science and Urban Economics* 37: 375–398.

Reese, L. A., Rosenfeld, R. A., 2004. Local economic development in the United States and Canada: Institutionalizing policy approaches. *American Review of Public Administration* 34,3: 277–292.

Regalado, J. A., 1991. Organized labor and Los Angeles city politics: An assessment of the Bradley years, 1973–1989. *Urban Affairs Review* 27,1: 87–108.

Richardson, H. W., 1979. *Regional economics.* Urbana: University of Illinois Press.

Rigby, D. L., 2012. *The geography of knowledge relatedness and technological diversification in U.S. cities.* Unpublished paper, UCLA Dept of Geography. Delivered at the annual meeting of the Association of American Geographers, New York.

Roback, J., 1982. Wages, rents and the quality of life. *Journal of Political Economy* 90,6: 1257–1278.

Rodríguez-Pose, A., 2013. Do institutions matter for regional development? *Regional Studies* 47,7: 1034–1047.

Rodríguez-Pose, A., Storper, M., 2005. Better rules or stronger communities? On the social foundations of economic change and its economic effects. *Economic Geography* 82,1: 1–25.

Rodrik, D., Subramanian, A., Trebbi, F., 2004. Institutions rule: The primacy of institutions over geography and integration in economic development. *Journal of Economic Growth* 9,2: 131–165.

Rosenberg, N., 1982. *Inside the black box: Technology and economics.* Cambridge: Cambridge University Press.

Rosenthal, S., Strange, W., 2001. The determinants of agglomeration. *Journal of Urban Economics* 50,2: 191–229.

Roszak, T., 1969. *The making of a counter culture: Reflections on the technocratic society and its youthful opposition.* Garden City, NY: Doubleday.

Rothkopf, D., 2008. *Superclass: The global power elite and the world they are making.* New York: Farrar, Straus and Giroux.

Rubin, B. M., Wilder, M. G., 1989. Urban enterprise zones: Employment impacts and fiscal incentives. *Journal of the American Planning Association* 55: 418–431.

Rupasingha, A., Goetz, S. J., 2008. *U.S. county-level social capital data, 1990–2005.* University Park, PA: Northwest Center for Rural Development.

———, 2013. Self-employment and local economic performance: Evidence from US counties. *Papers in Regional Science* 92,1: 141–161.

Safford, S., 2009. *Why the garden club couldn't save Youngstown: The transformation of the Rust Belt.* Cambridge, MA: Harvard University Press.

Saks, R. E., 2008. Job creation and housing construction: Constraints on metropolitan area employment growth. *Journal of Urban Economics* 64,1: 178–195.

Samila, S., Sorenson, O., 2011. Venture capital, entrepreneurship and economic growth. *Review of Economics and Statistics* 94,3: 764–788.

Sampson, R. J., 2012. *Great American city: Chicago and the enduring neighborhood effect.* Chicago: University of Chicago Press.

Sapir, A., E., 1996. The effects of Europe's internal market program on production and trade: A first assessment. *Weltwirtschaftliches Archiv* 132: 457–475.

Save San Francisco Bay Association, 2012. *Our history.* http://www.savesfbay.org/history.

Saxenian, A., 1983. The urban contradictions of Silicon Valley: Regional growth and the restructuring of the semiconductor industry. *International Journal of Urban and Regional Research* 7,2: 237–262.

———, 1994. *Regional advantage: Culture and competition in Silicon Valley and Route 128.* Cambridge, MA: Harvard University Press.

———, 2000. *The origins and dynamics of production networks in Silicon Valley.* SSRN Scholarly Paper No. ID 1512273. Rochester, NY: Social Science Research Network.

———, 2002. Silicon Valley's new immigrant high-growth entrepreneurs. *Economic Development Quarterly* 16,1: 20–31.

———, 2006. *The new argonauts: Regional advantage in a global economy.* Cambridge, MA: Harvard University Press.

SCAG (Southern California Association of Governments), 1984. *Profile of an economic transition: A status report on the Southern California economy.* Los Angeles: Southern California Association of Governments.

———, 1993. *Regional comprehensive plan.* Los Angeles: Southern California Association of Governments.

———, 2007. *State of the region report.* http://www.scag.ca.gov/newsandmedia/pages/publicationreports/aspx.

Scalice, G., 2009. Personal interview, March 6. San José: Semiconductor Industry Association.

Schoeni, R., Dardia, M., McCarthy, K., Vernez, G., 1996. *Life after cutbacks: Tracking California's aerospace workers.* Santa Monica, CA: Rand Corporation.

Schumpeter, J., 1934. *The theory of economic development.* Cambridge: Cambridge University Press.

Sciesi, M. J., 1991. Designing the model community: The Irvine Company and suburban development, 1950–1988. In R. Kling, S. C. Olin, and M. Poster, *Postsuburban California: The transformation of Orange County since World War II*, 55–91. Berkeley: University of California Press, 55–91.

Scott, A., 1993. *Technopolis: High-technology industry and regional development in Southern California.* Berkeley: University of California Press.

———, 1999. The US recorded music industry: On the relations between organization, location, and creativity. *Environment & Planning A* 31,11: 1965–1984.

———, 2002. A new map of Hollywood: The production and distribution of American motion pictures. *Regional Studies* 36: 957–975.

———, 2004. The other Hollywood: The organizational and geographic bases of television-program production. *Media, Culture and Society* 26,2: 183–205.

————, 2005. *On Hollywood: The place, the industry.* Princeton, NJ: Princeton University Press.

————, 2010a. Jobs or amenities? Destination choices of migrant engineers in the USA. *Papers in Regional Science* 89,1: 43–63.

————, 2010b. Space-time variations of human capital assets across US metropolitan areas 1980 to 2000. *Economic Geography* 86,3: 233–249.

Scott, A. J., Storper, M., 1987. High technology industry and regional development: A theoretical critique and reconstruction. *International Social Science Journal* 112, May: 215–232.

————, 2009. Rethinking human capital, creativity and economic growth. *Journal of Economic Geography* 9,2: 147–167.

Scott, M., 1963. *The future of San Francisco Bay.* Berkeley: University of California, Institute of Governmental Studies.

Siegfried, J., Zimbalist, A., 2000. The economics of sports facilities and their communities. *Journal of Economic Perspectives* 14,3: 95–114.

Simonson, G. R., 1968. *The history of the American aircraft industry: An anthology.* Cambridge, MA: MIT Press.

Soja, E. W., 2010. *Seeking spatial justice.* Minneapolis: University of Minnesota Press.

Sonn, J. W., Storper, M., 2008. The increasing importance of geographical proximity in knowledge production: An analysis of US patent citations, 1975–1997. *Environment and Planning A* 40,5: 1020–1039.

Stangler, D., 2013. *Path dependent start-up hubs: Comparing metropolitan performance, high tech and ICT startup density.* Kansas City, MO: Kauffman Foundation.

Starr, K., 2006. *Coast of dreams: California on the edge, 1990–2003.* New York: Vintage Books.

————, 2011. *Golden dreams: California in an age of abundance, 1950–1963.* Oxford: Oxford University Press.

Stekler, H. O., 1965. *The structure and performance of the aerospace industry.* Berkeley: University of California Press.

Storper, M., 1995. The resurgence of regional economies, ten years later: The region as a nexus of untraded interdependencies. *European Urban and Regional Studies* 2,3: 191–221.

————, 2005. Society, community and economic development. *Studies in Comparative Economic Development* 39,4: 30–57.

————, 2010. Why does a city grow? Specialization, human capital or institutions? *Urban Studies* 47,10: 2027–2050.

————, 2013. *Keys to the city: How economics, institutions, social interactions, and politics shape development.* Princeton, NJ: Princeton University Press.

————, 2014. Governing the large metropolis. *Territory, Politics, Governance* 2,2: 115–134.

Storper, M., Bocci, M., 2008. *Metropolitan economic growth: Three theories in search of evidence.* Barcelona: Aula Barcelona.

Storper, M., Christopherson, S., 1987. Flexible specialization and regional industrial agglomerations: The case of the U.S. motion picture industry. *Annals of the Association of American Geographers* 77,1: 104–117.

Storper, M., Salais, R., 1997. *Worlds of production: The action frameworks of the economy*. Cambridge, MA: Harvard University Press.

Storper, M., Venables, A., 2004. Buzz: Face-to-face contact and the urban economy. *Journal of Economic Geography* 4,4: 351–370.

Sturgeon, T. J., 2000. How Silicon Valley came to be. In M. Kenney and R. Florida, eds., *Understanding Silicon Valley: The anatomy of an entrepreneurial region*. Stanford, CA: Stanford University Press.

Sutaria, V., Hicks, D. A., 2004. New firm formation: Dynamics and determinants. *Annals of Regional Science* 38,2: 241–262.

Thisse, J.-F., 2010. Toward a unified theory of economic geography and urban economics. *Journal of Regional Science* 50,1: 281–296.

Thomas, W. F., Ong, P., 2002. Barriers to rehiring of displaced workers: A study of aerospace engineers in California. *Economic Development Quarterly* 16,2: 167–178.

Thompson, P., Fox-Kean, M., 2005. Patent citations and the geography of knowledge spillovers: A reassessment. *American Economic Review* 95: 450–460.

Tilly, C., 1986. *Big structures, large processes, huge comparisons*. New York: Russell Sage.

Tocqueville, A., 1830 (2000). *Democracy in America*. Chicago: University of Chicago Press. Originally published as *De la démocratie en Amérique*. Paris: Gallimard.

Turner, F., 2006. *From counterculture to cyberculture: Stewart Brand, the Whole Earth Network, and the rise of digital utopianism*. Chicago: University of Chicago Press.

U.S. Department of Transportation, 2011. *Tonnage of Top 50 U.S. Water Ports, Ranked by Total Tons*. Table 1-57. http://www.rita.dot.gov/bts/sites/rita.dot.gov.bts/files/publications/national_transportation_statistics/html/table_01_57.html.

Useem, M., 1984. *The inner circle: Large corporations and the rise of business political activity in the US and UK*. Oxford: Oxford University Press.

Vardoulis, B., 2009. Personal interview, March 13.

Verhetsel, A., Sel, S., 2009. World maritime cities: From which cities do container shipping companies make decisions? *Transport Policy* 16: 240–250.

Wachs, M., 1996. The evolution of transportation policy in Los Angeles: Images of past policies and future prospects. In A. J. Scott and E. Soja, eds., *The city: Los Angeles and urban theory at the end of the twentieth century*, 106–159. Berkeley: University of California Press.

Wade, R., 1990. *Governing the market: Economic theory and the role of government in East Asian industrialization*. Princeton, NJ: Princeton University Press.

Waldinger, R. D., Bozorgmehr, M., 1996. *Ethnic Los Angeles*. New York: Russell Sage.

Wallsten, S. J., 2004. Do science parks generate regional economic growth? In T. Bresnahan and A. Gambardella, eds., *Building high-tech clusters*, 229–279. Cambridge: Cambridge University Press.

Walker, R. A., 2008. *The country in the city: The greening of the San Francisco Bay Area*. Seattle: University of Washington Press.

Walrod, W., 2009. Personal interview, February 13. Irvine, CA: Orange County Business Council.

Whittington, K., Owen-Smith, J., Powell, W., 2009. Networks, propinquity and innovation in knowledge-intensive industries. *Administrative Science Quarterly* 54,1: 90–122.

Woo, M., 2009. Personal interview, January 30. Los Angeles.

Woolcock, M., Narayan, D., 2000. Social capital: Implications for development theory, research, and policy. *World Bank Research Observer* 15: 225–249.

World Bank, 2002. *Local economic development: A primer.* http://www.worldbank.org/urban/led.

———, 2009. *World development report: Reshaping economic geography.* Washington, DC: World Bank.

Woronkowicz, J., Joynes, D. C., Frumkin, P., Kolendo, A., Seaman, B., Gertner, R., Bradburn, N., 2012. *Set in stone: Building America's new generation of culture facilities, 1994–2008.* Chicago: University of Chicago, Harris School of Public Policy, Cultural Policy Center.

Yamamoto, D., 2007. Scales of regional income disparities in the USA, 1955–2003. *Journal of Economic Geography* 8: 79–103.

Yochum, G. R., Agarwal, V. B., 1987. Economic impact of a port on a regional economy: Note. *Growth and Change* 18,3: 74–87.

Zak, P. J., Knack, S., 2001. Trust and growth. *Economic Journal* 111,470: 295–321.

Zhang, J., 2003. *High-tech start-ups and industry dynamics in Silicon Valley.* San Francisco: Public Policy Institute of California.

Zook, M., 2002. Grounded capital: Venture financing and the geography of the Internet industry, 1994–2000. *Journal of Economic Geography* 2: 151–177.

Zysman, J., Cohen, S., 1988. *Manufacturing matters: The myth of post-industrial America.* New York: Basic Books.

Index

Page numbers followed by "f," "t," or "m" indicate material in figures, tables, or maps. "LA" indicates the Los Angeles city-region. "SF" indicates the San Francisco Bay Area city-region.